William Henry Drummond

The Large Game

And Natural History of South and South-East Africa

William Henry Drummond

The Large Game
And Natural History of South and South-East Africa

ISBN/EAN: 9783743386365

Manufactured in Europe, USA, Canada, Australia, Japa

Cover: Foto ©Andreas Hilbeck / pixelio.de

Manufactured and distributed by brebook publishing software (www.brebook.com)

William Henry Drummond

The Large Game

ROUGH NOTES

ON

THE LARGE GAME

And Natural History of South and
South-East Africa.

EARLY MORNING ON THE BANKS OF THE NKWAVUMA

THE LARGE GAME

And Natural History of South and
South-East Africa.

FROM THE JOURNALS OF THE HON. W. H. DRUMMOND.

EDINBURGH: EDMONSTON AND DOUGLAS.
MDCCCLXXV.

PREFACE.

THE chief points, it seems to me, on which the public have a right to expect information in a Preface are three, viz., the author's reasons for, or object in, writing the book, what knowledge he possesses of his subject, and what help, if any, he has received from others.

It had always struck me that, with one or two noteable exceptions, the books hitherto published on African sport were to a great extent mere illustrated game-books, telling indeed the quantity and quality of the game which the writer or his companions had killed, but not giving such particulars as would enable the untravelled reader to bring every occurrence vividly and truthfully before his mind's eye; and when I found that others in this country agreed with me as fully as those amongst whom I had hunted had always done, I determined to note all the details that my journals or memory could supply which in any way bore upon the subject of large-game shooting in South-Eastern Africa, or upon such points of Natural History in connexion with it as had come under my own observation, and the result has been these pages.

It has been my principal object to write for the information of such of my fellow-sportsmen as may be tempted to pay a visit to this, the finest game country in the world, and I have attempted to give them as good an idea as is possible on paper of what they may expect to find when in pursuit of each of the large animals they will find there; and should what I have written prove of *practical* use, even in a single instance, I shall have had my reward. It is, however, necessary for any one who, taking these pages as his guide, goes out to South Africa to shoot, to bear two things in mind: firstly, that day by day, almost hour by hour, and with ever increasing rapidity, the game is being exterminated or driven further back, and that on the ground about which I write, where I have seen almost countless herds of buffalo and antelopes of various kinds, their numbers have very seriously diminished; and secondly, that my experiences are merely those of one individual, and that, as I have elsewhere remarked, different people in the same country, and under apparently similar conditions, often arrive at widely different results, a fact that I hope such of my critics as I may have the misfortune to differ from may take into consideration.

The experiences upon which my book is founded extended over a period of some five years, ending in 1872 (though one or two incidents belong to a prior period), during which time, to all intents and purposes, I lived amongst the natives and the game, rarely, except when visiting the colony to dispose of cattle or hides, and to lay in a fresh stock of goods, sleeping under other covering than that of heaven, with the distant muttering of the lion or the mournful howl of the prowling hyena as my lullaby; and I can truthfully say, that the memory of those five years, spent in that wild land under the shadow of the Southern Cross, is a very pleasant one.

It is perhaps as well to mention at once, that, except at very short ranges, I can lay no claim to being a good rifle shot, and that whatever success I may have had as a hunter was entirely due to what I learned from professional natives, who, though as a rule very ordinary shots, make up for every deficiency by their wonderful skill in still hunting and in tracking, their capacity to undergo great hardships and fatigues, their exhaustive knowledge of the haunts and habits of the game, and their resolute perseverance in its pursuit. I possessed a great advantage in, from the commencement, thoroughly understanding their language, and in being naturally able to undergo at least as much fatigue and hardship as they could; experience gradually did the rest, and in course of time I was able to find, follow, and approach game with so much certainty as to more than compensate for the deficiencies of my shooting.

About Natural History as a science I know, I am sorry to say, little or nothing, and therefore whatever I have said on the subject must be taken for what it is worth, though I may mention that I have been careful to exclude everything but what has come within my personal knowledge. For this reason it has often been difficult for me to identify from the scientific name and description animals and birds with which I was practically well acquainted, and of which I knew the local or native name.

Regarding the Illustrations, my thanks are due to that able artist, Mr. Edward Hodges, to whose skill and untiring patience it is owing that the imperfect materials with which I supplied him have assumed a shape which I venture to hope may meet with the approval of such of my readers as may happen to be conversant with the objects depicted; as also to Mr. James Drummond, R.S.A., the accomplished Curator of the National Gallery of Scotland, to whom I am indebted for the sketch of the "Isles of the West;" nor while on this subject can I do less than acknowledge the great courtesy with which all my views have been met and forwarded by every one within whose province it lay to assist me.

As the contents of this book do not refer to a single journey, but are the accumulated experiences of very many, often over much the same ground, it has not been deemed desirable to do more than append a sketch or outline map of the country I passed over, which, however, I have attempted to render as perfect as possible.

It would be unjust to the memory of my late friend, Mr. Leslie, were I to omit to mention that to his great knowledge and experience I owe much of whatever may be of value in these pages, and that to his kindly placing at my disposal during my expeditions the large number of hunters and natives in his service, I owe many of my opportunities for observation.

With these few words of acknowledgement and explanation, I place my first book in the hands of the public, upon whose verdict it now depends whether it shall also be my last.

W. H. DRUMMOND.

Appin, *March 30th*, 1873.

"The Isles I love best are the Isles of the West
Where men speak the Gaelic tongue."

CONTENTS.

CHAPTER I.
BUFFALO.

Hunting camp in Eastern Africa,	p. 1, 2
Troop of impalla,	3
Water-antelope,	3
Saved by a rhinoceros-bird—Buffalo bull,	4
Difficult position,	5
A mud-bath—A foolish shot,	6
Following the spoor,	8
The reeds,	9–12
Death of a solitary,	13
Best place for buffalo-shooting—Good day on the Nkwavuma,	14
Anecdote of a lion,	15
Two old bulls,	16
The "strong names,"	16
A valuable hint,	16
Following a wounded buffalo,	17
Its death,	17
A tremendous fusilade—Three troops of buffalo—Curious scene,	18
Large buffalo cow,	19
Shooting a rhinoceros-bird—Danger in the reeds,	20
A furious charge,	21
Surrounded by buffalo—Honesty of the hunters,	22
Twenty-nine buffaloes killed—Curious spectacle,	23
Combat between two bulls,	24, 25
Breeding season,	26
Two curious assertions of native hunters,	27
Anecdote of a hunter—The Pongolo,	28
Picturesque encampment—The "impalla-catcher,"	29
Catching a buffalo calf,	30
A miserable coward,	31
A serious injury—Species of buffalo,	32
The Bombo mountains—The grey monkey—A magnificent view,	34
A curious cover — Remarkable strength of the buffalo,	35
Description of a forest buffalo—Good days and bad days,	p. 36
Superstition of the native hunters,	37
Extracts from my Journal,	38
A herd of buffaloes fording a river—A deadly shot,	39
Safe under the massive roots of a fig-tree,	40
Finishing off a bull—Tenacity of life in large game—Blood-marks on the spoor,	41
Catching sight of the herd,	42
A vicious charge,	43
Killing a cow,	44
Natives holding themselves responsible for their master's safety,	45
The orthodox manner of following the spoor,	46
Difficulty of tracking,	47
Wounded buffalo at bay with dogs,	48
Wonderful pluck of a native,	49, 50
Instance of an unprovoked charge—Terrible wound,	51
Miraculous recovery,	52
Anecdote of a native hunter and a buffalo,	53, 54
Personal narrow escapes,	55
Unpleasant predicament,	56
Killing a buffalo with spears,	57
Adventure with a solitary bull,	58
Called by the rhinoceros-birds—The first two shots,	59
The Nkwavuma,	60
I am knocked down and trodden on—Shamming death—Final escape and victory,	61–63
A shot at a critical moment,	65
Habits of buffaloes,	66–68
A stunned bull,	69
Anecdote of a rogue,	70, 71

CHAPTER II.

RHINOCEROS.

The Black Umfolosi,	p. 72
Sufferings from thirst,	73
Shooting an antelope,	74
The camp charged by a rhinoceros,	75, 76
Tracking its spoor—Firing a volley—Its cunning,	77
Its death,	83
Number of species in Africa,	83
Description of,	84-86
Waterholes,	89
Quantity and variety of game which frequent them,	87, 88
Watching them at night,	89
A troop of lions during a thunderstorm,	90
Watching a waterhole for two nights and a day,	90
Large bag,	91
The duiker antelope,	92
A herd of koodoos,	93
Stalking a rhinoceros by moonlight,	94
An unpleasant predicament,	95
Sleeping in a tree,	96
A black rhinoceros,	97
The ititihoya plover,	98
A herd of rhinoceros,	99
Causes of missing,	100
Finishing off a wounded one,	101
Vegetable caves,	102
The lair of an upetyane,	p. 103
An excited animal,	104
A herd of wild pigs,	105
The leopard's victim,	106
Risking a long shot,	107
Hyenas,	108
A large herd of buffalo,	109
A stratagem,	110
The hardening of bullets,	111
Effects of soft and hard bullets,	112-114
The best bore for guns,	115, 116
Capturing a young rhinoceros,	117-119
Habitat of the different species,	120, 121
My first introduction to a kulumane,	122
Forming an ambuscade,	123
A broken-legged cow,	124
The habitat of *R. Keitloa*,	125
Shooting one with a single ball,	126
General habits of the rhinoceros,	127
Best place at which to aim,	128
Savageness of *R. bicornis*,	129
A hunter killed,	130
A black rhinoceros spares a baby,	131
Two thousand men put to flight by one,	132
An African scene,	133
Personal adventure with one,	134
An ill-famed spot,	135

CHAPTER III.

ELAND.

Return of a hunter,	138
The honey-bird,	139
The honey-hunter,	140
A troop of elands,	141
A trying race—Running down an eland,	142
An old blue bull,	143
Species of eland,	145
The striped variety,	146
A great herd,	147
An unexpected shot,	148
Tribute to native hunters,	149
A disputed buffalo,	150, 151
How to make a waterproof hut,	152, 153
Travellers' mats,	154, 155
On the march,	156
The sassabi,	157
Quantity of game,	158
A long shot,	159
A beautiful picture,	160
My last bullet,	161
A pleasant surprise,	162
Extermination of the eland,	163
Their breeding season,	164
A gallop after a young cow,	165
The gun break back,	166
An ugly fall—Pace of an eland,	167, 168
Swaziland,	169

A waggon encampment,	. p. 170	An enormous bull, . p. 175
Starting for a final day,	. 171	A nasty collision, . . 176
Driving a herd, . .	. 172-174	An unusually large bag, . 177

CHAPTER IV.

ELEPHANT.

An African summer's evening,	. 179	Reward for our exertions, . . 198
The great reed fields, . .	. 180	A determined charge, . . 199
A herd of rogue elephants, .	. 181	In hiding—Hunter's Law, . 200, 201
Lost in the reeds, . .	. 182	Finding a herd, . . . 202
An oasis, . . .	. 183	A beautiful sight, . . . 203
A lonely camp, . .	. 184	Killing a bull, . . . 204
Noises of the night, . .	. 185	Breaking up the carcase, . . 205
A tuskless cow, . .	. 186	Killing with a single bullet, . 206, 207
Finding my way out, .	. 187	Driven out of the jungle, . . 208
Shooting a hippopotamus, .	. 188	Concealed under a fallen tree, . 209
The signal gun, . .	. 189	A furious herd, . . 210-212
Hard work attendant on elephant-shooting, . . .	. 190	Districts frequented by elephant, . 213
		Umzila's country, . . 214, 215
The spoor of an old bull, .	. 191	Danger encountered in elephant-shooting, . . . 216
A miserable night, . .	. 192	
In want of food, . .	. 193	Rogue elephants rare, . . 217
Crossing the river, . .	. 194	The "horse-sickness," . 218, 219
Heavy rain, . . .	. 195	Best marks to aim at, . . 220
Still on the spoor, . .	. 196	Protest against the wholesale destruction of elephants, . . 221
The first shot, . .	. 197	

CHAPTER V.

LIONS.

Moving the camp, . .	. 222	Account of a hunter—Lioness with three cubs—Another instance of self-possession, . . . 241
Country bordering the Pongolo,	. 223	
Choosing a new site, . .	. 224	
Arrival of the hunters, .	. 225	Man killed by a lioness—Unexpected encounters, . . 242
The hunting-song, . .	. 226	
Rejoicings over a dead lion, .	. 227	Running away, . . . 243
A native hunter's story, .	. 228, 229	Instantaneous death, . . 244
Night in the tropics, . .	. 230	Instance of a lion attacking a human being—Camp on the Nkwavuma, 245
Attack of a man-eater, .	. 231	
Its death, . . .	. 232	A herd of buffalo, . . . 246
A man killed, . . .	. 233	Meeting a lioness, . . . 247
A fellow-stalker, . .	. 234	Tambuti grass, . . . 248
A buffalo attacked by lions, .	. 235	Lion and lioness—Umdumela speaks to the lion, . . . 249
Mutual fear, . . .	. 236	
Man-eating crocodile, . .	. 237	The lioness goes away, . . 250
Man's life saved by his dog, .	. 238	Tracking the lion, . . . 251
Prowess of the African lion, .	. 239	Anecdote of a lion—Two men killed, ... 252-254
Instance of self-possession, .	. 240	

CONTENTS.

Man-eaters—A man-eater which had killed thirty or forty individuals, p. 255
Great strength of a man-eater, . 256
A dark night, ... 257
Beating up the country, . . 258
Taking up the spoor, . . . 259
A village turns out to hunt the man-eater—Waiting for the spies, 260
Entering the jungle, . . . 261
Turning a somersault, . . 262
Firing a volley, ... 263
Fighting the lion with assagais, . 264
Death of the lion, . . . 265
Performing the bravery dance—Slaughtering two oxen to celebrate the victory, . . . 266
A contest among the hunters, . . 267
A midnight visitor, . . . 268
Return of the lioness, . . . 269
The path of the Nkwavuma—Meeting the man-eater in the dark, . 270
Making a new camp, . . p. 271
Waiting for the man-eater's return—Shooting at it in the dark, . 272
Finding the lioness dead, . . 273
Disturbing a lion, . . . 274
Instance of the folly of pushing a lion to extremity, . . . 275
Death of an obstinate hunter—A beautiful sight, . . . 277
Encampment on the Black Umfolosi—Watching a lion family feeding, 278
Trying to catch a lion's whelp, . 279
Lion attacking a buffalo, . . 280
Remarks on the food of lions, . 281
A hunter sleeping inside a dead rhinoceros, ... 282
Shooting two lions dead in the dark, ... 283
Anecdote of a Dutch hunter, . 284
Most likely places to find lions in, . 285
Best places to fire at, . . . 286

CHAPTER VI.

LEOPARDS.

Different species of leopards, 288, 289
General resemblance to a lion, . 290
Habits of the ingwe—Hunting the leopard on the Pongolo, . . 291
A surprise—Killing the leopard, . 292
Leopards gambolling, . . . 293
A beautiful skin—The river Tugela—On the track, . . . 294
Goat killed by a leopard, . . 295
Dangerous work, ... 297
Lying in wait, ... 298
The Bombo Mountains—A watch hut, ... 299
Instinct of the leopard, . . 300
The maned leopard, . . 301, 302
Great resemblance of the maned leopard to a lioness—Stalking a maned leopard, ... 303
A tempting shot—Death of the two leopards, ... 304
Seven men mangled by a single animal, ... 305
Man-eating leopards, . . . 306
Species of hyena—Habits of the hyena, ... 307
Damage done by the hyena—Hyenas attacking human beings, . 308
Anecdote of a hyena—Hyena seizing an infant—Cowardliness of, 309, 310
The wild dog, ... 311
Wonderful skill of a pack of wild dogs, 312
Wild dogs hunting an old gnu, . 313
The different species of wild dog, . 314
Unexpected meeting with a pack of wild dogs, ... 315
The jackal—Its beautiful skin, . 316

CHAPTER VII.

HUNTING WITH DOGS.

Makambi's black dog, . . . 317
Native breed of greyhounds, . . 318
Novel mode of buying a dog—I commence coursing, . . . 319
Description of a native hunting party—A performance by the head of the hunting party, . 320
Lying in wait—Slipping the hound, 321

CONTENTS.

The death—A curious incident, p. 322
A tremendous bound—A free fight among the natives, . . . 323
Curious mode of treating the conquered, ... 323
A furious animal, ... 324
The Noodsberg—An oribi caught by dogs, ... 325
A great disappointment, . . 326
A novel mode of hunting the oribi, 327
Death of Usipingo—A great temptation, ... 328
Hunting the impalla with dogs, . 329
Coursing the Vaal and roi raebok, . 330
Hunting wild pigs, . . 331, 332
Killing with the spear, . . . 333
Wonderful length of the boar's tusks, ... 334
Different kinds of pigs, . . 335
A curious mode of exit, . . . 336
An immense boar, ... 337
A dangerous wound, . . . 338
Killing a baboon, ... 339
Disagreeable resemblance between a baboon and a human being—The blue gnu, ... 340
Baiting the gnu with dogs—A vicious rush—A clever dog, . . p. 341
A beautiful scene, . . . 342-344
A picture worthy of Landseer, . 345
A dangerous shot—Frightening the crocodiles, ... 346
A hunting party given by Prince Usibepe, ... 347
A koodoo bull—A mad gallop—Unpleasant proximity of the Prince's bullets, ... 348
Great heat of the native huts, . 349
Dangerous proximity to a lion, . 350
I accidentally shoot my dog, . 351
The hartebeest — Coursing them with greyhounds, . . . 352
A curious freak of nature, . . 353
A great disappointment, . . 354
An exciting scene, ... 355
A chase, ... 356
Necessary qualities of a good horse, 357
A long ride, ... 358
Horse, dog, and antelope are all dead beat, ... 359
I resolve never again to ride a hartebeest down, ... 360

CHAPTER VIII.

ANECDOTES OF ANTELOPES.

Skill of the gnu in the use of its horns, ... 361
Stalking the gnu, ... 362
Wriggling up to a herd, . . 363
Shooting an old bull gnu—A terrific thunderstorm, ... 364
Wonderful tenacity of life among antelopes, ... 365
Different species of zebra, . . 366
The water-antelope, . . . 367
A curious shot, ... 368
Antelope browsing in a curious manner, ... 369
The Drachensberg Mountains—Bushman's River, ... 370
Scenery of the Free State—A picturesque fire, ... 371
Magnificent spectacle, . . . 372
My first antelope, ... 373
African chamois, ... 374
Anecdote of a Dutch Boer—A first-class liar, ... 375
Galloping antelope down on horseback, ... 376
Come to grief, ... 377
The Nyala antelope, . . . 378
Various species of antelope, . . 379
A narrow escape, . . 380, 381
Charge of a wounded nkonka, . 382
A first-rate shot, ... 383
Setting traps for leopards, . . 384
Trap carried off by an antelope, . 385
Following its track, . . . 386
Turning the antelope—A fatal accident, ... 387
Driving the antelope out of the jungle, ... 388
Fight between two nkonkas — Fight between an nkonka and a leopard, ... 389
Following the leopard, . . . 390
The red buck, ... 391
The blue buck—The most enjoyable method of hunting the blue buck, 392

Difficulty of attaining absolute noiselessness in tracking, p. 393	Tenacity of life in the duiker—The roi raebuck, . . . p. 399
Hunting with beagles, . . . 394	The ant-eater, ... 400
The steinbuck, ... 395	Digging it out of a hole, . . 401
The Vaal raebuck — The klipspringer, ... 396	The porcupine — The cane-rat — A dainty addition to an African bill of fare, ... 402
The reed-buck—Its habits, . 397	
The duiker—Its great daring, . 398	Hunting the cane-rat, . . 403-405

CHAPTER IX.

GAME BIRDS.

The ostrich—Its feathers, . 407	The guinea-fowl — Its different species, ... 415
The pauw—Its different species, . 408	
Difficulty of killing it, . . 409	Treeing the young brood, . . 416
Its habits and modes of living, . 410	The several varieties of plover, . 417
The bustard, ... 410	The several varieties of quails—The snipe, ... 418
Its different species, . . 411	
The dikkop—The wild turkey, . 412	The different varieties of geese—The varieties of duck, . . . 419
The snake-bird, . . . 412	
Superstition of the natives with respect to it, ... 413	The pigeon, ... 420
	The goat-sucker — Its resemblance to the woodcock, . . . 421
The partridge — Its different species, ... 413, 414	The Cape-lark—The crested-crane, . 422

APPENDIX.

I.—MAMMALS,	425
II.—BIRDS,	427

LIST OF ILLUSTRATIONS.

EARLY MORNING ON THE BANKS OF THE NKWAVUMA,	*Frontispiece*
THE YOUNG RHINOCEROS IN CAMP (p. 119),	*Vignette*
THE ISLES OF THE WEST,	PAGE xii
BUFFALO'S HEAD (*Bubalus caffer*),	xix
SASSABI (*Bubalus lunata*),	xxi
SKULL OF AFRICAN BUFFALO (*Bubalus caffer*),	1
"THE RISING MOON THROWING A FLOOD OF LIGHT OVER HIS IMMENSE PROPORTIONS,"	14
"IT NOW CAUGHT SIGHT OF THE BOYS,"	65
HEAD OF RHINOCEROS (*R. bicornis*),	72
HEAD OF RHINOCEROS (*R. Keitloa*),	136

LIST OF ILLUSTRATIONS.

HEAD OF ZEBRA (*Asinus zebra*), .	PAGE 137
" THE OLD FELLOW TAKING HIS OWN LINE,"	142
HEAD OF ELAND (*Antilope Oreas*),	178
SKULL OF ELEPHANT (*Elephas Africanus*), .	179
" HE WENT A LITTLE DISTANCE OFF AND STOOD,"	200
" ITS TRUNK COILED ROUND THE BRANCHES OF A TREE,"	206
HEAD OF LION (*Felis leo*),	222
" SILENTLY AND QUIETLY HE MOVED DOWN,"	254
" IT WAS THE LIONESS,"	272
HEAD OF LIONESS (*Felis Leo*), .	287
ARD WOLF (*Proteles cristatus*),	288
" TREACHEROUS, COWARDLY, AND SAVAGE,"	307
HEAD OF BLESBUCK (*Damalis albifrons*),	316
HEAD OF WILD BOAR (*Phacochœrus Æthiopicus*),	317
" THE BOAR WAS STANDING FACING THE DOG," .	333
" ON A SMALL SAND-BANK STOOD THE TWO NOBLE KOODOO BULLS AT BAY,"	344
HEAD OF GNU (*Catoblepas gnu*), .	360
HEAD OF IMPALLA (*Antilope melampus*), .	361
" PERHAPS THE MOST BEAUTIFUL OF ALL THE ANTELOPES IS THE NYALA," .	378
" THE LARGEST AND FINEST OF THEM IS THE REEDBUCK,"	397

LIST OF ILLUSTRATIONS. xxi

HEAD OF REED-BUCK DOE (*Eleotragus arundinaceus*), . PAGE 405

GROUP OF OSTRICHES, . 406

THE CRESTED PAUW (*Eupodis cristata*), . 407

GREAT CRESTED CRANE (*Balearica pavonina*), . 423

SKETCH-MAP *at the end of the Volume.*

SASSABI (*Bubalus lunata*).

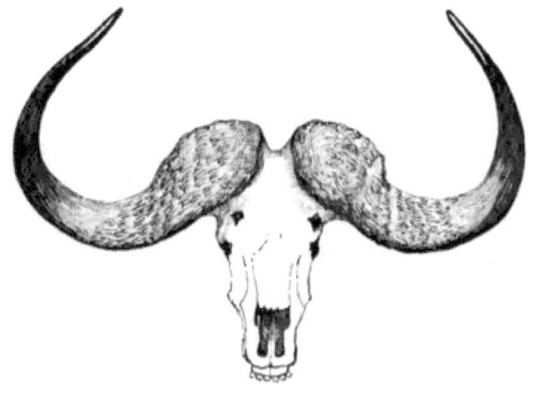

CHAPTER I.

BUFFALO.

The morning star was sufficiently high to enable me to tell that dawn would soon make its appearance, as I got up from my rude bed in camp, and, with some little trouble and a good deal of grunting on his part, succeeded in rousing my gun-bearer.

No more picturesque scene could be imagined than that by which I was surrounded as I sat smoking by the ash-covered embers, waiting for the native to get my gun and cartridges. A rough, though tolerably high fence of thorn enclosed a space round the flat-crowned mimosa-tree, through whose roof-like branches the stars shone down upon us, and under which, in every variety of posture the great heat could induce, lay about twenty Kaffirs, their guns and assagais beside them. On the side on which I slept a dried buffalo-hide had been thrown to protect me from the heavy night-dew, while two or three propped up formed a screen for the now smouldering fires which guarded the entrance. On the ground outside, and strewed all about, were hides and skins, horns of various kinds, and innumerable relics of departed dinners, in the shape of marrow and other bones, while a few yards off the dim shadows of great masses of buffalo-beef could be distinguished, hung out of the reach of prowling hyenas or jackals on an adjacent thorn-tree. Several dogs lay curled up at their master's feet, giving an occasional howl as they were kicked away by the hot and restless sleepers.—Such was our hunting camp during the summer of 1870 in the far interior of Eastern Africa.

Outside all was perfectly still and calm, not a breath of air stirring, and nothing to break the silence but the occasional mournful howl of a passing wolf. It was so light that once or twice I went out fancying that dawn was breaking, and at last, tired of waiting, I started. The country around was a dead flat, unbroken for hundreds of miles, and covered with thorns of every variety, here and there deepening into almost impenetrable thickets, or opening out into treeless glades. About a mile off was the Unkomati, a river of considerable size, along the banks of which I now went; for as all game comes down to drink about dawn, I was certain to find plenty of antelopes, and at that early hour I was not unlikely to come across the larger and more rare animals.

As soon as I could see the sight of my gun I left the Kaffir behind, as, though they are sometimes capital spoorers, following a track as if by instinct, they are at the same time as often careless; and absolute noiselessness, especially when the game is still on the move, and consequently more watchful, is the great point to be attained. After telling him to come to me if I fired, I crept on through the low scrub, stealing along the narrow game-paths so as to avoid the rustle of the grass, and in a few minutes I saw something red moving among the trees, and stopped to watch it. It turned out to be a troop of impalla coming back from water, and making for some of the grassy glades. There might have been seventy or eighty of them picking their way along in Indian file, nibbling here and there, but always moving, and seeming like a troop of ghosts in the dim twilight and silence. I had, however, plenty of meat in camp, and being also unwilling to disturb any larger game that there might be within hearing, I waited unseen till they had all passed and then proceeded.

Several times I came across different herds of the same antelope moving out of the hot thickets which lined the river, but for some time I saw nothing else. At last I made out a black shadow standing in a clump of bush, which practice told me was a water-antelope, and as it, at any rate, would be worth killing, and there was a strip of thorns which would conceal me till I was within twenty yards of it, I got into them and made the best of my way towards it. I reached the spot without making any noise sufficient to disturb it, and on peering through the bushes I saw that it was a bull, and at once covered it, and should have killed it in another second, when suddenly the harsh "tcha, tcha" of the rhinoceros-bird broke the silence, and as my eye followed the sound it rested on the massive grey head of an enormous old buffalo bull, which, the remainder of its body concealed by a bush, was standing looking about him some two hundred yards off, probably wondering what had caused the bird, which from its elevated position had no doubt seen me, to utter the warning cry, which, for that day at least, had saved the water-antelope's life.

In a few minutes he walked out into the open, and commenced feeding, enabling me to see that I had to deal with an old "rogue," or solitary bull, of no common size or age. His immense horns, which from the eye to the back of the head formed a solid rugged mass, impenetrable to bullets, were so worn down at the ends that their natural curve had almost disappeared, and they now stood out nearly at right angles from his forehead. His skin, never very thickly covered with the dark brown hair that clothes these animals, had become through age perfectly nude, and was of a shiny slate colour, except where a remaining fringe formed a black line along his withers and back. His immense neck, rivalling that of the elephant in thickness, so took off from the size of his head, that by comparison it seemed quite small, while the roundness of his great carcase proved him to be in the highest condition. A flock of upwards of a dozen of the red-beaked rhinoceros-birds were seated all over him, some contentedly on his forehead and horns, others running about with their quick starling-like movement in search of the great grass-ticks on which they live.

I was in a most difficult position, and did not know very well what to do. If I disturbed the antelope the buffalo would undoubtedly take the alarm; while, as the thicket I was in ended here, I could not tell how to get nearer to him without doing so; but ultimately I decided to remain where I was and watch. I waited, I should think, more than half an hour, during which the buffalo had moved up towards the other end of the open, and as I feared that when he had done grazing he would take himself off for many a weary mile to some shady spot he knew of, where the breeze might cool him during the mid-day heat, and give me hours of patient tracking to undergo before I could again overtake him, I became impatient to get rid of the antelope. If I could but induce it to move, it would soon take itself off to another thicket and leave me at liberty, so in despair I tried to frighten it. First I whistled softly, causing it to look about uneasily, though it did not stir; then I tried to imitate the growling of a lion, though I doubt if it recognised the resemblance. However, it walked out, came straight to me, and stood not a yard off, evidently without an idea of where the sound had come from. When I whistled again it saw me, and disappeared with a rush, luckily in the direction I had come from, and away from the buffalo.

I could still see the latter at intervals between the trunks of some large water-loving trees which surrounded and partially concealed a water-hole, and as by making a slight detour I could gain the shelter of an evergreen bush which stood within a few yards of it, I at once started to do so. I went as rapidly as possible across the open, but became cautious as I neared the bush, for I had just heard the rhinoceros-birds rise, shrieking, and a heavy gurgling sound made me imagine that the bull must be enjoying a mud bath. Immediately on gaining the desired shelter I peeped round it, and there, sure enough, was the unwieldy animal kneeling in the hole, one side already plastered over with black slimy mud, which, if left to itself, would soon cake and protect him from the bites of the enormous gadflies, which, despite the thickness of these animals' hides, are one of their chief pests during summer. He was in a capital position for a shot; but, just as I raised my gun, he rolled over on to the other side, and wallowed about, forming a deep hollow in the soft mud, and at last extricating himself with a jerk, he came out dripping with mire, and approaching a tree not five yards from me, began to scratch his neck against it, presenting his forehead towards me.

In the centre of every bull buffalo's head there is a parting, or furrow, where the horns scarcely join, and in which a bullet will very often prove immediately fatal, and though it never exceeds a quarter of an inch, and in the present animal was, from his great age, scarcely perceptible, a fancy seized me to make the attempt, as, if I was successful, I should kill him on the spot, and escape the work and danger I should otherwise have to undergo. Just glancing round, therefore, to see where I should make for afterwards, I took aim and fired, at the same instant springing to the other side of the bush, clear of the smoke. As I did so I heard the crack of the ball, and then a singing in the distance told me that it had glanced off; but I had no time to think about it then, for almost instantly the head of the old bull appeared through the smoke, which hung heavily on the thicket. Fortunately the bush was thick and the branches strong, and he was unable to force any more of his body through; and as he jerked himself clear again, I made a rush to a small thorn-tree close at hand and clambered up. I do not think he saw me, and I was by no means sorry at the time, for I didn't place any very great reliance on the stability of my refuge; but he was evidently much put out, and made several blind charges before he galloped off, accompanied high in the air by his shrieking bird-followers.

There was no doubt that I had made about as complete a mess of it as I could well have done. The buffalo had gone, perfectly uninjured, and thoroughly roused, and it was impossible to say how far he might go before he stopped, besides which he would be sure to take precautions against surprise, and would remain suspicious of the slightest sound during the remainder of the day; and it was the more annoying that had I only taken time and put a well-aimed ball into or behind the shoulder, I should have been sure, if I did not kill him on the spot, to do so within a circle of a mile or so. However, there was no help for it, and I patiently waited for my Kaffir, who must have heard the shot.

He soon made his appearance, and then I had to undergo the categorical cross-questioning to which even a native chief, under similar circumstances, would have been equally subject.

"What did you fire at?"

"Buffalo," was my curt answer.

"You missed it," with a grin. "Wau! what a spoor

it's got; where was it? where were you? where's it gone? Wau!"

As I knew perfectly well that no silence could be hoped for until I told him all about it, I did so amid his astonished ejaculations of "Wau!" and then, after satisfying himself by examining the spoor as to where the charge had taken place, and with his sharp eyes detecting a splinter of horn on the ground where the bull had been standing when I fired at it, and after casting a wondering look or two at the tree I had climbed, he turned to me and asked, "Shall we follow it?" and on receiving an affirmative reply, he at once took my gun from me, struck the spoor, and went along it at a rapid walk.

For the first hour no word was uttered, the native, his curiosity once satisfied, completely absorbed in the work of tracking. The buffalo had galloped steadily up the river, avoiding the thickets, and in the long grass his trail was quite plain. At last he reduced his pace to a walk, and entered a small thorn jungle, through which, taking my gun, I followed him in person, until he left it and again struck across an open, where the shorter grass and sun-baked soil, combined with the faint impression he made when walking, taxed the united powers of both of us to keep the spoor. It was mid-day before we reached the next cover, into which he went; it was a large one, with cactus for underwood, and heavy timber at intervals, and we had no doubt but that he would lie down in some part of it.

Up and down we followed the spoor of the restless brute, finding many spots where he had stood, sometimes in gloomy caves formed by the cactus, where the sunlight never rested, or in shady recesses under an impenetrable tangle of thorns, or by the side of some great tree, against which the mud resting on the bark showed that he had been rubbing. Several times the rush of a disturbed bush-buck, or, in the more open parts, of an impalla, sent my heart into my mouth, for it is nervous, uncanny work silently moving through these deep half-lit masses of vegetation. Once the Kaffir touched my shoulder and pronounced the magical word "imbubi;" but it was no lion, but a great wild boar, whose tawny-coloured hide gave it in the gloom a certain resemblance to the king of beasts. Up and down, and up and down we wandered, the spoor forming never-ending circles and mazes, sometimes so involved that we were fain to leave it and let him go; sometimes we sat down for a few moments while the native solaced himself with snuff, but we did not despair, and followed on, though the difficulties were such that it was nearly four o'clock before we found that the buffalo had left the jungle on the side next the river and had entered the reeds. These, which here form a border to the river of some sixty or seventy yards in breadth, are so dense as to effectually conceal an animal a yard off; they grow to a great height, often upwards of twenty feet, and so closely together that, unless some large animal has already passed, it is often difficult for a man to crush through them. Buffalo, the only game, except water-antelopes and lions, which ever enter them, form in such places as they constantly visit a net-work of narrow paths, generally running parallel to the river, and in some districts, especially those which are liable to be much disturbed, herds lie in them during the day, though, generally speaking, they form a cover used only for shelter, unless by a solitary bull or a sick beast, and as a refuge when pursued by lions or human beings. No place is more shunned by the professional hunters, who are shooting for hides and not for sport, and—from the total absence of trees, the close proximity at which you must fire, and the unpleasant chance of stumbling upon a lion, or, what is even more to be dreaded, a buffalo with an old wound—the bad name it bears is not altogether undeserved.

We were standing by the bank, just after making the discovery that the spoor had gone in, when suddenly the "tcha" of a rhinoceros-bird was heard in the air above us, and on looking up we saw that it was flying high above the reeds in search of game. All at once, when nearly abreast of us, it made a hover, then a sudden downward slant, and lighted on a reed, from which, a second after, it hopped down, no doubt on to the back of some animal lying there; probably the very one we were after.

This at once decided me to go in, about which I had hitherto rather hesitated; and I did so after making my Kaffir climb up a great fig-tree, from which he would have a good view of what went on, and would be able to see by the waving of the reeds where the buffalo was, should I unfortunately disturb it before getting a shot, and then be able to direct me by his shouts. The one thing necessary in the reeds is noiselessness. It is not by any means easy to prevent them rustling, or occasionally a dry one breaking, but it must be done, or there is far more chance that the buffalo will kill you, especially if already wounded and enraged, than you it. As an old and very good hunter of mine used to say, "You ought to kill with a single bullet." Wounded game undoubtedly expects to be followed, and in such cover as this has the advantage of being motionless, and ready to detect the faintest sound that will give it a clue to its enemy's whereabouts, and will enable it to expect his appearance in a given direction, and while the hunter advances blindly it will remain quiet, patiently listening to every step, until it either sees him or the shaking reeds point out his exact position, when it suddenly and unexpectedly charges, and, as the numerous accidents prove, too often successfully. In more open cover it is generally possible to make a circuit, and approach the animal from a direction contrary to that from which it came; but it is impossible to do so in the reeds, for the spoor once left, the chances are very faint of your ever finding the animal again, and therefore you are forced to follow its trail wherever it goes until you find it, and in this lies a great part of the danger.

The buffalo had in this case made use of a track by which the game went down to water, and when near the river had turned into another narrow path which ran parallel to it, thereby enabling me to proceed much faster and with less chance of being heard than if he had forced a path for himself, more particularly as the reeds were in many places unusually thick, probably not having been burned for a long time, and so overhung the path that it was absolutely dark, and like going through a tunnel. After having been an hour inside, during which time I had not accomplished over two or three hundred yards, I came to a mud-hole straight across the track. I had already passed several of these places, which are hollows which the river on every inundation fills with soft mud and water, and are occasionally ten or twelve feet deep, but I had found means to get across them; this one, however, extended into the reed thicket on each side, and as it seemed deep, from the amount of mud the animal had taken out with it on to the opposite side, and as it was too broad to jump without noise, I preferred entering the reeds, dense as they were, to the chance of getting bogged, and disturbing everything within half a mile in my efforts to flounder out. So, as silently as might be, I searched for a crossing, opening up the obstructing reeds with my gun, and taking ten minutes to every two yards. The hole only extended a short distance, and just as I passed the end of it I heard the faint twittering of the rhinoceros-birds—a sound which I recognised as one made by them when sitting contentedly on an animal's body after satisfying their hunger, and which did not seem to proceed from more than a couple of yards off. It was an anxious moment, and for a second I wished myself outside in safety. Undoubtedly a buffalo, if not a lion, was close to me, and such of the former as lie in the reeds are equally formidable antagonists with the latter. I remained still for a second or two, and then, gathering courage, I stole on as if my life depended on my not even making a rustle; inch by inch I got nearer, till the twittering became so loud that I knew in another second I must see the game. Another pause, and then, with a steady hand, though my heart was thumping against my ribs in such a fashion that I half feared it would be heard, I put aside a few more reeds, and found myself unperceived so close to the mighty head of a buffalo, that had I stretched out my gun the barrels would have pressed its forehead. It was no time to hesitate, for at any second the rhinoceros-birds might discover my presence and give the alarm, so, aiming through the intervening stalks, I covered the centre of the forehead and pulled the trigger, bounding at the same instant into the reeds, so as to be out of danger of a charge. The birds rose screaming, and by the heavy struggling and crashing that I could hear I knew that the bull was endeavouring to rise. The thumping and noise lasted a minute or more, and then I heard the low death-bellow, without which no buffalo draws its last breath; so, rising, I approached the spot, though still cautiously, and saw that my huge antagonist was indeed dead.

It was the largest bull that I ever saw, and the mark of my morning's bullet proved it to be the same that we had been following all day. His horns met in the centre, in a way that I never saw equalled either before or since; and it was a matter of far greater surprise that the last ball should have penetrated to the brain than that the former should have failed to do so. The amount of weight that he carried on his forehead was wonderful, for the mass of horn that protected it, and which was nowhere less than an inch thick, unless in the centre, extended from the back of the head to within a few inches of the nose, completely overhanging the eyes, and measured over two feet in breadth. His neck, as he lay dead, came above my knee, and my efforts to move his head to enable me the better to examine the bullet-marks were totally unavailing. He had no tail, and hardly a hair on his body, but was, as I had noticed in the morning, extremely fat. He formed a grand picture as he lay there in the silence, with the rising moon throwing a flood of light over his immense proportions, while I waited for the return of the Kaffir from camp, where he had gone to get help to break it up.

The best buffalo-shooting is undoubtedly to be found in the reeds, particularly when a herd has taken refuge in them; for on such occasions none except the one fired at will stir, and sometimes not even it, unless to charge, and in consequence a very large number of shots may often be fired at them in a limited time. When hunting on the Nkwavuma in 1870, I had a good day in the reeds which are found in the upper parts of that river. Two Dutchmen were staying with me at the time, and as I am not fond of hunting with a large number of people, I had gone out accompanied by a single hunter, leaving the main body to go with them. We took our way up the banks of the Nkwavuma, partly in hopes of crossing the spoor of some troop that might have been drinking, and partly on the chance of any old bull or wounded animal that the rhinoceros-birds might point out to us in the reeds that bounded and concealed the winding stream. High banks, clothed with dense evergreens, confined what must at some remote period have been the bed of a very considerable river; and as these bushes, on one side at least, were a very favourite resort for the smaller herds of buffalo, I undertook the task of examining them, while the hunter skirted the reeds on the opposite side.

In some places the reeds came close up under the banks, and the belt of bushes dwindled down to a few trees; and as I passed such a spot the fresh spoor of a lion descending towards it put me in mind of a story I had lately heard from the Bombo Kaffirs about one of their number, who, when out hunting, accompanied by a

"THE RISING MOON THROWING A FLOOD OF LIGHT OVER HIS IMMENSE PROPORTIONS"

little boy, had sat down here to rest, and, sitting on the edge of the bank, had allowed his feet to dangle down. As the boy afterwards related, he suddenly saw a lion below them, and while he was still speechless with terror he saw it jump up, as a cat would at a low-flying bird, and catching his companion's feet in its fore-paws, drag him shrieking down. His cries soon ceased, and the scared little nigger, terrified out of his senses, made the best of his way from the ill-omened spot. It is only an instance of one out of hundreds of similar stories that might be collected from these natives relative to their losses from wild beasts.

I had gone about a mile when I crossed the spoor of two buffaloes, seemingly on their way to water, and turning off, I followed them down through the reeds to where they had drunk. I found that they had crossed over, and in consequence had to do so myself. This is a point in which the unshod native possesses a marked advantage. Much valuable time is often consumed in taking off one's shoes and stockings, and if, in the hurry of the moment, one neglects to do so, the continual squish-squash of the water afterwards makes a noise anything but conducive to silent stalking. I found that the best plan was to make two great gashes in the sides of my shoes, which allowed the water to escape at once, as, even if there are no rivers to cross, as is often the case in Africa, the heavy dew wets almost equally as much. On resuming the spoor I found that the buffaloes, after quenching their thirst, had gone into the reeds, so, making one or two well-known bird-calls to inform my companion of my whereabouts, and also that I was "on spoor," I followed them in. In ten minutes I had reached a portion of the cover where the game was fond of lying, and was momentarily expecting to find them, when suddenly there came the noise of breaking reeds, followed by a shot on the outside, and almost simultaneously I heard the native shouting out the "strong names" of his gun—a sort of semi-religious observance rarely omitted after a successful shot. On making my way out, I found one of the bulls lying dead, and was told that the pair had tried to break, but that the other had turned back at the report, and was still inside. I immediately went after him, and, aided by the openness of the reeds, which were much broken by the numerous herds of buffalo that frequented them, I soon came upon him standing, half-facing me, about fifteen yards off, and gave him a shot in the shoulder. Of course I cleared out of the smoke and reloaded, even although I could hear him crashing in the opposite direction. This is a thing that one should invariably do on principle, ridiculous as it may occasionally appear to be running in one direction while the game is making off in the other; and more lives are annually lost by its neglect than by any other accident. I never knew but one old experienced hunter, though it is the common fault of beginners, who did not do it, and that was my present companion, and that he had hitherto escaped may be traced partly to luck and partly to his remarkably fine shooting and steadiness of nerve, though I feel no doubt that ultimately, if he remains a hunter, an accident will be the result of his omission of this common precautionary measure. It is useless to trust to the ear to tell you which way the brute is going, for, besides the fact that a charge is made so suddenly that an instant's hesitation is fatal, it is curious that for a second or two one is unable to judge whether the sound is receding or approaching.

On again taking up the trail, I found that the animal was bleeding heavily, and in another ten minutes I again saw its black form looming through the stalks not many yards off, and at once fired, as it does not do to give them time to consider whether they will charge or not, but is better, by the infliction of a fresh wound, to make them resume their flight. This time it broke cover, and received my companion's fire, who had a splendid chance at it not ten yards off in the open, on which it took to the dense evergreens which lined the bank; and as a bull buffalo after its second or third wound proverbially becomes very dangerous to follow, great caution was necessary in doing so.

My companion took up the spoor, while I kept parallel to him a few yards on one side, and before many minutes had passed we heard its laboured breathing close by, though we were unable to see it from the thickness of the bushes; at last, however, I caught sight of it lying under a large tree, and fired at its ear, the only result being a shake of the head; I next ineffectually tried the shoulder, and getting emboldened, I then foolishly walked up to it with my empty gun, under the belief that it could not rise. The moment, however, that it caught sight of me it struggled up, and I might have paid dearly for my rashness had not Umdumela, who had occupied my vacated position, at once brought it down with a well-aimed shot.

While engaged in finishing this last buffalo we heard a tremendous fusilade going on up the river, as many as thirty or forty shots having been fired since we quitted the reeds, and as there did not seem to be any more fresh spoor about, we made the best of our way in the direction thus indicated. Half an hour at a steady trot brought us in sight of the Dutchmen's party, from which it proceeded, and we were at once told that no less than three troops of buffalo had been forced into the reeds, that the firing we had heard was while they were engaged in driving them in, and that, although there were a considerable number wounded, only three had been killed.

The scene was a curious one, and well worthy a description. The river-bottom was here about a quarter of a mile broad, and extended for about a mile in a straight line; it was filled to within ten yards of the banks—which were clothed with the densest jungle—with a level sea of waving reeds, in which the buffalo were standing; on each side stood a Dutchman, attended by a little knot of favourite hunters, the remainder of whom, to the number of about forty, lined the whole banks. Several rhinoceros-birds were hurrying about, alighting in the reeds, or rising with their harsh cries, unwilling to be driven from their food, while high aloft were circling a number of black dots—vultures—who had already scented the coming slaughter.

It spoke volumes for the dread in which the reeds are held that out of some fifty hunters certainly not more than ten, if so many, were inside, the remainder waiting without for anything that might come their way, but as far the best shooting was to be had inside, Umdumela and I hesitated no longer than was necessary to understand the position, and to gather what information we could as to the whereabouts of the different herds. It was no use to follow spoor, unless we should happen inside to come upon any that was unmistakably fresh, for so many buffalo had been moving about that morning that it would only delay us to do so,—so we simply went in and used our eyes; and as it was more than probable that if we found any, we should find a group of at least three or four together, we did not separate, though it is more usual to do so in such cover. Two guns cannot, indeed, in general, work well together, unless game is very plentiful, as the one leading will get all the chances, while his follower will have the pleasure of watching him fire, and of helping to finish off the wounded game, besides occupying the most dangerous position, for it is almost invariably the second or third of a line who gets caught when a charge takes place.

We almost reached the other side before we came across anything, and then a buffalo started from within a few yards of us, but, as we did not see it, we went outside, intending again to enter the reeds a little higher up. Just as we did so a small troop of eight or ten broke below us, and after a smart run we both got a distant, but ineffectual, shot. Resuming our original intention, we were walking up outside, when a very large buffalo cow, attended by a flock of rhinoceros-birds, came out, running across, upon which Umdumela, who was nearest, fired, and I made a rush to cut it off, but after a couple of hundred yards it suddenly pulled up, and wheeling round faced me; the spot was perfectly bare, not even a shrub anywhere about;

and I, in common with those who were watching and who now began to shout to me, fully expected a charge; however, I ran on, and was greatly relieved, as well as astonished, to see her lie down, evidently unable to go further. On getting close, I noticed through the long grass that her ears were still moving to and fro, and aware of the danger of going too near a buffalo when not quite dead, I made it a certainty by a bullet in the shoulder before I did so. I found on examination that the first shot, which we had both imagined to have been a miss, had entered at the flank and driven forward, a wound more often immediately fatal than almost any other; while mine had killed a rhinoceros-bird, which, even in death, had remained perched on her shoulder.

In the meantime the firing, both in the reeds and on the banks, had become continuous, and on re-entering the former we came upon several hunters loudly disputing for the possession of a cow which lay at their feet, perfectly riddled with bullets. Passing them, we proceeded down the lanes the game had formed, and in a very few minutes Umdumela, who was leading, raised his gun. I stepped on one side while he fired, and as soon as we could hear which way the animal was going, I passed him—gathering as I did so that he had fired at the haunches at three yards distance—and kept on down the lanes, which were here very numerous. Suddenly, on glancing round to the right, I saw a cow not five yards off, standing by one of the island-like clumps of reeds which separated the intersecting paths, quietly watching me. It was an instance of the danger undergone in such cover, as, had it charged the moment it saw me, I must inevitably have been caught.

As it was, I instantly fired into its chest and dropped it, bellowing, and then retired to the banks of the stream to load. Meanwhile Umdumela had come on, and after firing a second shot, joined me. He had seen two buffaloes—a bull that he had last fired at, and which had moved further back, and the first one, a young cow, which was standing a few yards beyond where mine was lying. While he loaded I advanced again, and catching sight of his cow I brought it to the ground, standing as I did so within a few feet of my own, which struggled up at the shot, and took my second barrel to keep her down. Three more hunters then came up, attracted by the firing, and finished these two off, and while we were turning them over, and examining the bullet-marks to see whether they had been previously unwounded, one of them, hearing us say that there was a third buffalo standing a little further in, went after it unperceived by us, and the first intimation we had of his having done so was the report of his gun, followed by loud and repeated grunting on the part of the bull, and every evidence of a furious charge having been made. Of course a simultaneous rush was made in the direction, and we found the man knocked down, and rather shaken, but otherwise unhurt. Nothing annoys native hunters so much as one of their number being injured, and the bull was followed with as much haste and noise as if it had been a harmless antelope, the result of which was that he charged us before we saw him, and it was only by luck that one of the half-dozen bullets hurriedly fired at him was successful in stopping him.

After this we again crossed the river, and commenced to search the opposite bank, Umdumela keeping near the water, and I going further in. After about half an hour had passed I heard him fire, and then his voice calling to me to look out, and in a moment more I could tell by the crashing and noise that a large herd was coming straight towards me; hardly an instant elapsed before I found myself, having taken refuge in a thick tuft of reeds, completely surrounded by the galloping animals, which, on both sides, almost touched me as they passed. Of course, I fired right and left, and as soon as I could recover my senses I shouted to those outside to be on the lookout also. I had hardly reloaded before I heard a volley and much shouting in the direction in which they had gone, and on forcing my way through the reeds I found three buffaloes standing in different parts of the open, and one dead, while scattered about were a dozen or more hunters busy loading, each, when he was ready, firing at the wounded one nearest to him, until they severally dropped, after receiving from six to ten shots apiece, while the one I took in hand charged viciously at every discharge, driving every one from the open, and only fell after six bullets from me and at least an equal number from the hunters. The next thing to do was to go back on the spoor of the herd and see whether either of the ones I had fired at had been left behind, but, though plenty of blood besprinkled the reeds, they had been able to keep with the rest. However, on returning outside, the hunters one and all disclaimed having fired at the heifer which had dropped dead, and, as there were fourteen or fifteen of them, and only three other buffalo killed, it said a good deal for their honesty; and as on examination only one wound was found, I concluded that she belonged to me, a supposition which was afterwards confirmed by my bullet being cut out of her.

As the camp was several miles off, and the sun on the verge of setting, we soon afterwards left the spot, though there were no doubt many buffaloes still standing in the reeds. Our numbers had been increased by several of our bearers in search of meat, and by some of the Bombo Kaffirs who were out trapping, and had been attracted by the firing, so that the line which I headed homewards amounted to not far short of a hundred men, and their triumphant hunting song could be heard far and wide, causing many a troop of gnu and zebra to raise their heads in astonishment and watch us as we passed. Every hunter wore at his belt the tails of all he had killed, and those who had none, and they formed a good proportion, were loud in their explanations and excuses.

Only twenty-nine had been brought to bag, though several hundred shots must have been fired; but when it is taken into consideration how seldom a single ball kills these large animals, and the excitement and consequent missing a scene of this kind was sure to produce, such a number as twenty-nine cannot be considered bad, and is, indeed, considerably the largest I have ever seen killed on one day. My own case might be instanced regarding the number of shots fired relative to the number killed; my share on this day being three head, while I had fired no less than eighteen shots, few, if any, of which had missed.

The very next day after this I witnessed a rare and most curious spectacle—a combat between two buffalo bulls. Many hundreds of the Bombo Kaffirs had arrived in the morning, some bringing maize-beer, maize, millet, and other grains to exchange for meat, but mostly to carry off whatever we might leave; and as all the hunters had to return with them to the scene of yesterday's shooting, to see that their hides were properly looked after, I went out by myself, merely accompanied by a boy of ten or twelve, then acting for my water-bearer who was laid up with fever. It was a tremendously hot day, and I could see no fresh spoor, so, soon after noon, I lay down under the shade of a euphorbia, thinking I might rest a little until the cooler afternoon should bring the water-antelopes out of the reeds and thickets in which they lie. Of course, I dropt off asleep, and did not awake until I was roused by my boy shaking me. "What's the matter?" I asked as I rubbed my eyes. "There's something going on over there," he answered, and then I noticed for the first time that the little fellow looked very frightened. He had hardly uttered the words, when there came a tremendous thud, and then a loud clattering sound, seemingly arising from some thickets a few hundred yards off; I had never heard anything like it before, nor had the boy, though he had been born and bred among game, and it was his ignorance of the cause that was making him frightened; so when I heard it again I took up my gun, gave him a hoist into the tree, telling him to keep quiet till I came back, and went to look. The sound was repeated at short intervals, and as I got nearer I could distinguish the tramp of heavy hoofs, so that I was not altogether surprised when I saw what it was.

On looking through the edge of the last thicket which concealed them, I saw two buffalo bulls standing facing each other with lowered heads, and, as I sat down to watch, they rushed together with all their force, producing the loud crash I had before heard. Once the horns were interlocked they kept them so, their straining quarters telling that each was doing his best to force the other backwards. Several long white marks on their necks showed where they had received scratches, and blood dripping down the withers of the one next me proved that he had received a more severe wound. It was a magnificent sight to see the enormous animals, every muscle at its fullest tension, striving for the mastery. Soon one, a very large and old bull, began to yield a little, going backwards step by step, but at last, as if determined to conquer or die, it dropt on to its knees. The other, disengaging his horns for a second, so as to gain an impetus, again rushed at him, but, whether purposely or not I could not tell, it did not strike him on the forehead, but on the neck, under the hump, and I could see that with a twist of his horns he inflicted a severe wound. However, instead of following up his seeming advantage, he at once recoiled, and stood half facing his antagonist, who, getting on his legs again, remained in the same position for several minutes, and then with a low grunt of rage, rushed at him. This time he was not met, and his broad forehead struck full on his rival's shoulder, almost knocking it over. The old bull then went a few yards off and stood watching the other for fully a quarter of an hour, when he walked slowly away in the opposite direction. Unfortunately, as it turned out, I did not fire at him, thinking one would be enough for me to manage; but the moment it disappeared the other lay down on the spot where it had been standing, and stealing up behind the shelter of a neighbouring thorn, I fired at its shoulder; it only made an ineffectual struggle to rise, and then I went up closer and closer, until I could see the back of its head, and shot it through that part into the brain. On examining it I found a deep hole in the upper part of its chest, and on the ground there was such a pool of blood as showed that one of the great arteries had been severed. It was otherwise slightly scarred on the neck, but there was no other wound of importance, though I believe that this one was sufficient in itself to have caused death. When it was afterwards cut up I noticed a slight discoloration of the brain, but my last bullet was sufficient to account for that.

Fights of this description, though probably not unusual, are rarely witnessed, and I should judge that any fatal results from them were most uncommon. The horn of the buffalo is not suited from its curve for stabbing, and unless their skull gets injured in their furious onsets, as I have heard of its doing, no very severe wounds are likely to be effected. I also believe that had the older bull been conquered, or, perhaps, after being conquered on several similar occasions, that he would have become an outcast from the herd, and would have joined the ranks of "solitary" or "rogue" bulls; and it is probable that this is the case with all those species of large game amongst which we find similar exiles.

These animals breed during summer, and most of the young calves are running by their mother's sides at the end of February. I have never heard of twins at a birth, though as in most points they closely resemble domesticated cattle, I can see no reason to doubt it. For about ten days after the young calf's birth, the mother separates from the rest, and after hiding her offspring in the long grass, remains within a quarter of a mile or so, visiting it at short intervals. As soon as it is strong enough to follow her she rejoins the herd, but hangs about the outskirts without entering it, and when danger threatens usually leaves the calf in some shady out-of-the-way spot, and provides for her own safety, sometimes when wounded entirely deserting it.

I remember once shooting a cow which had no vestige of an udder, and though this took place on the 16th May 1871, yet she proved to be heavy in calf. I fancy that she must have been born so, as no hyena would have had the daring to attack a buffalo, though they not unfrequently seize cattle by this part and tear it away. If so, it would seem to bear out two assertions that I have heard native hunters make, and the latter of which I quite agree with ; one being that the calves suck any of the cows which may happen to have milk, without reference to which has given them birth, and that if the mother happens to be killed, or, as in this case, has no milk, her offspring is adopted by the herd; and the other that, as with cattle, a certain number have their young at irregular periods, though the greater part calve at a certain fixed time.

A cow with a young calf is the most dangerous animal of the kind that can be met with, as indeed I have personally good cause to know. I remember in 1869 seeing from a considerable distance a hunter of mine catch a young calf which got up out of the long grass in front of him; the little beast immediately commenced to bellow lustily, and I saw the mother emerge from a thicket about a hundred yards off, and trot down—evidently in fear of being heard if she galloped—until within ten yards of him, when up went her tail, and, lowering her head, she charged, giving him the first intimation of her presence, as he afterwards said, by a grunt of rage as she reached him. She struck him low on the back with her forehead as he was stooping over the calf, and her horn caught in the belt which supported his bandolier, and by this she swung him round until it broke and he fell behind her. Then, without bestowing further notice upon him, she commenced licking her calf, in which operation I found her still engaged some five minutes after when I came in sight, having hurried down to the man's help. On seeing me she faced round, and I shouted to her to go away, for I didn't want to shoot her, and after some hesitation she disappeared with her calf in the thicket beyond. The man fortunately was more frightened than hurt, but had very wisely shammed extinction for the time.

The only serious injury I ever received while hunting was from a vicious old cow with a calf, and it happened towards the end of autumn, when the calves are mostly strong and well able to keep up with the rest of the herd, so that the one in question must have been born late. I was encamped on the Pongolo river at the time, and a most picturesque encampment it was. There were seventy hunters, and between thirty and forty bearers and servants, and they had built dozens of little grass huts round the great camp, which, in itself, was merely a thorn-fence protecting two sides, while a high bank that restrained the river when unusually flooded formed its back, and over which the branches of some trees which grew above were pulled down so as to form a sort of network supporting a number of hides which did duty for a roof. From these branches were suspended almost everything that could be thought of by the South African hunters,—bandoliers, powder-flasks made of buffalo-horn, hunting-knives in sheaths made of a buffalo's tail, hunting-charms, coats—mostly old red regimental ones, or military great-coats,—blankets of many colours, native dresses of wild cat or antelope skins, calabashes of all sizes, containing buffalo or rhinoceros fat to be taken home to the owner's wives, and sundry other articles of native manufacture or use, not to mention the number of bright gun-barrels which were placed against the bank, or hung by loops of hide from the branches above, or the dozens of assagais and sticks that accompanied them. At night this was lighted up by a number of great fires in front of the main camp, while every one of the little beehive erections had its own fire before the entrance, round each of which were grouped a number of natives employed in telling hunting stories, or in chanting hunting songs, in the intervals of leisure afforded by their principal occupation of eating the meat roasting on sticks at every fire.

I had left here early in the morning accompanied by two hunters and a gun and water-bearer, and after wading across the river we had found the spoor of where a large herd of buffalo had been feeding during the previous night, and this we followed until about noon it led us into a dense ukaku thicket. This, which is as often known as "Bamba 'mpalla," or the impalla-catcher, from its being supposed that that antelope is sometimes caught in it, is formed of a species of thorn-tree armed with myriads of tiny curved thorns, every one of which curves in a different direction, and which, growing very close together, seldom much exceeds seven or eight feet in height. Progress through it, even to the naked savage, is a matter of no small difficulty, while to the European, except at the expense of having his clothes torn off his back, it is almost an impossibility, unless he be, as I was, clad entirely in soft, close-fitting leather, which, however, is so dreadfully hot as to be all but unwearable. On entering it we found that the herd had separated, and I followed the larger spoor with one hunter, while Umdumela took the other. The portion I went after had merely made a detour, and on reaching the spot where they had joined the rest I saw that Umdumela had already passed, and in a few minutes I heard him fire, and then the angry grunt of a charging buffalo. Hurrying up, we found him standing over the carcase of a three-parts-grown bull which he had shot, and in a state of considerable excitement and anger at having been viciously charged by one that he had not meddled with, and which he had barely managed to escape by dodging among the bushes. He said that it was a cow, and as I remembered having seen the track of a young calf when we were following them, I suggested that it was probably its mother, and after a careful search we hit off the young one's spoor and soon had it safely secured; and as I thought it seemed old enough to do without the maternal milk, and wished to get some to take out to the colonies with me, I sent my gun-bearer away with it to camp, before following up the herd. This we had to do for some hours, as they had been shot at a good deal, and were not inclined to stop soon when once they were disturbed; but at last we heard them breaking through the bush on the outside of which we were, and a smart run to cut them off ensued, in which I was able to pass the others and to be within two hundred yards when, after galloping through a small open in view, they pulled up and faced round to have a look at us ere they took refuge in the next thicket,—a pause that I took advantage of to fire both barrels at them. I had hardly expected to do anything, as I had a smooth bore; but was agreeably surprised on reaching the spot to find a drop or two of blood on the spoor, and just inside the thicket to find a young bull lying dead, while the continuation of the blood-marks showed that both bullets had taken effect. After again following them for over an hour, during which they turned and twisted in and out of the numerous Bamba 'mpalla thickets, we found them enter one of rather greater extent; and as I had somehow got last, on seeing an opening parallel to the one down which we were going, I struck into it, hoping to get on faster. Just at this moment the buffalo could be heard breaking in front; and finding that I had got into a *cul-de-sac*, I had to turn back and follow the others, which I did at a run. Suddenly I heard a shot, and a buffalo charging, and quickening my pace, was in time to see the second hunter—a miserable coward—throw his loaded gun down and climb into a small tree. Everything in front of him was concealed by the smoke; but just as he left the path his place was occupied by a buffalo's head, the owner of which instantly catching sight of me, came on with a grunt. I had neither time to fire nor run before it struck me on the left knee, causing excruciating pain, and hurling me violently on my back. The brute passed over me, paused, turned, and again lowering its head, rushed at me, but Umdumela, who had run forward with his unloaded gun, seeing how matters were, and catching sight of the other hunter's gun on the ground, snatched it up, and put a bullet of six to the pound through her shoulder, making her stumble as she reached me, and after running about ten yards, drop dead.

On attempting to move I found that my knee was seriously hurt; and on ripping up the trousers we found the knee-cap had been thrust up out of its position, and that the small bone or knuckle immediately below it was fractured, while the whole of it was tremendously bruised.

For weeks after I could not even turn my leg without assistance, and was slightly lame up to last year, and even now cannot trust the sinews above the knee for any unusual exertion. There was little doubt but that the brute was the same cow whose calf we had found, as she proved to be in milk; and that she was not the one I had already wounded was proved by there only being a single bullet-mark, Umdumela having fired at another, and this one having as before at once charged him.

Only one species of buffalo (*Bubalus Caffer*) is found in the southern part of Africa (though another, differing principally in the shape of its horns, is met with further north), and it appears from the accounts of travellers to exist all over that continent. Slight modifications, however, are found in size, and in the shape of the horn,—the few buffaloes that inhabit the heavy timber jungles being unusually large, having blacker hair, and more widely-spread horns. Such, indeed, seems to be a general rule when animals of the same species are found both in the forests and in the thorns; several other instances occurring, among which the Nkonka, or male bush-buck, may especially be noted. A herd of buffalo, or, more correctly speaking, several herds, that exist in a district known as the Umbeka, on the north-east of Zululand, are famed as having a tinge of red in their colour, and as being smaller and more dangerous than any others. This last is a peculiarity that I shall again have occasion to notice with regard to the smaller of two species, or even the smaller variety of a single species, the smallest species of leopard, lion, rhinoceros, and crocodile, all being the most savage. No two buffaloes, even in the same herd, are ever exactly alike, and I never yet saw two pair of horns of precisely the same shape—a fact that has been noticed by Dr. Schweinfurth with regard to the Central African hartebeest and eland.

They are not, as I have said, found in any great numbers in the forests, preferring the more open thorns, where better feeding and equally good shelter is combined; but still they do exist, to a greater or less degree, wherever there is cover for them, and I have come across them in the most unlikely spots, as, for instance, in the great forests which cover the top of the Bombo mountains. This range, whose name literally means "the bridge of the nose," is a wall-like obstruction which gradually rises from the sea at St. Lucia Bay, and, running about N.N.E., attains to a height of some seven thousand feet, dying away in a number of irregular hills to the north of Delagoa Bay. It forms a natural boundary between Zululand, Swaziland, and part of the Trans Vaal republic on the one hand, and Nozingile's Amatonga, and that portion of the Abakwandwandwe tribe that followed the fortunes of Sotyongane's son, Mawewe. Much of its summit, which is an irregular table-land, broken up by perpendicular ravines and glens, is covered with large tracts of heavy timber forests, the home of the grey monkey (Insimango), whose skin, having a considerable marketable value among the natives, is yearly sought after by professional hunters. Several small tribes inhabit it, who pay tribute to the more powerful nations between whom they lie, and whose territory is generally decided by the natural divisions formed by the seaward passage of the rivers Umkusi, Pongolo, Nkwavuma, Sutu, Mbuluzi, and Mbululzane.

On one occasion I had to ascend it, for the purpose of seeing one of these chiefs about getting me a supply of carriers, and while sleeping at his kraal several of the natives—whose one idea on seeing a white man is to persuade him to shoot meat for them—assured me that buffalo were to be found in the adjoining forests, and as I had never shot one in such cover, I consented to go after them next morning. Our way, in the first instance, led along the top of the precipitous face up which I had clambered, often on my hands and knees, the day before, affording me a most magnificent view of the thorn-covered flats below, through which the broad Sutu gleamed as the morning sun struck upon its waters, while great patches of jungle, that I knew to contain twenty or thirty acres, seemed no bigger than a single tree. Opposite rose the irregular grey hills of Swaziland, while far off to the south could be distinguished some of the cone-like peaks which rise from the Zulu boundary. After passing along this edge we entered a deep defile, steep and stony, from which we emerged, after hard climbing, only to enter a similar one, until, after many hours' unsuccessful search for spoor, I sat down, fairly tired with so much unwonted climbing under the glaring sun, and told the Bombo Kaffirs who accompanied me that I did not believe that there were any buffaloes, and that unless they first found the spoor I should not stir from the spot on which I was, except to go home when it got cooler. On this, several of them started to examine the ground, and in about an hour one came back to say that he had found the fresh tracks of a solitary bull; and on accompanying him to the grassy slope on which he said that it had been feeding, I found that he had spoken the truth, and at once followed it into the jungle, where it had next gone.

This cover was quite different from any that I had before been in. The trees were huge thorns, very short and thick-stemmed, and throwing out long bare branches within a foot or two of the ground, which interlaced with those coming from the neighbouring trees in such a way as to form in many places an impassable barrier. All these were again bound together by a network of tough monkey-ropes, which twined in and out among them in the direst confusion. It shows the remarkable strength of the buffalo that he had been able to quietly walk through all this, snapping branches and creepers as if so much pack-thread; while it was only in single file, and treading where he had trod, that we could follow him at all. For three hours we kept upon his spoor, during which time he was twice disturbed, and once I fired as I caught a glimpse of him. He made no attempt to break, but on reaching one end of the cover turned back towards the other; and no doubt while following his spoor I must have more than once passed within a few yards of him standing concealed in the thickets, for the jungle, though long, was quite narrow. At last, towards sunset, when I was thinking of leaving him, two or three dogs which had just arrived with a hunter of mine, getting his wind as he approached the part where their master was standing, rushed in at him, and as he was probably much out of temper at having been kept moving so long, he at once went to bay; and while I was still a long way off upon the spoor, and from the denseness of the thicket was unable to increase my pace, I heard three shots at intervals, and found on getting up that the hunter had killed him. He turned out to be an unusually large-boned, though thin, animal, and his horns were remarkable for their great breadth and spread.

On this day, as on many others, I was out from sunrise to sunset without ever having a shot, unless the glimpse I once had of him can be called so. Good days there certainly are, but the bad ones preponderate; and many a time I have come empty-handed back to camp after an absence of from twelve to sixteen hours, occasionally without firing a shot, and so done up from the heat and want of water, that, although in nine cases out of ten I had not broken my fast since the previous evening, I was unable to eat, but, throwing myself down, would sleep till the following morning. Luck in large game-shooting comes most irregularly : sometimes for weeks you can kill nothing; you wound game almost daily, planting your balls exactly where you intended, but the animal always succeeds in making its escape. At last luck changes, and for an equal period your most hurried shot inflicts a mortal wound.

As an instance of this, I remember that in 1871, from June 12th to the 26th, I never bagged a single head, though I was out daily, had many fair chances, and severely wounded many animals. On the 27th I killed a buffalo, on the 28th three, on the 29th one, on the 30th a rhinoceros and a zebra, and so on, with occasional blank days, for several weeks. All the native hunters recognise these alternations of good and bad fortune, and ascribing them to the anger of the inhabitants of the spirit-world at some omission on their part, they usually sacrifice a sheep or a goat, and anoint their weapon with its blood. This produces the expected effect often enough to confirm their faith, as, their shooting having been demoralized by an idea that they cannot kill anything, the mere fact of their being reassured frequently brings about the desired result. The following two extracts from my journal will tend to show what even buffalo-shooting entails, and it must be remembered that other kinds, especially elephant-shooting, are far harder work.

"*October* 17, 1870.—A tremendously hot day. I left the place where we had been sleeping just as dawn was breaking, being anxious to catch the game on the feed, as there was no meat in camp, and we had all slept supperless. We struck the spoor of a herd of buffalo about sunrise, and from that time till late in the afternoon we continuously followed them, sometimes in view, though unable to force them into cover. We had not a drop of water, and my tongue and mouth were so dry that I could hardly speak, and the blood kept surging up into my head in such a way that I momentarily expected sunstroke. Within an hour or two of sunset we forced them into the Daka (a large jungle), and Mainga wounded a bull, which we succeeded in killing almost by starlight. We had then to break it up to get at the meat, and did not reach camp (about twelve miles off) till past ten o'clock—all this time without water. I drank gallons when I got in, but was too tired to eat, and went to sleep."

The next entry is shorter, but still to the point :—

"*November* 14, 1871.—The weather is fearfully hot. I hunted the whole day, leaving before dawn and getting back after dusk, and never got a shot, though I was 'on spoor' the whole time. Usikoto (my gun-bearer) broke down, and we had to leave him. Makumbi (a hunter), whom we left, quite done up, about five miles off, has not come in yet, and only Umpin'wembazo and myself, out of six men, got home together. On reaching camp I immediately went to sleep on the ground, but awoke hungry half an hour ago (10 o'clock P.M.)."

The largest number of buffaloes that I ever killed in a single day was only four, and one wounded and got next day, though I have heard of as many as eight or nine; such days, however, must necessarily be rare, not indeed from want of buffalo, but on account of the average length of time it takes to kill each, which cannot be much less than two hours. On the one in question I was accompanied by a number of natives who had come from their kraals, a distance of thirty or more miles, to ask me to shoot meat for them, and early on the morning of the following day a troop of buffalo having been observed to go into a thicket on the other side of the river, I sent them all across to try and drive them to the fords, at each of which a gun was stationed, and I had hardly reached one of the best, to the no small disgust of the man who had already chosen it, and who naturally enough feared that I should take most of the shooting, when a loud shouting on the opposite bank was succeeded by the cry of "Look out below," and in another second a herd of buffalo, their heavy gallop sounding above the roar of the river, came straight to the ford. The pass by which they would be forced to ascend on our side was very narrow, and from the height of the banks there was no other mode of exit, so, saying to the hunter to let them get through the deep water before we fired, so that they should not turn back, I took out half a dozen cartridges ready for use, and waited. They came into the water with a rush, but the current was too strong and rapid to be trifled with, and they soon steadied into a walk, and after passing through the deepest part their chests began to show above water. "Take the outside one on your side, and I will on mine, aim low and don't waste your second barrel—fire," and away went the bullets across the water, his with a more deadly aim than mine, for the one he fired at made a heavy plunge, and then floated, kicking, down the stream, while mine, struck by the ricochet, for I had aimed too low, reared up, and bounding forward, came on with the rest.

Before, however, it had done this, the sight of my gun

had rested upon another, and with greater success, for it was left, after a short struggle, standing alone in the water. The herd had almost reached the shore before I had got my next cartridges in, but they were much nearer, offering magnificent shots, and both bullets told loudly, though without visible effect. I had then just, and barely, time to reload before they were within fifteen feet of me, thundering up the banks on which we were, and as I raised my gun I heard a report and saw one drop in its tracks, shot, as we afterwards found, through the brain. My first ball I aimed at the head of a bull on whose chest a white mark showed where he had been already wounded, the second, with the muzzle of the gun almost touching it, into the shoulder of a cow. Neither fell, and knowing that my position, with an empty gun, was one of great danger if any of them chose to turn, I made one bound over the perpendicular bank, up a narrow path in which they had come, and found myself in half a minute safe under the massive roots of a fig-tree from which the water had washed out the soil. Here I loaded, and was soon after joined by the hunter. The first thing we saw that had to be done was to secure the buffalo that had floated down the stream before it reached the still waters where crocodiles were plentiful; and as some of the natives had already made their appearance on the opposite bank, my hunter, calling to them for assistance, at once plunged in after it, while I, sitting down and taking deliberate aim, tried to finish off the one I had wounded, and which was still standing where the others had left it. It was not more than thirty yards off, with the water covering about half of his chest, and I aimed the first two shots at his forehead, producing no effect, except to make it slightly shake it, as if bitten by a fly. No less than seven shots did I fire, the last five striking it fair on the chest, without its taking any more notice of it than if it had been inanimate, and then at the eighth shot, which struck it just in the same place as the others, he sank down with a low moan, but without kick or struggle, and was borne away by the stream. This is a trait of wild game that I have noticed in buffaloes, elephants, and rhinoceros, most generally with females; after getting into a certain state, generally, I think, produced by lung-shots, sometimes standing up and sometimes lying down, they will not die, and no amount of shooting seems to hurt them, at least they give no outward sign of its doing so, nor does it seem to at all hasten their end. I have found from experience that, with an animal in such a state, it is best to sit down quietly and have a rest, or a pipe, for half an hour, and before the end of that time it will probably be dead.

Numbers of natives had now come up, attracted by my repeated shots, and, calling my hunter back, I left them to do the skinning and to carry the hides with my share of the meat to camp, as payment for the remainder. On taking up the spoor of the herd, a little examination showed three distinct blood-marks; but as they were all going together we followed the broad trail, one on each side of it, so as to notice if any of the wounded separated. There was scattered thorn all about; but the nearest cover sufficiently strong to hold buffalo was nearly a mile away, and for this they were evidently heading; however, before we had gone half that distance, we saw one lying in the open, and after a cautious approach, we discovered that it was dead. It turned out to be a cow, one of those that I had fired at in the water, with a ball in her chest; and cutting off the tail as a trophy, we passed on and soon reached the cover. Just on its outskirts we found that one, and that the one that was bleeding most, had separated from the rest and had entered it alone, and the question arose whether we should follow it up first, or go in after the herd. I wished to do the former, and my hunter the latter. He, very naturally, wanted to find fresh buffalo, as those already wounded belonged, by hunter's law, to me, and as I did not care much, and felt pretty sure that the one that had separated would not go far, I agreed to follow the herd.

This we did; but as soon as we got inside we found that another of the wounded, which, by the blood besprinkling the twigs and leaves, we could tell was the cow which I had shot in the shoulder, had also separated; however, we kept on after the main body, and after following them through all their devious wanderings with the utmost caution—for the bush was composed of ukaku thorn, and there was not a tree in the whole of it where one would be safe—we came upon them standing in a little thicket on the outside of, and separated from the rest by a couple of yards of open. We both caught sight of their black shadows simultaneously, and crouched, and then, instinctively, without a word, each glided to opposite corners of the bush, so as to command a second shot when they broke; and I, the quicker of the two, took aim at the black mass—one could not distinguish which was head and which was tail—and fired first. Of course I jumped clear of the smoke, and as I did so I heard that vicious grunt that has heralded death to so many hunters, and a bull made a vicious charge into it, while I could hear the other buffaloes breaking on the opposite side. I had waited until he had passed me, and was just going to fire again when he wheeled and came towards me, causing me to think that he had seen me. This was probably not the case; most likely he was going to follow the rest; but thinking so made me fire hurriedly and bolt. I missed him clean, and when he noticed me I heard him utter that murderous grunt again. Bolting out through the open, I made for the little thicket where the herd had been standing, and diving in, dodged round, and threw myself down flat, meanwhile thrusting cartridges into my gun. As the brute followed me I heard my companion, who had luckily been unable to get a shot at the others, fire, and saw it make a heavy stumble as the ball struck, then another shot, and with a crash it fell within a few yards of me. I lay motionless, watching its head, uncertain whether it could rise again; but the moment the hunter's ramrod was heard at work it got up, and standing still, turned its head round in the direction of the sound. This was my opportunity, and aiming at the ear, I pulled the trigger; down it came again, stunned; but as I was too well acquainted with the thickness of a buffalo bull's skull-bones to fancy that he was dead, I jumped up, and running round behind it, I put the other barrel through its brain from the back of the head—the most deadly shot there is.

A careful examination of all the bullet-marks made us think that this was the bull that I had wounded at the river, though it was rather uncertain; as, if I had wounded it when I fired into the bush, and if I had not missed it, as the whistling of the bullet made me think I had, with my second barrel, then the full number of shots would be accounted for, even to their position; but as we could find no trace of blood on the spoor of the herd, and as it was certain that the wounded bull had come so far with them —for we found plenty of evidences of its presence in the thicket—we inclined to believe that, so far, we had accounted for all those first fired at, and that none had gone away wounded.

Skirting the bush, we now went round it, and took up the spoor of the cow, and in a few minutes I sighted her lying down about ten yards off, and in a good position for a shot. Motioning to the hunter to come up, I pointed to her, and whispering "Fire in half a minute," cautiously stole a little on one side to where I could get a good chance at her if she tried to rise after his shot. Just as I reached the spot he fired, and whether the bullet struck a twig or what, it missed the buffalo clean, and went away singing in the distance. Up struggled the cow, evidently very stiff, affording me a lovely shot, which I took advantage of, and kept her where she was, and he, running in with his second barrel, finished her on the spot. Hanging my fourth tail on my belt, we proceeded to search for the fifth and last, though the sun was now rapidly declining and we should have to hurry if we did not wish to have our long walk to camp in the dark, never a very pleasant thing in such a country, and especially disagreeable now on account of the number and daring of the lions. The spoor of this one, which was of the largest size, was easy enough to follow from the amount of blood on it, and I proceeded rapidly, thinking of the setting sun, till suddenly I heard a shot behind me, and the unmistakeable grunt, and wheeling round I just caught a glimpse of a buffalo's stern disappearing through the bush. On going back to where the hunter was, he began to blow me up for going on so rashly and so fast, asking me if I didn't know that he was responsible for my safety when he was with me, and what business had I to go rushing into danger when he was there for the express purpose of doing so?

This is no exceptional language. Many and many a time my hunters have besought me not to go into some danger, such as following a wounded buffalo up in reeds, or in such thorns as these, urging upon me in the coolest manner that it wouldn't so much matter to myself if I was killed as to them, because the white men on their return would hold them responsible for my safety, and besides, as one muttered *sotto voce*, "You owe us a lot of wages, and who would pay us if you go and get killed?" Beginning then in this way, he went on to say that he had followed me slowly, paying more attention to the thicket on each side than to the absolute spoor, and that a few seconds after I had passed he had seen the head of this buffalo protruding from a bush, evidently watching me with mischief in its eyes, that he had instantly fired, drawing its attention from me, and causing it to charge the smoke.

The first thing we did was to proceed to the spot where it had been standing, and the pool of blood on the ground showed that it was undoubtedly the one we were in search of, which, doubling back on its spoor, had taken up its position with the view of attacking any one who might follow it; and I had reason to be thankful that I was not alone, as my carelessness had placed my life in jeopardy. We then went after it again, proceeding, however, after the lesson we had received, in the most orthodox fashion. This consists in one man following the spoor, while the other keeps parallel to him a yard or two distant, carefully searching all the thickets and gloomy recesses where a buffalo might conceal itself, so that the undivided attention of the spoorer, who is most in danger, may be wholly given to his work, and in the case of a charge upon either, one may be in safety and able to use his weapon with effect. In the above way, then, we tracked it right through the bush, but as our progress was very slow from the caution necessary to be used, the sun was setting as we found that it had gone out and taken to the open, heading for a cover some half-mile off; so we retraced our steps and covered over the three killed with branches to keep the vultures off, as well as to scare the hyenas by causing them to think that some trap was concealed, and then made for camp well satisfied with our bag of six buffaloes.

Next morning, it being the general opinion of the hunters that the one we had left could not go far, we took up its spoor where we had left it. A disturbed or wounded buffalo always gallops in the open, and it was therefore easy for our numerous party, consisting of myself, a hunter, a gun-bearer, and three men to carry the hide and meat, to follow it so far; and even after it had entered the cover we experienced no difficulty until after we had found the place where it had lain down; but as here the last signs of blood ceased, and the spoor soon crossed and mingled with others of the same date, it became very hard to distinguish it. In cases of extreme difficulty like this the following plan is pursued : one man takes up the track, having a companion on each side of him, a yard off; none of the three ever speak, but so long as the one in the centre retains it he keeps up a low cracking of the finger and thumb, and when he loses it makes a louder crack, and with a motion of the arm indicates the direction he thinks it has taken; hardly a second elapses, if the men are good spoorers, before the cracking is taken up by one or other of those on the flanks, upon which the man in the centre immediately changes his position and goes on the outside of the one who has recovered it, and so they proceed across all the most difficult ground, which is generally open, until they reach cover, and then resigning the now plainly visible spoor to one of their number, the other two skirmish on either side of him, seeing that he is not taken by surprise, and ready to help him when necessary. This we had now to do, and it made our progress exceedingly slow, as sometimes the track was all but invisible, and in many places was so mixed up with others, that to avoid losing it altogether, we had to trace it even on our hands and knees, step by step. There is no work connected with hunting so tiring as tracking; the slow pace, the continuously bent head exposing the bare neck to the scorching rays of the sun, and the necessity of being always on the watch for a sudden charge, being so wearisome that it requires all the excitement of the find and subsequent action to atone for it.

The spoor led through several dense covers, where we

momentarily expected to find the animal, but, probably wishing to cool itself in the river, it kept on, and at last crossed at a deep and nasty ford, where it was with great difficulty that we could keep our footing. The water was low, and on the opposite side several hundred yards of shingle absolutely concealed the track; this again was bounded by one of those dense masses of overgrown evergreens that line most of the river-banks. As, however, it was only ten or twelve feet broad, and the buffalo had already passed through so many places where it might naturally have stopped, we did not imagine that it would remain here, and sending the hunter on the outside to search for the spoor leaving it, I went below, and in a few minutes found where it had gone in.

After following it for some twenty yards I came to a place so dense that I could not easily force my way through, although the buffalo had done so, and as there was a small opening immediately beyond, I came outside again, intending to pick up the spoor on the other side. Just as I did so, one of the dogs ran in, and instantly a yelp, followed by a grunt of rage, and by the heavy breaking of the branches, showed that we had at last overtaken it. Away went the unarmed natives to the trees for shelter, and as I ran up the open I caught sight of the brute charging my hunter, with half-a-dozen dogs jumping round it. I had no time to fire myself, but just as the animal seemed to me to have reached him he did so, and jumping round the bush by which he was, he threw himself down, while the buffalo, passing through the smoke, galloped into a thorn thicket one or two hundred yards off, where it came to bay with the dogs.

Leaving the hunter loading, I ran on, and getting to a small tree some twenty yards off, from which I could see it, I fired both barrels at its shoulder, the second bringing it to its knees. The dogs soon roused it from this position however, and as I was in my turn loading (I had a muzzle-loader, my breech-loader being out of order), my hunter came up, and on my pointing out the animal, passed on. He had almost reached the small tree for which he was making when it caught sight of him, and at once made a determined charge; he knelt down, and, levelling his big elephant-gun, waited, with a coolness and pluck that would have done credit to any European, till the animal was positively within a yard of him—until, indeed, it lowered its head, which a buffalo never does until it is almost within striking distance of its enemy—and then fired, at the same time bounding with wonderful activity on one side, while his adversary, struck in the centre of the forehead, fell lifeless on the spot.

On counting the bullet-marks we found five fresh, exclusive of the last, four of mine and one other, and no less than four old wounds partially healed, at once accounting for the bad temper the brute had displayed. On cutting it up we also found three of the old bullets, one of which, seemingly of eight to the pound, had passed through from side to side and stuck in the skin. It had probably been severely wounded in the first instance by that very ball, and after being followed up, and three more put in it, had succeeded in making good its escape for the time.

It would be incorrect to describe the buffalo as the most dangerous of all African game, though it has been stated to be so, and several authors, principally those accustomed to shoot from horseback, and to whom the

D

idea of following a wounded buffalo into the thickest cover it can take to is therefore a strange one, as it can only be done on foot, have mentioned their fear of it; and undoubtedly more lives are annually lost in its pursuit than in any other kind of hunting; but then it must be remembered that for one man who especially goes after elephants, rhinoceros, or other game, there are ten who make buffaloes their sole object. Generally speaking, they do not charge until after they have been wounded, though the contrary is occasionally the case, and I have personally known one instance of it. Another instance was related to me by my friend the late Mr. David Leslie, whose experience in such matters was very great, and who within a few weeks of his death had offered to write it down for me for insertion here. As, however, he was never able to do so, and as I have both heard the story from him and from the principal actor in it, I am able to give the more salient points from memory.

Mr. Leslie, who, in addition to his other valuable qualifications as a traveller and pioneer through the savage tribes of South-Eastern Africa, among whom he obtained great power and influence, for the use of which in her interests the colony of Natal must always remain his debtor, was a keen sportsman and a first-rate shot, and on one of his expeditions in the interior was out buffalo-shooting in the bush known as the Umbeka, which I have already mentioned as being the home of some herds of very small and vicious buffalo. The bush itself is chiefly composed of cactus underbrush, which forms the densest and most impenetrable cover imaginable, and in which it is utterly impossible to see an animal a yard off, and through which it is equally impossible to go except along the paths the game has formed. It is also exceptionally dangerous, for, while presenting from its thickness and the poisonous properties of its thorns, an impassable barrier to a human being, it is at the same time no obstacle whatever to any animal sufficiently large to be dangerous.

Mr. Leslie was accompanied by his chief hunter Untabine, and by several natives, and had tracked a herd of buffaloes into this bush, through which they had followed them, and had at last wounded one. This Untabine followed, while Mr. Leslie with some of the natives went after the others which were standing scattered through the bush, but they had not separated many minutes before the voice of the former was heard as if in pain, and Mr. Leslie, running back and up the path he had taken, saw him lying under the cactus, while a buffalo cow was trying to raise him sufficiently to enable her to use her horns.

The path happened to be nearly straight, and he was thus enabled to see what was going on at such a distance that no certain aim could be taken; but as no time was to be lost if he wished to save the life of the man, who was an old and valued servant of his, he at once pulled up and fired, and by great good luck the bullet, entering behind the shoulder, passed through the upper part of the heart, and the animal, staggering away, fell dead in a few steps. On going up to the man Mr. Leslie found that the brute had thrust its horn in between his shoulders, and that its point had come out on the opposite side under the right breast, from which latter wound his lung was protruding. This he pressed back with his hand, and closed the wound over it to the best of his ability by the insertion of two long thorns, and then he had the man, who was in the greatest agony, carried to camp, some miles off, where both wounds were sewed up. No one had for a moment imagined that such an injury could end otherwise than fatally, but to the general astonishment he gradually recovered, and after five or six months was able to go about again, ultimately getting perfectly well, and retaining no trace of his accident other than two tremendous scars.

Subsequently I hunted a great deal, when staying in my friend's camp, with this very man, and have heard from his own lips how it occurred. He said that he was following the track of the wounded animal up this narrow path, guarded on each side with walls of cactus, and that he suddenly heard a grunt close beside him, and as he turned round to look he saw before him a buffalo in the act of lowering its head. Escape was impossible, and almost instantly it accomplished its purpose, rendering him partially insensible from the sharpness of the pain, and he remembered little more until he was being carried home. It was found that the cow was unwounded, and that therefore its attack was a totally unprovoked one; and the instance is valuable as showing both how accidents may occur in spite of all forethought and skill—for this man had few equals as a hunter—and what a native may go through and yet live.

I remember another instance of the wonderful power the natives seem to possess of recovering from wounds which we should deem fatal, which was related to me by the hero of it, and whose scars left no doubt of the truth of his story.

He was a Zulu, a nation justly famous for their courage, and was noted, even among them, for his daring and success as a hunter. In point of fact he used to do what no European, nor, indeed, any one to whom life had any value, would care to do—namely, to hunt and kill all the dangerous game without better arms than a few spears, a sorry weapon to depend upon to turn a charging buffalo.

A book might be filled with his hairbreadth escapes and other hunting anecdotes that I have heard him tell, and on this occasion, on which he cannot be said to have escaped with anything but life, he was hunting, as he generally did, with only two or three dogs for companions. After following the spoor of a herd of buffalo for some time, he succeeded in crawling up very near, and in severely wounding one which was on the ground, and in planting another spear in it as it rose, and, after a chase of a mile or more, his dogs brought it to bay in a small open surrounded by thorn-trees, of which the native took advantage to endeavour to approach within the distance at which he could effectually hurl his spear. Unluckily, however, the buffalo saw him, and as is usual when baited with dogs, it at once left them and charged their master, who, throwing his spear into it, turned and made for the nearest tree, but, his foot slipping, was at once overtaken and tossed, the horn of the enraged animal striking him on the thigh. As he descended it again caught him, this time stabbing him in the side and tossing him so far forward that he fell on a thorn-tree, a broken stump of one of the branches of which caught in the wound in his thigh, and held him dangling there for several minutes, which, though the saving of his life, must have seemed an age to him as he swung about head downwards. The buffalo, missing its victim and constantly baited by the dogs, in the meanwhile moved its position, so that when the flesh gave way and he fell, it did not see him, and gave him time to crawl with what remaining strength he had left under the shelter of a friendly shrub, which concealed him when it, still unsatisfied, came back in search of him before finally taking itself off. He told me that his bowels were protruding from the wound in his side, and from the position and great size of the scar I could believe it, and that his thigh was dreadfully torn, as it must have been, for it still had a hole in it into which I could almost place my fist, and that he was eight or nine miles from the nearest village, and twelve or fourteen from his own home. It was a position in which most men in utter despair would have lain down and awaited death; giving in, however, must have been, from the way in which he spoke, the last thing that he thought of. He bound up the edges of the wound in his side with some of the long Umqokolo thorns every native carries in his hair; he fastened his belt above the one in the thigh; and then, slowly but surely, he made his way homewards, sometimes lying for an hour or two in a semi-conscious state, but on waking up always resuming his journey, till at length, more dead than alive, he reached the nearest kraal, which, very fortunately for him, for it is otherwise very doubtful whether they would have allowed him to enter, belonged to his uncle. He hovered between life and death for a long time, but his vegetable diet and healthy life turned the scales, and he lived to enter my service, having become a refugee from his native country, and he still hunts, though with the gun now, as much and as pluckily as ever.

Personally I have had fewer narrow escapes than most

men who have shot an equal number of buffaloes, though of course I have been often enough charged, but a tree or a bush, or an effective shot from some one else, has always averted the danger before it became very imminent; and on the only two occasions on which I have been overtaken by a buffalo, not counting the time the cow caught me, and which I have already mentioned, I was fortunate enough to get off with a few severe bruises. On the first I was out pig-sticking with a large pack of dogs, not far from the river Mbuluzi to the north-east of Swaziland, an amusement I had lately taken to. Our party, consisting of about a dozen men, was armed solely with spears,— for though I know it was unwise with such weapons to go out hunting in a country where there were plenty of lions and leopards, yet as I could not restrain the men from firing at the pig, I made the few hunters that chose to come on their idle days leave their guns behind. We had seen a troop of pig go into a small thorn thicket, and had instantly cheered the dogs in after them. The moment they got inside they gave tongue, and, as the muttered roar of a buffalo (when not uttered aloud) slightly resembles the grunt of a boar, I fancied that they had one of the latter at bay, and kept shouting to the dogs, hoping that they would force him out. It is probable that the buffalo, already enraged by them, was attracted by the noise I made; at any rate, the first intimation I had of its presence was its nose protruding within a yard of me, as he made a furious charge out, uttering the now unmistakable roar which has such a savage vindictive sound. My only chance was to throw myself flat, and as I did so it leaped over without touching me. It was instantly followed by all the dogs, and after running half a mile pulled up in the bare open.

It was anything but a nice position, for a buffalo baited by dogs will come at the first human being it sees, especially an old solitary bull like this; and when I considered that these same bulls have been known to take over thirty bullets, in good places, before succumbing, I hesitated about attacking it with spears only. However, I did not see how I could get the dogs off, and as there were a few stumps of trees scattered about, one of which was within ten yards of the animal, I thought that if I could reach it I should not have a bad chance; for, unless it made a headlong charge, when no dogs could stop it, it could not budge far with a pack of thirty baiting him, and I could severely wound most animals at ten yards' distance. So I collected all the heaviest spears which my people had with them, and making them spread round in a circle so as to distract its attention from me, I started towards it, keeping the thorn between us. I had almost gained its shelter when it saw me, and bellowing with rage, charged. I had often been told by older and more experienced hunters what one ought to do under the circumstances in which I now found myself, and, though it was embarrassing, I tried to carry out their instructions. I threw myself flat on my side, taking the longest stabbing spear—a very formidable weapon, as sharp as a razor—into my right hand, and lay still. He came on until he almost trampled upon me, when, probably having just opened his eyes and missed me, he pulled up, and then, suddenly catching sight of my position, he lowered his head and again came on. With my full strength I stabbed him in the nose, the long iron blade going right through it and pricking him in the chest, while he struck me heavily with his horn-covered forehead, and his hoof trod on the fleshy part of my left arm, causing the most horrible pain. But the nose is a tender spot, and he sprang back, and stood looking at me with his savage bloodshot eyes, which peered from under the mass of horn which almost covers the face of an old bull.

I wasn't altogether at ease about the result, but I knew that so long as I kept perfectly still and flat he couldn't stab me with his horns—their formation prevented that, and I trusted in my spear still. He made another rush, but not such a determined one, and again feeling the assagai point, he retreated on one side, but soon returned; this time coming from behind, and catching me between the shoulders. Finding he did not get pricked here, he absolutely kneeled down, knowing that he could not get at me in any other way, and began to pound me on the back with his forehead. The blows were very heavy and jarring, and I felt myself fast losing consciousness, when one of the dogs,—all of whom had been baiting him unnoticed the whole time—smelling the blood on his nose where I had stabbed him, pinned him by that delicate organ, and soon brought him on to his feet again, though in getting up he trod on me for the second time. The Kaffirs also ran in shouting, and one got near enough to send an assagai into the brute's ribs, on receiving which he made a blind rush, and I took advantage of the respite to gain the friendly shelter of the tree. I was not much hurt, though considerably shaken, and as the buffalo's evil genius made him come and stand directly underneath me, I took advantage of the chance, and with both hands and all my force drove one of the great spade-like spears right down into his vitals. He made a short rush, stood still, trembled, and then fell on his knees, on seeing which we all ran up, and stabbed him again and again as he attempted to regain his feet and bellowed with ineffectual anger, until, after displaying that wonderful tenacity of life which has been so often noticed, he ceased to struggle. None of the dogs were hurt, and except my left arm, which the weight of the brute had made into a sort of jelly, I was none the worse of it.

About two years afterwards I had a very similar adventure with a bull, differing, however, on the latter occasion, in my being alone, without dogs, and armed with a gun. It occurred in the reeds at the Nkwavuma, close to which stream my camp was at the time situated. I had not, contrary to my usual custom, gone out before dawn, but being knocked up and lame from two very hard days I had had, I did not get up till after sunrise, and then, lightly attired in a shirt and a pair of shoes, I went down to the stream to bathe. In the uninhabited game districts one rarely goes ten yards from camp without a native attendant, generally a small boy who follows one about and does any trifling services that may be required. It is not a custom of European introduction, but performed voluntarily by the natives, who are accustomed to pay the same kind of respect to their chiefs, and treat their temporary master as holding a similar position. Another habit that becomes a second nature in such countries is to take up one's gun even when merely going a few

yards, it being quite uncertain what one may meet or
see even in so short a distance, and it therefore becomes
as natural to carry a gun as to put on a cap when going
out. On this occasion, then, though only going to bathe
some fifty yards from where a campful of people were
assembled, I was both accompanied by a boy and carried
my gun; but on arriving at the place, finding that I had
forgotten to bring any soap, I sent him back for some,
and in the meantime sat down to wait for his return. He
had not been gone half a minute when I heard the chirping of some rhinoceros-birds within a few yards of me in
the reeds, and thinking that they were probably settled
on a water-antelope, I went in towards them, and in three
or four minutes came upon a buffalo so standing across
one of the game-paths as to present me with its shoulders,
while the other parts of its body were concealed. I made
a careful shot, to which he fell; but before the smoke
cleared he rose and made off, and I, after reloading, took
up the spoor, which I found all covered with blood. It
took me a long time to come up with him again, although
he had not gone far, but the reeds were thick, and I had
to be very careful in going through them for fear of noise.
At last I saw him about three yards off, half-facing me,
and instantly fired at the point of his shoulder. He, however, noticed me as I pulled the trigger, and charged, and
I only escaped by a couple of feet or so, he passing me
within that distance. People not accustomed to positions
of this kind may very naturally ask why I did not use
my second barrel; but a very little experience of buffalo-
charging soon teaches the absurdity of attempting to do
more than avoid the first rush, which is made so instan-

taneously that one has rarely time to do more than jump a yard or two on one side, where, however, more especially in reeds, one is as safe as if ten times the distance off. If the buffalo afterwards turns and comes back to look for you, or should there be an open beyond your concealment, then your second barrel comes into play; but in my experience, when a buffalo does charge, unless from a very considerable distance, any time put off and lost in thinking of firing a second shot at it is extremely likely to be fatal to the hunter.

After passing me I heard the brute wheel, and again head down stream, until I lost the sound of the breaking reeds. It is a curious trait of large game that after the first rush their passage becomes inaudible, even though it be through the thickest of thick jungle. The sound does not even gradually die away, but suddenly, while yet quite loud, it ceases to exist; and yet, as the spoor afterwards shows, the animal is still going at full speed. On resuming the track I found that the buffalo was losing more and more blood, and by the way he put down the near fore-foot I felt sure that his shoulder was broken. Of course I had to be more cautious than ever, particularly when I found that he crossed and recrossed the Nkwavuma, probably for the sake of cooling himself, but which had the effect of bringing me into view while I was in the water, when he might be watching me from the opposite reeds. The stream is not broad, and for the above reason I never crossed it exactly in his footprints, but either above or below, until, on coming to a place where a small island divided it, and where the opposite bank was so high that I could not be watched, I took straight across. It struck me afterwards that I must have made a considerable noise in the water, as it was deep and rapid, and the slippery stones caused me to make more than one heavy plunge; but one is more careless when the sound of running water seems to drown whatever noise you make, and on getting out I at once clambered over the bank, not anticipating danger, but, from the force of habit, with the gun at the charge and ready for use. As my head rose above the bank the first thing that I saw was the buffalo's horns, which instantly disappearing, gave place to his tail. He had not turned round, but, lowering his head while he raised his tail, was in the act of charging. The distance was so short, scarcely more than a yard, that I had no time to put the gun to my shoulder, but, shoving it into his face, I pulled the trigger, and threw myself headlong under a mass of those water-loving bushes which may be found in Africa, as in England, in the swampy places by a river's banks. It was no good, though. He put his head through the smoke, saw that I wasn't in the water, and turning round, discovered me, and with a savage grunt again lowered his head. Luckily for me I had thrown myself so far under the thickest of the overhanging branches, that he was forced to pull up, treading, however, as he did so, on my leg, and striking me with his head high up on the thigh. Then he retired backwards and charged again, not treading upon me, but again hitting me with his head, after which he began poking me with his nose, trying his best to shove me on against the branches, and so enable him to get his nose under me, and allow him to raise me to a height at which he could use his horns. He had already attempted to use them, but, unable to get them low enough, took this method of raising me.

It was the most dangerous movement of his whole attack, for I particularly wished to sham death, and at the same time had to resist his shoving with all my strength; however, I succeeded in retaining my position without any apparent movement, and in a few minutes he desisted. The next thing he tried, probably with the idea of ascertaining whether I was really dead or not, was to lick me over with his file-like tongue, an ordeal which, as in several places it nearly rubbed the skin off, was most trying to undergo without moving, and one which apparently satisfied him that he had killed me, though I have no doubt that he also felt very sick from the effect of his wound, the blood from which had perfectly covered me, for after standing motionless watching me for some minutes, he at last turned away, and, to my great delight, re-entered the reeds. I lay perfectly still until he was completely out of sight, for I could not reach my gun from where I was, and then rising and loading the discharged barrel, I also disappeared in the reeds. I had not gone in on his spoor however, but crossing above it (for the island was small), I skirted along outside to see if he had gone out, and on finding that he had not, I again entered exactly opposite to where he had gone in, and after moving quietly forward for a few minutes I saw that I had acted rightly, for I could see his black outline lying down, with his head turned in the direction in which he had come. He was not in a satisfactory position for a telling shot, and as I had no desire for a repetition of the late scene, and wanted this bullet to end the matter,

I slightly shook the reeds, in the hope that he would rise and afford me a good chance. This, however, having no effect, I took a dry reed and broke it, with a like result. I now felt pretty sure of how things were, though not quite, and to make certain I threw the broken pieces on to his body, and that failing to rouse him, I went up and found him, as I now expected, stone dead, his last thought evidently having been to lie so that he would front any one who followed him.

I was just in the act of severing his tail, when I heard my Kaffir name shouted, and on forcing my way through the reeds I found a couple of hunters, accompanied by the little boy whom I had sent for soap, come after me. I had forgotten how peculiar my appearance must be, having nothing on but a shirt completely saturated with blood, much of which had run down into my shoes, while a few daubs ornamented my face, with no hat or cap on, and my long hair waving over my shoulders; but the hurried way in which the men came across, and in an evident fright asked me where I was hurt, reminded me, and I eased their minds by jumping into the river, and there removing the stains.

Though I have often, as I have already mentioned, been indebted to others for a saving shot at a critical moment, it has rarely fallen to my share to be in my turn of equal service to them, and I only recollect one occasion of the sort, and then each of my two barrels prevented a wounded buffalo from doing damage. The animal in question had been fired at by one of my hunters at dusk, close by a water-hole, which they were both approaching with the same thirsty intent, and, according to his account on his return to camp, it was so hard hit that its escape was only owing to his fearing to follow it up in the rapidly-increasing darkness, and, as he expressed himself certain that his bullet had struck about the shoulder, and that the animal was lame, we concluded that he had broken that limb, and that it would be in consequence incapable of going far, and therefore decided to go after it and finish it off next morning before separating for the day's hunting. The spoor was soon found; and as we fully expected to discover the brute close by, we followed it with great caution through the denser thickets, until, its lair of the previous night having been passed, and on seeing that the track—now of the early morning—led out into the open, where, despite the shelter of a few thorn-trees, it could not well conceal itself, we pressed forward as rapidly as possible. The ground was hard and the grass short, rendering spooring so difficult that before long our party was considerably scattered, many of us doubting whether the marks which the others were still slowly deciphering were indeed those of the buffalo of which we were in search, as we fancied that it was too severely wounded to have left the coverts.

Just at this moment a thorn a couple of inches long, hundreds of which covered the ground, ran into the sole of my foot, through a weak spot in my shoe, and as I staggered about on one leg trying to pull it out without leaving the point in, I heard a volley to my right, and on looking up, saw a buffalo running across me about two hundred yards off. Out came the thorn, without the point of course, and away I went as hard as I could race after it. There was a hunter and two boys further to the

"IT NOW CAUGHT SIGHT OF THE BOYS"

left, and consequently much nearer to the buffalo, but even they would not have succeeded in cutting it off had not a dog that accompanied the former run in, biting at its heels. This provocation brought it round at once with a vicious grunt, and a second afterwards the dog was lying on its back yelping, while the bull with nose in air came straight back at the hunter, who, instead of taking time and giving it a ball in the centre of the chest at a few yards' distance, which would probably have stopped it, fired at once, and, foolishly aiming at the head, the bullet merely grazed one of the horns, upon which he immediately betook himself to the nearest tree. Just as he seemed out of the reach of the buffalo, now not a yard off, the branch to which he was clinging broke, and down he came half way, his legs hitting the astonished old bull in the face, who, though unable to stop at the second, had evidently seen its adversary's predicament, and wheeled round to have another go in at him. At this moment I was about five-and-twenty yards off, still running, but at once pulled up and let drive at the brute's shoulder as it came round, causing it to again turn its attention in my direction. It now caught sight of the boys,—who were unarmed, except with spears, charged determinedly after them, and, as there were no trees near enough to save them, and no one but myself had a loaded gun, would no doubt have caught them, had I not shouted to them to run past me, and when the animal arrived in pursuit exactly opposite and not five yards from the bush behind which I was, I luckily dropped it dead with a ball through the top of the heart. On examination we found that last night's bullet, instead of being in the shoulder, had merely passed through the hind-leg about half an inch above the hoof, causing the animal to limp a little, but in no way disabling it, a fact about which the hunter had to stand a considerable amount of chaff before the day was over.

It is most difficult to ascertain to what age buffalo live, though, as old solitaries have been known as such for twelve years, it is probable that, unless cut off by some of the numerous accidents that they are liable to, thirty years would be under the mark. At the same time, it is impossible for me to do more than guess, as among the many hundreds that I have seen dead, there was not one that had come to its end through natural causes; and lions alone are a sufficient explanation of this, as any sick, disabled, or weak animal becomes their certain prey. Gradually and by degrees they are decreasing in numbers, and retiring further and further back, decimated by the hunters' guns, until, in a few years I expect that a buffalo will be as scarce as an elephant now is. They have only two enemies, man and lions; but as the former follows them through the live-long day, often wounding when he does not kill, and the latter takes up the chase at nightfall, and unless he catches one does not retire till daybreak, while both occasionally change their times,—the lion, pressed by hunger, following them during the day-time, while the hunter spends the night in ambush near their drinking-hole,—it is not to be wondered at that in places where, even in my own day, herds varying from ten to a hundred were common, there are not now ten head in all to be found.

Their habits are in general much the same as those of

other large game. They graze, lie down, and go to water at regular intervals during the twenty-four hours. About sunrise they drink a sufficient quantity to last during the long hot day, and then make their way to wherever they may have determined to sleep. This in summer is generally on the highest and most breezy spot to be found, under the shelter of two or three trees; in winter, in the thick jungle. They do not lie further from water than possible, as the moment the sun goes down, often before, they go straight to refresh themselves with a bath and drink before feeding, which they continue to do till soon after midnight, making the most horrible maze of track imaginable. They then rest and chew the cud for some time, getting up and continuing grazing until it is time to revisit the river or hole, and so onward to their lair. It is a common practice among hunters when in the neighbourhood of any rising ground, to ascend it at early dawn, and if there are buffalo about they have a good chance of seeing them making for the spot they will lie in during the day.

It is of the greatest importance to the hunter to know such of their habits as will aid him in finding them. By practice it becomes easy to decide whether the spoor in question be that of the morning or evening march to water, or whether where they have been feeding was before they lay down or not; and on this being correctly done depends whether you have to follow the track for five or six hours, or find them in one; and ultimately, whether you have a good day and several shots, or no time to follow them after they have been once disturbed. In the hot weather their morning journey is usually a long one.

It is not easy for them to find a sheltered yet cool place, and even when one does come upon them lying in the shade, it is a difficult task to drive them into thick cover, an almost impossible one with a small troop of ten or twenty head. The great herds take it very coolly, often allowing a hunter, especially a European, to walk within 150 yards of them, standing in a mass with lowered heads, evidently not quite sure whether they need take the trouble to run; but they soon tire when once started, and make for shelter. They stand in the same way when they see a lion; but it is curious that, as far as men are concerned, there is really no danger of a charge. As a rule, without exception I believe, unless after nightfall a buffalo will never attempt to advance upon any one out of a herd in the open. Even when wounded, it is a sign that they are altogether done up if they separate from the rest where there is no cover, and the real character of the animal does not show itself until, after much hard and very hot work, you have forced it to take to its strongholds, the thorn thickets or the reeds.

A bullet entering anywhere may produce a mortal wound, so much depends on the angle you fire from, but still there are certain spots better than others. Generally speaking, at the shoulder if it is broadside, in the flank when three parts turned away, and at the root of the tail when stern on, are all dead shots. Under some circumstances the head presents the best mark. The cow has a broad forehead, in almost any part of which a bullet is fatal on the spot, as also behind the ear; but it must be remembered that they carry their heads straight out, and unless feeding or standing square to you a ball is apt to glance. A bull, on the contrary, is quite invulnerable in this part of the body for all practical purposes. I have seen them shake their head when hit in the ear, as if stung by a gnat; and though there is a place just above the eyes, between the horns, an inch or two long by half an inch broad, it is the merest chance if they drop to a shot aimed there. You may, however, stun a bull by a ball in the head, and I remember a case in point. I had got close to one in thick jungle, and aimed at the ear, bringing it down on the spot; and thinking it was dead, both I and the Kaffir who accompanied me sat down to respectively take snuff and to smoke. After a few minutes we heard it breathing heavily, and I went up and, to make sure, fired point-blank into the other ear. The breathing ceased, and I returned to finish my pipe. After another five minutes, I rose and commenced loading, but had only got the powder down, when the brute jumped up and ran between us; luckily, however, too dazed to take any notice. We never saw it again, though we followed it for some distance, and I have little doubt it recovered. There are plenty of other instances of stunned buffalo getting up long after they were supposed to be dead. It has even happened that the hunter has cut off its tail as a trophy and as a proof that he had killed it (the usual thing to do), and has gone to camp for help to break the animal up, and on his return found it gone, and I once heard of one that got up while they were cutting its chest open to see whether it was fat.

A buffalo will often get away with a broken shoulder, especially if broken high up, but never, or rarely, when it is the hind-leg that is injured. The best place to finish them off when unable to rise is in the brain from behind, between the horns.

I have before remarked the wonderful tenacity of life these animals display under wounds of the most fatal kind, and another instance of it occurs in my journal for 1871, which so well illustrates it that I will give it here :—

"*June* 3*d*.—They found an old rogue buffalo in the Daka to-day—a most ill-tempered brute. I was sending two messengers into Zululand, and while passing through that bush on their way, it repeatedly charged them, driving them up trees, and preventing their getting through, and it was with some difficulty that they managed to get back and report to us; but as soon as Dupre heard it, he at once started in pursuit, accompanied by four or five hunters, all sick men, who for that reason were at home, leaving me much disgusted at having to stay behind (I was at the time laid up with the injured knee I have already mentioned). They had no difficulty in finding the spoor, but such an account of the ferocity of the animal had been given by the two boys, that all the hunters disappeared in the first few yards—got lost, they said—except one. He, a very plucky fellow, accompanied Dupre, and they had not gone far before the brute charged him. He waited until it almost touched the muzzle of his gun, until, in fact, it lowered its head to toss, and then pulled the trigger, but the gun missed fire, and it was only by Dupre's firing in the nick of time that he escaped being gored, and was only knocked down; the animal staggering forward and coming to its knees before it went on. Unfortunately the man was a good deal bruised, and Dupre had to assist him to camp, instead of following the buffalo as he would otherwise have done ; but as it is unsafe for the boys to go in even to fetch firewood, it must be killed to-morrow.

"*June* 4*th*.—Dupre and all the hunters went into the Daka after that brute of a rogue. They scattered all over the bush, and at last three of them found it, after a long hunt, lying concealed close by where three paths met. It instantly charged, and they fired in succession, the first two bullets not making the slightest impression. The last man, or rather boy, for he was only fifteen, being a favourite of Dupre's, had a double rifle, and fired right and left, bringing it down the second shot. It is very rarely that a buffalo will keep on charging straight in the face of well-directed bullets, such as these were, but, as the hunters said, this one wanted to kill a man before it died. It was found to be one wounded by Shuga on the 5th of last month. His bullet of six to the pound had gone right through the body, and was cut out of the skin on the opposite side, having penetrated the stomach and liver, in consequence of which the whole of the intestines were rotten and most offensive, and no doubt it would ultimately have caused its death, though the length of time, a whole month, shows how tough it was."

Many other instances have come to my knowledge, sometimes of their making a fight of it for some time after they had got a ball through the heart, sometimes of their recovering from wounds which are usually considered certain death, and it is not an uncommon thing to extract half a dozen old bullets from the body of one when killed, some of them having evidently been there for years.

CHAPTER II.

RHINOCEROS.

ONE day in spring, when although, and perhaps because, we had as yet had no rain, the heat was more overpoweringly great than it was in summer, four of us found ourselves late in the afternoon on the brink of a small waterhole, and in a few seconds afterwards each individual was lying in the deep mud which surrounded the lukewarm and beastly stuff that, though composed of every nastiness under heaven, we dignified with the name of water, and which we were at that particular moment only too glad to get.

We had left our camp on the Black Umfolosi on the previous morning, and had gone to sleep at a place some twenty miles distant, where the native who guided us had assured us we should find plenty of water, as well as the buffalo we were after; but on getting there at sunset we found the hole dried up, only about a breakfast-cupful of liquid mud being procurable after digging as deep as we could without a spade, and in consequence we were forced to sleep the whole night, and hunt the whole of the next day without a drop to drink, until, when nearly exhausted after upwards of thirty hours without being even able to moisten our tongues, we had seen the fresh track of game that ultimately landed us at this water-hole.

It was already so late, and the sufferings we had all undergone without water under that broiling sun had so fatigued us, that it was determined we should sleep where we were, and not attempt to reach camp that night, especially as, having killed nothing, and there being plenty of fresh spoor about, we were in no particular hurry to return now that we had found water; all places being much alike to hunters so long as there is game to be found. Two of my comrades therefore started off in different directions to look for food, and I did the same, as soon as I had pointed out to the boy who carried my mat the spot to form the camp in.

At first I followed some of the buffalo-tracks which were so numerous, but after going a little distance I found that they joined, and the footprint of one of the hunters warning me that he was already after them, and that it would be useless for me to go further, I turned off into the thickets and glades in search of anything that might be feeding, and just at dusk I saw a white cocked-up tail about twenty yards off. The thicket was too dense for me to see anything more, and covering it, I fired without any idea of what the animal might be. As the smoke cleared I ran forward and saw an nkonka, or male bush-buck, running round in a circle, evidently stupified by the shot, and as I had learned by dear-bought experience that they are nasty beasts for charging, I thought I would rather waste another bullet than go up to it as it was. I afterwards found that the first ball, entering exactly where it was aimed, had pierced right through the animal and had come out at the chest. It fell to the second, and then I had the hard task of carrying it to camp, and as an nkonka is generally supposed to be a good load for two, and I have seen four men carrying the larger specimens found in the heavy timber jungles, it may be imagined that my chest and arms ached for some time after I had thrown it down. It was lucky that I had come across this antelope, for half an hour after my return the two hunters came in empty-handed, saying that the herds of buffalo they had respectively been after had not remained in the neighbourhood, but had crossed the open and gone in the direction of the hills; and indeed in this hot dry weather they would be sure to make for the highest ground, only coming down to drink.

Our camp was a primitive one in all ways, for I had been guided in choosing it chiefly by the sight of a dead tree, the nearness of which would save our one boy a good deal of trouble in getting firewood. I had not, however, while doing so, altogether forgotten my wood craft, and from the other side of the umtombe tree under which it was placed, it was impossible to see our camp-fire, so that whatever game might come to the water-hole to drink during the night would not be disturbed by its glare. Several small bushes grew round the trunk of the tree, and those in the centre had been cut down and added to the others, and when the fire was lighted and the shoulder and legs of the nkonka stuck on sticks round it to roast, it did not look by any means an uncomfortable sleeping-place, nor unpicturesque with the flame gleaming on the barrels of the guns standing against the tree, and lighting up the whole interior, while it made the enclosing bushes look the blacker and thicker by contrast.

In about an hour the first shoulder was done, and the boy brought it to me and stuck it up in front of me by means of the stick which had already been supporting it while roasting, and I, drawing my hunting-knife, and sharpening a stick for a fork, was just in the act of breaking my fast for the first time that day, when I heard a sudden succession of puffs, like a train just starting, and could distinguish the heavy foot-fall of some animal. In a second everybody was on his feet, and in another we were all scrambling up the tree, I, I am sorry to say, still holding on to my shoulder of antelope, and oblivious of the fact that I had left my gun down below. We were barely in time; indeed, if the rhinoceros had charged straight up to the tree it must have caught me, but it was not necessary to go very high, and I was soon able to watch its movements. Hardly ten seconds had elapsed since I had heard the first warning puff, and now our fire was scattered in every direction, and the vicious animal was stamping upon it and everything else it saw, and squealing with rage the whole time. The meat had disappeared, some of it trampled into the ground, and some thrown yards away by its feet; two great burning logs of wood were smoking on the top of my spread-out bed, and even from where I was I could smell the smouldering blankets; the remains of my water-calabash were lying in every direction, and everything in camp, save my gun, which the brute had not so far touched, was more or less destroyed. It was enough to try any one's temper, and I asked the man next me if his gun was loaded, and on getting an affirmative answer, I told him to pass it over to me, and propping myself up against the trunk to prevent myself being knocked down, for it was an elephant-gun of six to the pound, I aimed at the shoulder of the trampling and squealing beast, and pulled the trigger. A stillness followed the report for a second, and then a heavy thud, and after that violent struggles on the ground. The other hunter had a double-barrel, and emptied both of them into the struggling mass below him, but despite the shots the brute regained its legs, and went away the moment after it did so; its vicious temper much sobered by the treatment it had received. Ours were not, however, improved by the incident, and it was all I could do to prevent one of the hunters, who was almost speechless with rage at losing his supper, from giving chase on the spot. We had, it is true, the satisfaction of knowing that the upetyane, for it was one of those vicious representatives of the 'Black' species, had received a wound that would to some extent punish him for his unprovoked attack, but a shoulder of antelope was not much among four famished men, for of course I shared it with the others, and the loss of my water-calabash was a serious one where it could not be replaced.

I rather over-slept myself next morning, for the sun was just rising when I awoke, and I found that the two hunters had started a few minutes previously on the spoor of the rhinoceros. It was not difficult to follow them, as the heavy dew on the long grass showed very plainly where they had passed; and as I could do so at a run, while they had to slowly pick out the toe-marks of the animal, which, despite its great size, makes but a faint spoor on the hard ground, and as the dew had since fallen, rendering it all the more difficult to do so, it was not long before I overtook them. The beast was not bleeding, as indeed we had not expected, the thick indiarubber-like skin closing so quickly over a wound as to make bleeding, except in rare instances, next to impossible; but it was unsteady in its gait, and in more than one place the marks on the ground showed that it had come to its knees. We therefore fancied it could not go far, and hunted with the greatest caution through the thickets into which it had entered, even though the general opinion was that we should find it dead.

We passed several places where it had stood under the trees, and at last we came to where it had lain down, and where we could see that it had passed the night, and had not left until daybreak. The spoor was now easy to follow; indeed, it was not necessary to look at it much, for once assured we were following the right animal, the broad trail of where it had brushed the dew off enabled us to go after it as fast as we liked. There was no question either of whether we should find it alive or not, as, facing the open, it had gone straight across, a distance of some two miles, heading for a line of thick bushes that bordered an old water-course beyond, and if it had strength to do this, there was no doubt it would also have strength sufficient to make itself very formidable when we found it. As we neared the edge of these trees, the wind, which had hitherto been coming in little puffs from every point of the compass, could be felt blowing on our backs, rendering it no longer safe to follow the animal by its spoor, and we had therefore to turn off, and, keeping well out on the flat, to go down the water-course for half a mile, and then, crossing it, to go for about three times that distance up it, when we concluded that the rhinoceros was probably lying somewhere between us and the spot at which its spoor had entered, a mile lower down. The fringe of jungle which bordered the water-course on either side was nowhere more than thirty yards across, and though, as in all semi-moist positions, there were a good number of evergreen bushes, which made some spots very gloomy and dark, yet on the whole it was pretty open, and had a fair sprinkling of trees easy to climb, and sufficiently large to protect one even from so powerful an animal.

It was decided that I and one hunter should search the ground on the side on which it had entered, while the other should keep parallel with us on the opposite side as well as he could, and that, if possible, whoever found it first should warn the others of his having done so by making the bird-call in common use among hunters, and on this understanding we entered the thicket. When we had gone about half a mile, my companion, who was nearer the water-course than I, called me with a low whistle, and on going to the spot I found him bending over the fresh imprint of a rhinoceros's foot, though he was uncertain

RHINOCEROS.

whether it had been made by the one that we were after or by another. I was, however, able to set that question at rest at once, as one of the toes of the wounded beast was unusually small, and this was undoubtedly the same animal.

It had come from below, and here, turning on its track, had gone back again—a manœuvre that proved to any one who had before seen instances of this animal's cunning that it was thinking of lying down, and was taking this precaution in case any one should follow it. The other hunter was soon brought to our side by means of a whistle that resembled the accentuation of the words, "Mena, nangu'mzila-bo," "Here, here's the spoor," and leaving him to do the tracking, we searched the ground on either side, but a few yards in front, until the low chirp of a rhinoceros-bird struck our ears, upon which we left the spoor, and, joining, stole up towards the sound. Guided by the continued chirping, we kept on until I made out the loom of the animal lying in a bare spot in the shade of a thick thorn-tree. There was another thorn-tree between us and it, and, motioning to the Kaffirs to follow me in single file, I glided towards it, sheltering myself behind its trunk, and hardly daring to breathe for fear of disturbing the watchful birds. At last we all three knelt down behind it, not ten yards from the unsuspicious brute, and, in the lowest of whispers, I told the one who had a double-barrel to fire at it as it lay simultaneously with myself, so that we should all have a shot left when it rose. It was lying on its knees, nearly broadside to us, its long protruding snout turned in the direction of its upward spoor, and its bare black hide glistening where the sun's rays, penetrating the thick thorns, danced upon it. I aimed at the shoulder, it being so near that I could pick out the exact spot that I thought would be fatal, while my comrade took it in the head, having a crotchet that there was some vulnerable spot there.

Smoke always hangs long in jungle, but the moment after we fired our ears warned us, and we sprang into the tree with our second barrels undischarged, while the other hunter, who had waited to plant his ball in the brute's chest, barely escaped by dodging to one side of the tree as it passed on the other. There was just time to send another bullet after it before it disappeared, and then we all got down, and, after reloading, prepared to follow it. This was all very well so long as it kept galloping; but when, after about half a mile, it reduced its pace on entering a large thorn jungle to a walk, and began to stand about, come back on its spoor for ten yards, make short parallel lines, and, in a word, do everything that its cunning suggested to lead us astray or within its reach, it became frightfully dangerous, and after a short time its spoor became such a labyrinth of converging circles, some larger and some smaller, that, besides the difficulty it caused in tracking it, it made the risk to ourselves so great that I thought it my duty to ask the men whether they cared to go on, and though they both answered in the affirmative, they urged the advisability of our leaving it alone for a while, so as to allay its suspiciousness, and allow time for its wounds to get stiff. To this I agreed, though rather doubtful whether any lapse of time would make an animal with seven balls in it much less suspicious, suggesting that meanwhile we should make sure that it had not left this jungle, and that they should walk round on one side while I examined the other, and this being decided upon, we separated.

I had not gone very far when I came across a track, which a few seconds' examination proved was that of the identical animal, which, after leaving a maze of spoor that would take hours for us to unravel, had taken itself straight off to another cover, to which I at once followed it, only to find that after standing about in several places it had left it also, and gone on. No doubt the pain it was in rendered it restless, and as in the direction it now took there were only a few scattered bushes for some miles, I thought that the chase seemed likely to be a long one. On reaching the first clump, however, I found that it had stood there also for some time, and had wandered about round it, probably with the intention of lying down; though it occurred to me that its taking to the flat might be only a stratagem, the better to enable it to see any one approaching, and that I ought to be careful in going near similar places.

It was indeed lucky that the thought had entered my mind; otherwise it is more than probable that I should have walked heedlessly on, never dreaming of any danger in the open, until I had placed myself within its reach; for, as I got near the very next clump, it struck me that the shadow was unnaturally deep in one spot, and there being no tree of any size closer in I sat down by the one by which I was, and, after watching the suspicious place for some minutes, I determined to try the effect of a shot, as, even if I was mistaken, it would serve to guide the

F

hunters to me. I therefore covered the blackest part of the shadow and pulled the trigger, and in another second the rhinoceros, for it had been it after all, was charging straight towards me. There was no particular hurry, as the tree was an easy one to climb, and I waited until it was within fifteen yards before I fired again; the white flake on its chest where the big bullet had already entered serving as a mark. I could hear the clap of the ball as it struck, but it did not take the slightest notice of it, and for the third time I had to take refuge in a tree. This time, however, it did not go so far, but pulling up when about three hundred yards off, it walked under a thorn and stood, its wounds at last evidently beginning to tell upon it.

At this moment I saw the two hunters hastening towards me, having heard the shots, and I had to jump down and wave and shout at them before they saw the danger they were running into, though, even when they walked up to a tree within two hundred yards of the beast, it remained quiet and took no notice of them. The moment I was loaded I went towards it; there were two trees intervening, one about half way, the other fifty yards nearer, and it was an anxious moment as I crossed the open towards the first, for had it charged then, it must have caught me. Just as I gained the shelter, the hunters, who had probably been waiting for me to do so, fired, neither of their bullets, however, touching the animal, and only causing it to wheel half round with a stamp of its foot and bring its body broadside to me. I knew that I could hit it from where I was, but one hundred and fifty yards is a long way in firing at large game, and I thought I would try and reach the next tree, and so lessen it by a third before I made the attempt; so, stealing out for a few yards, I made a sudden rush, and succeeded in my object, though it saw me, and probably feeling too sick for a downright charge, trotted out as if to meet me, halting when about half-way. It was now facing me, little more than fifty yards off, and covering the chest I again fired, this time bringing it to the ground, and before I reached the spot it had ceased to struggle. It is noticeable that this shot, so suddenly fatal in its results, was the third aimed at the chest, and it shows how little trust can be placed on a single bullet to stop or turn one of these animals, unless by accident.

It is not here necessary to discuss at length the as yet undecided question of the number of distinct species of rhinoceros found in Africa, though I hope to do so at some future time. As far as my experience and inquiries have gone, I believe, in accordance with the recorded opinions of most travellers and sportsmen who have given any attention to the subject, that there are four,—two of the so-called "white," and two of the "black." This distinction, however, of black and white, seems to me misleading and misapplied, all rhinoceros being of the same colour, namely, a peculiar shade of brown, or, if any difference does exist, it being in *R. bicornis* possessing a tinge of red. That to different observers, and in different localities, they do appear to be of different colours—Baldwin mentions a blue kind—is undoubted, but, except any slight variation that may locally exist, from the animal, as in Darwin's theory of protective resemblance, conforming to the prevailing colour of the district it inhabits, all such cases may be referred to outward circumstances, such as the position of the sun, or the kind of mud they may have been rolling in last, and partly, no doubt, to the age and sex of the animal. In exemplification of this I may mention that I have watched a bull of *R. simus* trotting past in the full glare of the mid-day sun, and it has appeared to me almost white, while after following the same animal up, and finding it feeding with the long shadows of evening on it, its colour has then seemed to be, as it really is, a deep brown.

These four species I would class as follows:—*R. bicornis*, otherwise known as the borele, or upetyane; *R. Keitloa*, the keitloa of the west, and umkombe tovote of the east; *R. simus*, the mohohu of the Bechuanas, and the umkave, or umkombe woqobo of the Amazulu and Amatonga tribes; and last of all the *Kulumane*, which, though I claim for it the position of a distinct species, and believe that I am able to fully prove that claim, has not as yet received a scientific name or recognition from naturalists. There is yet another species —the *R. Oswellii*, or kabaoba,—and if indeed it is not merely a variety of *R. simus*, as I am inclined to believe, it would follow that there are five kinds to be found on the continent.

The first two mentioned are those known as the "black," the latter as the "white." Of these *R. bicornis* (though why it should distinctively be named the "two-horned," when all African rhinoceros are equally so, is not very clear) is the smallest, most savage, and most to be dreaded. I consider it the most dangerous of all African game, and thousands of anecdotes might be related of its morose and vicious disposition, similar to the one already mentioned of its scattering my camp-fire.

R. Keitloa, which would better deserve the name of two-horned, as its back horn, which in other species is a mere stump, is in it of almost equal length with that in front, is a less common and better-tempered species, slightly differing in its conformation, especially about the head, from the last, which it also surpasses in size, though its chief characteristic is in the above-named peculiarity of the horns.

R. simus, the common white rhinoceros, is the largest of all, and is remarkable for the great length the front horn grows to, as well as for its gentle and inoffensive disposition. The kulumane differs from the other species in three important particulars: firstly, in its horns, which, though following the conformation of *R. simus*, never attain to the same size; secondly, in its measurements, which, while considerably inferior to those of the common white, are greater than those of the other two species, while it is to be noted that it possesses, though in a less marked degree, the long and prehensile upper lip which characterizes *R. bicornis* and *R. Keitloa*; thirdly, in its food, for, though preferring, as was to be expected from the formation of its snout, the young tender shoots and leaves of thorns, it also resembles *R. simus* in consuming large quantities of grass. In its disposition it would seem to combine the characteristics of the other species; seldom charging without provocation, but displaying great ferocity when roused, and it may also be said to be the most gregarious, herds of from five to fifteen being by no means rare. *R. Oswellii*, which in other points resembles *R. simus*, is considered to be a distinct species, from its front horn, which is straight and unusually long, pointing forward at an acute angle instead of standing erect from the snout, and is only found far to the north, though I have come across specimens presenting the same peculiarity in a modified form within three hundred miles of the coast.

No rhinoceros can fairly be called a handsome animal; its long protruding head and neck, the total length of which is almost equal to that of the entire body, with the horn—for the back stump may be ignored, and indeed is not visible from a front view—set, like that of the fabulous unicorn, in the centre, its great uncouth ears, and small cunning eye, the latter of which is placed far lower down than that of any other quadruped, and the unwieldy size of the great carcase set on such short legs, utterly depriving it of any claim to such a title. The great white species, however, which possesses all these characteristics in their least unpleasing form, and which in size nearly approaches to an elephant, is certainly a noble animal when seen, as it often is in undisturbed regions, quietly grazing amid all the beauties of tropical vegetation, lopping up with its tongue the rank grass in huge mouthfuls, and a whole flock of rhinoceros-birds perched, half asleep, or lazily picking off an occasional tick, on its broad back, while, it may be, a little hornless calf—a ludicrous miniature of its mother—runs between its legs, and is gently guided forward by the maternal snout. Such scenes often occur towards evening in the broad bottoms through which the rivers run, or on the edge of some water-hole to which the animal is going to quench its thirst after the long heat of the day.

Knowing no fear itself, and harmless towards all animals but man, it approaches the water in company with wild beasts of every description. Sometimes I have seen a troop of lions walk past an old bull with its mouth buried in the pool, and laying themselves down, commence to lap the water within a few yards of him, either party seemingly unconscious of the other's existence ; sometimes I have seen a herd of the beautifully striped koodoos spring away in alarm as their sharp ears caught the heavy footfall, only to return to the water as the grumbling ill-tempered upetyane came into sight, ploughing up the ground in long furrows as it pawed it with its foot, after the manner of savage bulls, but hardly making the antelopes stir as he walked past them into the centre of the pool, and, after drinking, began to roll in it, his great carcase forming deep hollows in the soft mud, and at times nothing but his hideous pig-like head protruding from the water. In winter, when most of the pools have dried up, and more especially in early spring, at the end of September or beginning of October, before the rains have come, and when the heat has already become great, the game congregates wherever there is water, and as rhinoceros are extremely fond of rolling in soft mud, it is to such holes as retain water that they go, in preference to the rivers. Gnu, zebra, eland, and other open flat-loving antelopes favour the same spots, and just as the sun is setting, or at early dawn, the most wonderful herds of mixed game may be seen converging from all points of the compass to some water-hole, perhaps the only one within a radius of twenty miles. Among the antelopes and zebra there is always a timid suspicion that their great enemy the lion may be concealed near the spot, and I have seen half a dozen rhinoceroses come down to the water in succession, drink and roll, and go away again; the white species to feed on the rich grass, often within a few yards of where I lay concealed, waiting for buffalo, and the others to seek their food among the dense ukaku thickets; while great herds of gnu and zebra, with perhaps a sprinkling of eland, stood three or four hundred yards off and watched them, fearful of approaching nearer so long as the wind, blowing from them to the water, put it out of their power to decide whether there was danger in so doing; and there they have stood almost motionless, too thirsty to graze, till near midnight, looking weird enough in the calm moonlight, till, their thirst conquering their prudence, they would come forward, halting every fifty yards, and even sometimes wheeling away in a panic that had originated with the gnu, till at last, as the foremost entered the water, those behind would quicken their pace, and jostling forward, the whole pool would be covered with them, the gurgling sound from hundreds of thirsty throats sounding strange in the stillness; then, unless—despairing of buffalo—I fired at them, the whole herd would retire, and, when the grass was good, feed all round me for hours, fresh troops occasionally arriving to quench their thirst, and sometimes the same returning a second time before going off to the great flats where they would spend the day.

Watching water-holes was always a very favourite mode of passing the night with me, especially during the warm spring evenings (for it is often chilly after the sun has set during winter), when there was sufficient moon to enable me to see. Many animals that one rarely comes across in the day-time, such as wild dogs, hyenas, leopards, panthers, jackals, and wild cats of many kinds, used to come prowling about, and there was always the charm of solitude and silence, broken only by the companionship of wild animals, and the many noises of a tropical night, while one never knew what game to expect, as, from the lion to the timid impalla, or little duiker antelope, all came at different times to drink, and, as the night is to much of the brute creation what the day is to us, many a curious scene has come under my notice, increasing my stock of natural history, while I have killed more game during these solitary watches than during all my other hunting put together.

There was one particular pool at which I spent many nights, sometimes when the moonlight was so bright that I could see the game approaching for several hundred yards, but more generally when I had only the light of the stars to assist my aim, while at others, when heavy thunderstorms covered the sky with black clouds, I could only see when the flashes of lightning lit up the scene. I found that buffalo and the larger kinds of antelopes avoided the water-holes during the bright moonlight, but that it made no difference to rhinoceroses and to the other kinds of antelopes, in common with the smaller carnivora, while the thickest of a storm was the time generally chosen by the lions to make their appearance. I remember once during a lull in a thunderstorm hearing the cat-like lapping of one of these great beasts, and when the next flash came, I saw three of them crouched flat on the bank still drinking. I levelled my gun at the spot, and waiting for the next flash, fired a snap-shot at the nearest, and when the lightning enabled me to look again, they had disappeared. I was sitting in the fork of a tree about six feet from the ground, and in about half an hour I heard a rustling at my feet which continued for some time, though, as the storm had passed, and it was pitch dark, I could not see what made it, but next morning I discovered by the spoor that it had been a lion, and on following it back, I found that it was the identical one I had fired at, and which, after making a detour, had come to pay me a visit, and must, from the way the grass was crushed, have been lying for some time within easy springing distance of me.

The pool that I have mentioned was one that, being fed by a spring, never dried up, and possessed such deep clear water, that the game came long distances to it, preferring it to the river, as being cooler. It was about fifty yards long, and surrounded by a fringe of thick evergreens, except at the upper end, where it was shallow and muddy, and where the animals entered it when they came to drink. My hiding-place was in the thick branches of a great cabbage-tree, just opposite the spot where the buffaloes generally stood when drinking, and about ten yards from where the rhinoceroses were accustomed to roll. On one occasion I remained here without moving for two nights and a day, sleeping in the shade at the foot of the tree during the noonday heat, and watching all night; a piece of sun-dried meat I had brought with me supplying me with food. This freak created great alarm in my camp, as I had left it at early dawn, before any one was awake; and though on the first night it was supposed that I had killed some game and was sleeping by it, yet when another day, followed by a night, passed without my appearing, the general idea was that I had met with some accident;

and when I arrived I found that every one had gone to search for me; and, as an instance of the wonderful spooring powers of some of the natives, I may mention that, the ground having been softened by a shower that had fallen the previous evening, one of them followed me through all the windings that I took while hunting on the day I left camp, and positively tracked me to the water-hole where I had been.

On this occasion I had unusually good sport, killing three rhinoceroses, two buffaloes, and a hyena, and wounding a water-antelope, that was afterwards got. I reached the pool towards five o'clock, and having noticed that there was a great quantity of spoor of all kinds of game that had been there on the previous night, and as I knew that the moon was nearly full, and as the wind was also favourable, I determined to watch that night, though, on most occasions when I did so, I brought, in addition to my double breech-loader of ten to the pound, a large-bored elephant-gun, that did great execution among rhinoceros and buffalo. Game might be expected to arrive at any moment after six o'clock; and so, after spending the interval in sitting at the foot of the tree, rising now and then to watch the flight of some rhinoceros-birds, whose cry high up in the air had caught my ear, and to notice with satisfaction that they were coming from the direction from which I expected sport, and that, after a short absence, during which they were probably drinking at the river, they passed back again, showing that they were returning to the game, having seen none nearer, I climbed up, and took my seat on the convenient arrangement of branches that had originally caused me to choose this tree, and having disposed the great cabbage-like leaves, from which it takes its name, so as to conceal me, I quietly waited.

In half an hour there was a rustle beside me, and a little duiker antelope, its grey skin shining like silver in the rays of the setting sun, stole down, and after gazing round it for a few seconds, stooped to drink, the reflection of its head and tiny horns being quite plain on the surface of the dark still pool, and then silently retired. A few minutes after another appeared on the opposite bank, followed by two more, and having satisfied their thirst, returned to nibble the young shoots of grass in the glades among the thickets where they lived. The next to arrive were a pair of reed buck, mother and calf, which had no doubt been lying in the long rank grass in the "vlei" beyond, and which, like all the smaller species of antelopes which inhabit the thorn jungles in common with the coast flats and the timber forests, were not nearly as large as those found in the latter places. The bush partridge, a species of francolin, had for some time been uttering their grating cry among the surrounding bushes, and now made their appearance to drink, while dozens of partridges of other kinds, mingled with turtle-doves and paroquets, and the little long-tailed pigeon, alighted on all sides, attracted by the common want.

Suddenly a commotion among them heralded the approach of something larger, though my duller organs had not as yet detected any sound; and in a few minutes a herd of koodoo walked up to the top of the bank and stood, scanning the ground—previous to descending,—for any sign of lurking danger. At last an old doe, as I could tell by her lighter colour and great size, walked forward, her great thin ears flapping as she moved, and the prominent eyes that are so remarkable among these beautiful antelopes visible even at this distance. She was followed by the whole herd, their movements possessing that wonderful stillness that induces in the observer a feeling that he is not looking at flesh and blood. Among them was only one bull, excepting a yearling with horns not larger than those of an inyala, who, though he had allowed the wary old doe to lead the way, no sooner saw her reach the water in safety than, using his magnificent horns to clear his path, he pushed his way through the rest, and advancing past them into the deeper water, stood, seemingly looking at his own reflection, within five yards of me. I could count every white stripe that marked his sleek skin, could notice the flaws in his horns where he had damaged them, either in fighting, or against a tree, and I could see every wrinkle and scratch in his great dark neck, and every line of his delicate limbs. It was a sore temptation, and at a later hour I should certainly have given way to it; but as I did not know what I might disturb, or how near the larger game might be, I allowed him to go unhurt.

Twilight in the tropics is of very short duration, and soon after this, the moon having not as yet risen, it became as dark as it ever is in that clear atmosphere, where myriads of stars of a magnitude unknown in this country cover the sky, and where the planets shine so brightly as to throw a distinct and dark shadow, so that, although I could now and then hear the rustling of small animals as they passed on their way to the water, I could not distinguish their outlines. Two hours passed like this, during which I amused myself by watching the huge bats and goatsuckers as they skimmed round me, and by listening to a great owl (*Bubo verrauxii*) that from some of the fissures of the mountain above me was imitating the cry of the leopard with such precision that no one unaccustomed to hear it could have detected the imposture.

I was, however, beginning to doubt whether I should see any game before morning, as the smaller animals had already mostly quenched their thirst, and there was no sign of the larger ones, when I heard a rumbling that I knew could only be produced by one of two animals, either an elephant or a rhinoceros, and as there had been no fresh spoor of the former about for some time, I rightly concluded that it was the latter. It seemed to issue from an open glade between two thickets about sixty or seventy yards off, and I waited for nearly half an hour, during which I again heard the sound once or twice, momentarily expecting to see the animal appear. At last, losing patience, and suspecting, as was really the case, that it had drunk at a smaller pool below me, and was now feeding, I got down from the tree, and, stealing round the edge of the water, I passed through the adjoining thicket, and crept forward to its edge. The moon had been up for some time, but was still looming large and misty through the moisture rising from the earth, and directly between me and it I saw the great black outline of a rhinoceros grazing broadside to me about forty yards off. I might no doubt have fired from where I was, but seeing by the long front horn that I had to deal with one of the white species, and noticing a shrub within a few yards of it, I determined to try and creep in nearer, as there was little fear of alarming it if I was careful, especially now when the watchful rhinoceros-birds were absent.

Ten minutes' crawling sufficed to place me under the lee of the shrub, which was of sufficient size to form a screen even when I should have to sit up to fire, and, still keeping my gun-barrels out of sight, as I was afraid of some gleam of the moonlight on them catching its eye before I was ready, I raised myself and looked through the intervening twigs. I had got near enough in all conscience, for I found its nose within a yard of my own, some slight noise I had made having struck its ear and caused it to wheel round. Of course, I remained like a statue, though I was nearer than I liked, the danger being that it might walk forward and come right upon me, when it would be difficult to say what even such an amiable-tempered animal as a white rhinoceros might do. They are always slow and deliberate in their movements, and this one stood there listening, while I could hear and almost feel its breath, till in my cramped position I would have given anything for just one kick. It would have been utterly useless to fire, for a rhinoceros, especially of the long-horned species, offers no mark whatever when it stands facing you with its head down, its chest being invisible, and, even if you were desirous of making the experiment of a shot at those well-protected spots, the horn guarding the brain and neck.

There was nothing for it but patience, and mine was pretty nearly exhausted before, to my great relief, it at last turned away, having heard something stirring in the thicket beyond. Fearing lest it should make some fresh movement, and so again conceal its shoulder, now in full view, I at once raised my gun, and hesitating for a second between the centre of the shoulder-blade and just behind it, I decided in favour of the latter and pulled the trigger, at the same time jumping clear of the bush and smoke, and throwing myself down in the open, where the grass was long enough to hide me. Loading as I lay, I watched the mighty struggles of the brute to rise, till, fearing it would succeed, I went up and fired both barrels, the first into the one shoulder, the second into the other, hoping in that way to at least disable it; and after waiting on the spot for ten minutes, I thought it unnecessary to do more, and returned to the pool.

Knowing very well that after all that noise I need not hope for anything to come for a long time, I stretched myself out as comfortably as the branches of the tree would allow, and placing my gun so that it could not fall, I tried to keep sleep off by thinking; however, I was tired, and the cool air and stillness made me drowsy, and before long I found myself sleeping in snatches, which at last ended in utter unconsciousness.

Some hours had passed when I next awoke, half falling off the tree before I remembered where I was, but the instant I did so the sullen gurgle of displaced mud warned me that there was something in the pool. Gently raising myself therefore into a sitting posture, I looked, and saw, for the moonlight was now almost as bright as day, a rhinoceros wallowing in the shallow water and mud, while its companion stood on the sky-line on the bank above. Looking more closely, while my hand sought my gun, I saw by their small size and diminutive horns that they were both upetyane (*R. bicornis*), a species against which, ever since I had been so roughly handled by one of them, I had always borne malice for their evil disposition and vicious propensities, and therefore, though their horns were utterly worthless, I was glad to get the opportunity. I could not at first decide which to fire at; for though the one in the pool was not ten yards off, yet it was lying in such a position that I doubted my being able to mortally wound it, while the other, unless it charged, would be out of sight the moment I fired and startled it; I therefore thought I would try a shot at the latter, which, though it was fully forty yards off, I could, from its prominent position, see almost more plainly than the other, and, resting the gun on a branch, I did so. The bullet told loudly, and the animal, puffing and snorting, disappeared, while the one in the water, springing to its feet, and sending the mud pattering among the surrounding leaves, trotted out, and then, wheeling half round, stood, evidently listening for some indication of my whereabouts. This I soon gave it, aiming as before at the shoulder, and bringing it to the ground on the spot, though, instantly recovering itself, it charged straight for the place where it had seen the flash.

Short as the delay had been, it had enabled me to load one barrel, and when it was within a yard of the tree I again fired down into its hump, making it swerve with the pain, and, losing its balance, fall bodily into the pond below. The water was deep, and it floundered about for some seconds before it found its feet, enabling me to reload, and to again plant my balls, right and left, in its shoulder, upon which it rushed off, scattering the water as it did so, and, going over the rise, was lost to view. While this had been going on I had an impression that I could hear distant squealing, such as these animals make only in their death-agonies, or when in very great pain, unless it be in moments of fury, but now in the restored quiet I could hear it quite distinctly, and I knew by it that my single bullet must have mortally wounded the first one. It would not, however, do to leave the brute squealing there for long, disturbing everything within hearing, and not impossibly bringing lions about, in which latter case I need not hope to see any buffalo, so, although I was rather nervous at the risk of coming across the other, which was very likely close by, and would not, I knew, spare me if it got the chance, I again got down, and proceeded in the direction of the cries. I had to be careful; the moon, shining brightly enough in the open, cast deep black shadows among the trees, and forced me to go forward foot by foot, sometimes standing more than a minute examining some dark recess before I ventured to pass it. The squealing of the animal, loud enough when I started, also gradually died away, until, ceasing altogether, it left me without any guide. However, I persevered, and, after going about a quarter of a mile, I saw a great shapeless heap by the side of a clump of bushes, which turned out to be what I was looking for, and, as it was quite dead, I made the best of my way back.

Nothing more disturbed the stillness of the pool until after the morning star had risen, when I heard the startled cry of the ititihoya plover, and knowing that it never stirs during the night unless almost trodden upon, I waited in expectation, and in a few minutes three old buffalo bulls, seeming almost white in the moonlight, came down to drink. Fancying that they would roll as well as drink, I did not fire at first, but when I saw that one, having satisfied its thirst, walked out, while the others stood with the water dripping from their mouths, only waiting to have another drink before they joined it, I delayed no longer, and taking the nearest one in the point of the shoulder—and it was almost opposite me, and not five yards off,—I dropped it where it stood. Its next companion, unawed by the sudden and loud report and the blaze of light, uttered a grunt, and, instead of taking to flight, charged straight out of the water, and tried to climb the bank on which the tree in which I was stationed grew, offering me, as it did so, a most beautiful shot at its broad chest. It was lucky for me that I was in a place of safety, for it did not even swerve when the ball struck it, but rushed past under me, breaking off one of the brittle lower branches in its way, and I saw no more of it.

Soon after this it became apparent that day was breaking, though for some time it was difficult to distinguish between it and the light of the moon, and some of the smaller antelopes were already making their appearance, when, hearing a noise at the further end of the pond, to which, as I had never seen any game drink there, my back was turned, I looked round and saw, to my surprise, the great heads and fore-quarters of several rhinoceroses protruding through the bushes, some drinking, and others standing still. I counted six, and from their numbers and short thick horns I knew that they were kulumane, making the third species I had seen that night. There was no good in my firing from my present position, as from the distance and the thickness of the bushes I could not make them out very distinctly, so I dropped down, and getting outside the fringe of bushes, would soon have got close to them, had not a seventh, which I had not seen, and which was standing with its head towards me, having probably finished drinking, and being on its way to feed, suddenly given the alarm; and though I fired as they trotted off at fifty yards, I believe I missed with both barrels, as I did not hear the clap of the ball following either.

Perhaps people who have never hunted large game may think that it would be almost impossible for any one who could shoot at all to miss such a mark as half a dozen rhinoceroses at fifty yards, but I assure them I have seen men come out from England, first-class grouse and partridge shots, and who were able to make wonderful practice with a rifle at a target with measured distances, but who could not for months kill more than an occasional head of the quantities of game by which they were surrounded; and I have seen rhinoceros missed clean, standing not twenty yards off, by men who could kill a couple of snipe right and left three times out of five. Judging the distance correctly is the chief stumbling-block in an atmosphere so different to that of Europe, and which, from its clearness, causes an animal at one hundred and fifty yards not to appear much over seventy, and the probable explanation of my missing these is that, deceived by the peculiar light of early dawn, I judged them to be fifty yards off, while they were perhaps eighty in reality.

There was, however, nothing for it but to return to my ambush, where I patiently waited till about seven o'clock without seeing anything worth firing at, and as the sun was by this time well up, and the game was retiring to their lairs, I descended, and, after having a bathe, during which I succeeded in moving the fallen buffalo, whose dying struggles had fortunately carried it into deep water, and towed it to the other end of the pond, where I covered it up with branches to keep the vultures from seeing it during my absence, I went off, in the first place, to visit the white rhinoceros cow that I had left still living, and then to see what had become of the upetyane at which I had fired so many shots, as well as the buffalo bull which had charged me. To my disgust I found that the former had got up and disappeared, though, from the marks on the ground, it was evident she could not go far as she was dragging one of her fore-legs, and in point of fact, I found her within a hundred yards of the spot, lying down, and rising with the utmost difficulty when I walked up. I settled her with three more shots, and then returned to the pool to take up the spoor of the other. It had gone away at a furious gallop, tearing up the ground, and smashing branches and small trees like reeds before it, and had kept up this headlong course for nearly a mile, when, reducing its pace to a walk, it entered an ukaku thicket, went straight through it, following the windings of an old game-path, passed through the next open, fully a mile broad, over which I had great difficulty in tracking it, and went into a large jungle that edged it; turning off at right angles to its former course, it then proceeded to make for the upper end, and after another mile I began to guess the spot it wished to reach. One part of this jungle was remarkable for having a creeper which, twining round the thorn-trees, formed a number of vegetable caves, so regular in their formation that, at first sight, it appeared to be impossible that it could be the work of nature, and that they must have been trained by the hand of man.

I had once before been there in pursuit of a herd of buffaloes, which we found lying in them, and at the time I had noticed that there were a great many rhinoceros spoors, both old and new, and several places in which they were evidently accustomed to lie, and as the direction this one was taking would bring it there in half an hour, I had no doubt but that it belonged to that spot,—as they wander so far during the night in search of food,—and was now, sick and wounded, trying to return there, perhaps expecting to meet its mate. As I proceeded I found that my conjecture was correct, and I also noticed several fresh spoors, and other signs that led me to believe that there were more rhinoceros in the neighbourhood, all by the smallness of their track belonging to the same species. On reaching the outskirts of the creeper-covered bushes I had to be very careful; indeed, the thought more than once crossed my mind of going back to camp and getting help before I prosecuted my search, and if it had not been so far I should probably have done so, as not only would the wounded one charge the moment it heard or saw me, but as there seemed to be so many about I ran the risk of being caught by one whose existence I knew nothing of, while intent upon following the other, and, added to this, I saw the fresh footprints of a lion, which might possibly be after my wounded rhinoceros, although I have noticed that it is generally rare to go far into the haunts of this species without finding that there has been a lion about lately.

However, I went on, the sole precaution I could take being silence, while I was often passing within a foot of a mass of tangle that, for aught I knew, might contain a rhinoceros or a lion. The feeling that one is passing thickets from which dangerous game may be watching you, especially when it is more than probable that it is so, and when one can do nothing whatever to mitigate the danger, is by no means a pleasant one, and before I had got far in I was wishing myself well out of it; indeed, I might have turned had I not thought it almost as dangerous to do so as to advance. In ten minutes I was in the centre of this patch, and still the spoor led me on until I began to hope that it would pass through, and that I should not have to tackle the most dangerous of African animals, rendered, if it is possible, more ill-tempered than usual by its wounds, by myself, and in the heart of its stronghold, when it made a sudden turn to the right, taking me past a dense wall of creepers.

I hardly know what tempted me to go and peer through them, gently passing my hand in, and moving them so that I could see a little, for I had not done it before, though I had passed dozens of similar places; but so it was, and there, scarcely a yard away, lay the great brute, its head turned to the entrance, opposite me, where it had gone in, and its side and hind-quarters towards me. It was no time for hesitation. I first glanced round for a tree, put the muzzle of the gun to the hole through which I had been looking, and, holding it at arm's-length, pulled the trigger, and then, nervous with the gloomy stillness of the spot, I climbed up into the tree without waiting to see the result of the shot, unfortunately leaving my gun at the bottom when I did so. I had hardly got into one of the lower branches before I could tell by the faint sounds of struggling in the thicket that I had no real cause for fear, and I was turning to come down again when I became conscious of an approaching noise of bushes breaking, accompanied by snorting and puffing, and in a few seconds a fresh rhinoceros made its appearance, evidently in the very highest state of rage and excitement at a gun being fired in this den of theirs. It soon got my wind, although it failed to see me sitting on a bare branch not two yards from its head, and went off in the direction I had come from, making a most tremendous noise, and tossing its head about in a very vicious manner, so that I judged it best to get out of the place as soon as possible; and as on going up to the wounded one I found it dead, my last shot having destroyed what little life was left, and there was nothing more to keep me, I made for the outside as fast as I could, only fearing, as was likely enough, that the brute might come back, and, striking my fresh trail, overtake me somewhere where I should not have the shelter of a tree; but I saw nothing more of it, and went straight back to the pool, arriving there shortly after mid-day; and after convincing myself that the wounded buffalo had not fallen in my neighbourhood, but that to kill it would entail a long and wearisome chase, the success of which was uncertain, I lay down under the tree and slept till evening, not awaking till the rustling of the long grass and leaves announced the arrival of the breeze which usually springs up at that time, and which is so refreshing after the furnace-like stillness and glare of the day. Rubbing my eyes, I climbed into my perch, and before long was surrounded by all the smaller animals and birds which had come to drink on the preceding night, and which, though I had seen them hundreds of times before, never wearied me in watching them. There was always variety. To-night a herd of wild pigs came rooting down the bank among the first arrivals, and remained in sight until dark, grubbing up the soil with their long snouts in search of the succulent roots on which they live, and among them was an immense old boar, with tusks forming three-quarters of a circle: one could not help being struck with the family resemblance he displayed both to elephants and rhinoceroses.

There was a large herd of impalla too, whose sleek skins, terminating in the purest white beneath, and set off by black points, and by a streak of similar colour that extends along the back, showed that they were now in the highest condition, as indeed at this time of year they always are. There was a little clump of bush standing alone on the flat above the pool, and as the herd retired, grazing as they went, a young ram went close to it. I was watching them at the time, admiring their graceful movements as, spreading out like a herd of sheep, they commenced feeding, though, as is the case with all gregarious antelopes, there was always some head up in search of any sign of danger, which, if seen, would at once have been announced to the others by a signal of alarm, resembling a suppressed sneeze, causing them to cease feeding, and to gaze in the direction indicated, from which, as has often been the case when I have been the cause of alarm, they would gradually edge away, although they could detect nothing, while, if the danger was palpable, they would assemble together, the oldest males still standing looking at it until the does and young ones had gone some distance, when they would join them, and, galloping away into the centre of the nearest plain, would resume their feeding unconcernedly, conscious of their safety in the bare open. The danger that now threatened one of them was, however, unnoticed by themselves or by me, until I saw a long spotted body spring out of the little clump of bush, and alight on the neck and head of the young ram that had gone so near it. The action was momentary, and the sudden change from the herd of antelopes peacefully grazing, with several wild pigs and a duiker in the foreground to a deserted flat, tenanted only by the leopard and its struggling victim, was almost theatrical. There were a few unavailing plunges, a half-choked bleat, and the antelope fell on the edge of the thicket in its last agonies, while the great cat never stirred from its original position, and never for an instant ceased tearing at its throat.

Although I was posted there for a precisely similar object to that of the leopard, while I had not even its excuse of hunger and necessity, I must confess the sight made me angry, and getting down, I went as near as the vegetation surrounding the water enabled me to go unperceived. Even here I was sixty yards off, though I was at the nearest spot to the clump in which concealment was possible, its very isolation having probably caused the leopard to choose it as making it a less suspected spot than a larger thicket would have been. It was also but an imperfect view of the animal that I could obtain through the long grass, and I hesitated considerably before I fired, not only doubting whether I could hit it at that distance, but aware that if I let it alone now it would go away before long, nay, might even come to the water to drink, and at any rate would enable me to hide myself during its absence in the clump of bush itself, and afford me every opportunity for a certain shot on its return; but my mind reverting to the tracks of a very large herd of buffalo which I had noticed when following the black rhinoceros, and which would in all probability come to drink during the night, I preferred to chance a shot now, rather than risk losing them while watching for it. I could just see its spotted skin crouched above the carcase, and, aiming low, I fired, the shot being answered by a low growl, while the animal bounded off, sufficiently in view to tempt me to try the other barrel. It however disappeared in the bushes, and I walked up and examined the impalla, finding no other wound, except some trifling scratches on the shoulders, but the one in the throat; and as it was not altogether impossible that the leopard might return after all, especially if it happened to be very hungry, and was unwounded, I did not attempt to touch it, but left it lying as I found it.

Soon after my return to the tree, however, I heard the melancholy howl of a hyena to leeward, growing louder and louder as the beast came nearer, and then, after suddenly ceasing, probably just when it caught the impalla's scent, I next heard it tearing at the carcase. It is curious how all creatures, whether birds or beasts,

that prey upon dead bodies, seem to become aware of
the existence of their food by some instinct independent
of their senses; it has been commented upon again
and again how vultures make their appearance in flocks
ten minutes after the game has fallen, when there was
not a single one in sight before; and in night-shooting,
though of course there are numerous exceptions, I have
often noticed how quickly hyenas and jackals would find
out anything I had killed, and how rapidly they would
congregate the moment a single one had discovered it; and
yet it seems certain that they do not call one another to
the feast, as they rarely howl except when in search of
prey, and quarrel and fight over every mouthful. To-
night was a case in point, and during the hours of darkness before the moon rose, I could hear them in increasing
numbers, snarling and crunching, and when the impalla
was finished, it being but a morsel among two or three of
them, it was evident enough by the sounds that they had
discovered the dead rhinoceros, and were trying their
teeth in its tough hide.

Once before the moon rose some large animal came
down to drink, but it was so dark that I could not even
distinguish its outlines from where I was, so I crossed
out into the open, and lay down flat, hoping that I
should be able to see it against the sky when it returned,
but the rhinoceros, as the spoor afterwards told me it
was, kept lower down and I missed it. However, as I
did not know this at the time, I waited, wondering what
was keeping it, till a low rumbling sound on the other
side attracted my attention, and in a few seconds I could
see—for though the moon was as yet invisible, it was up,

and it was not nearly so dark as it had been—the foremost of a long line of animals whose great size proved them to be buffaloes. They were approaching in single file, though in places there were three or four together, and before long the leading ones had passed, almost touching me where I lay. I at once decided not to fire until they had all gone down to the water, when, as I should be between them and the only way of egress, I should probably have time for several shots, so, remaining still, I attempted to count them.

There were sixty-seven in all, as well as I could make out, a large proportion of which were yearlings and two-year-olds, though among them were several large bulls, easily distinguishable by their massive fore-quarters and superior size. Ten minutes passed while I listened to the splashing of the water and to the gurgling of the soft mud as their heavy hoofs sank into it, and by that time the moon had fairly risen, enabling me to see pretty plainly, and then they began to come back again, though more irregularly than they had gone down. The first half dozen were cows and young ones, and close behind them was a large bull, which I picked out at once, and, waiting till he was within three yards of me, I knocked him over with the first shot, the echo of which had hardly broken the stillness before I could hear the whole herd thundering up the bank, and in a second more I was in danger of being crushed beneath their hoofs.

Jumping up, I levelled at the head of the nearest, the bright flash causing them to swerve, some passing on each side of me, and as I rammed fresh cartridges in I could tell by the sound that they had halted, and on turning round I saw them standing about seventy yards off, while on looking about I noticed that the bull I had knocked over had also disappeared. My first impulse was to run in and fire again, but while hesitating a low roaring caught my ears, and I could see that they were slowly advancing. I had heard this roaring before; it is a sort of suppressed sound, and peculiar to buffalo bulls when excited by the presence of a lion, and generally precedes a general charge upon the common enemy. I glanced behind me, the pool was thirty yards off, and the danger was every instant becoming more imminent, for the brutes, whether they mistook me for a lion or not, were evidently bent on mischief.

In this predicament it struck me to drop down among the long grass, and then crawl as rapidly as possible towards the pool, rightly, as it turned out, imagining that they would be puzzled by my sudden disappearance, and think that it concealed some stratagem. They were not now more than forty yards off, and I could already see that the front line was composed of bulls, so there was no time to be lost, and down I went, crawling away as hard as I could go, until, finding myself on the top of the bank, and not ten yards from the pool, I ventured to raise my head and look back. They were still standing where I had last seen them, so, aiming low, I fired both barrels in succession at the dark mass, bringing them down upon me like a troop of cavalry. Of course I jumped up, and took to my heels, easily reaching the tree in time to see them sweep round the head of the pool and gallop off in a cloud of dust in the direction they had come from. The next thing was to go and look whether they had left any wounded behind, and on reaching the spot I found a cow dead, shot through the brain by one of my last shots, while the two first, though neither were fired at over three yards' distance, had made good their escape. Nothing more worthy of note occurred that night. Some hyenas discovered the dead buffalo, and, as their teeth were able to penetrate the softer portions of its hide, and they would soon have destroyed it, I crept up and fired at them, killing one. Towards morning a herd of water-antelopes came to drink, and the one at which I fired, though it made off at the time, was found dead by the men I sent to skin the buffaloes, and to cut off the rhinoceroses' horns.

In all large game shooting, but perhaps especially with rhinoceros, the weight and the hardness of the bullet used is of the last importance, and much more depends upon it than would be thought, even by those who have had some experience, unless they have paid special attention to the proportions used, and have made it a practice to cut their bullets out, and notice what the effect of the concussion has been, both on the projectile itself, and also on the bones with which it has come in contact.

There are two compositions in general use for hardening balls in those countries where the game is of sufficient size to render it necessary, namely, lead and pewter, and lead and tin, to which may be added the occasional use of quicksilver. Formerly, lead and pewter was invariably used, in the proportion of about four of lead to one of pewter; but of late years tin has almost entirely taken the place of that compound. A bullet is generally considered at a proper state of firmness when the teeth will just slightly indent it, and one invariably sees native hunters applying this test to the first ball of a fresh casting. It not unusually happens, particularly in the more remote districts, that all hardening matter becomes exhausted, and one hears stories of canteens, tin cups, etc., being melted down as a makeshift; in such an extremity resort is had to fat—generally the hard tallow found about the intestines of a buffalo, or a water-antelope—a quantity of which is mixed with the liquid lead, and, further to harden them, each bullet as it is cast is immersed in cold water. The result of this is tolerably satisfactory, the firmness attained nearly equalling that of a mixture of pewter and lead.

It may be interesting to see what experience shows is the effect produced by bullets in different states of hardening. The object desired—and which is attained when exactly correct proportions are used—is that the ball, in striking a bone, should flatten sufficiently to prevent its boring through, should smash the obstacle sufficiently, while at the same time it must retain enough of the round form to obviate any chance of the increased resistance offered to the larger surface stopping its way, and thereby preventing its penetrating far enough. Such a bullet will often smash—I use the word in contradistinction to merely break—both the shoulders of a buffalo, and remain in the skin on the further side, or will penetrate a couple of inches into the enormous mass of bone which protects that animal's brain.

When no hardening, or an insufficient quantity, has been put in, the effect is that the whole force of the ball is expended on the first serious opposition it encounters. Should that chance to be strong enough to resist the shock, the bullet merely flattens itself, as it would against an iron target; though the stunning effect of such a blow is far greater than that caused by a hardened ball, a fact that has been discovered through game dropping more frequently to such a shot than when a better prepared missile has been used. When, however, the resistance offered is not so great, and the bone gives way, the smash that takes place is something wonderful. The flattened ball breaks up into innumerable fragments, which, by some unknown law of attraction, adhere to the bone, along which they run, rending and splitting it, until the ultimate result is very much the same as would be produced by a shell bursting. Of course, in such a case, the ball goes no further, and, though the animal is maimed, it is not vitally wounded. Firing unhardened bullets, as far as rhinoceros, hippopotamus, and elephants are concerned, is mere trifling—it may possibly amuse you, but it certainly cannot hurt them,—and even with buffalo, it will probably cause you to lose three-quarters of all those you may wound; though, on the other hand, it is decidedly to be preferred for lions, tigers, leopards, panthers, and such like animals, on account of the stunning and disabling nature of the blow on such comparatively small bones. There is a story told of an African native hunter, who affirmed that his soft lead bullet had rebounded from a rhinoceros's hide, and struck him in the face; and though perhaps this may be too gross an exaggeration to have ever obtained credence, yet some such idea was for a long time believed in, and even at the present day it is not impossible that some one may exist to whom it is news that an African rhinoceros's hide is easily penetrable by spears, not to speak of bullets, that is, so long as the animal is alive; for when the skin is taken off and dried it becomes so hard that it is even doubtful whether a hardened ball would then pierce it.

Generally speaking, it may be laid down as a rule, that whenever shells are found efficacious, hardened bullets will not only be unnecessary, but even not so useful, though to this buffalo prove an exception, as, at certain angles, it is possible to fire a shell into the vitals without meeting with any resistance sufficient to cause it to burst prematurely; while, when the part presented to the hunter entails the breaking of a large bone, a hardened bullet becomes necessary.

Too much tin is often accidentally added, and the result of so doing is diametrically opposite to that caused by its absence. The bullet will then penetrate through the bone as far as the projecting force will carry it, retaining meanwhile its exact spherical form. In a word, it combines the maximum of penetration with a minimum concussion. In proof of this it may be stated, that instances have occurred of the same bullet having been cut out of the carcase, and reloaded several times in succession, and having, in the hands of natives accustomed to stalk close, and make sure of their aim, killed several head of game without being recast. Indeed, were it not for the brittleness of overhardened bullets, they would be in general request for such shots as require great penetration; but, unfortunately, they cannot be depended upon, and often split and glance harmlessly off the first thing they strike. When fired at limbs, such bullets produce no great shock to the animal's system, generally only boring a hole through, and not breaking the bone, the practical result of which is that the animal will go ten miles further and stand double the number of shots—will indeed often go so far as to render it impossible to overtake it. Clean wounds are not so immediately disabling as those of an opposite nature, and though probably many, if not most, animals, that get away at the time, shot through and through, ultimately die, yet that is a very poor consolation indeed to the sportsman.

So much for the proper hardening of the bullets, their weight, which principally depends upon the size of the gun used, producing in its own way very similar results. The advocates of small bores say that their use requires more skill, while it makes the shooting neater and cleaner, and inflicts less pain. This must at once be allowed to be the case with all the small game, and even with many of the larger antelopes. It is undoubtedly far prettier work, and more sportsmanlike, to kill with a single ball, even though not larger than a pea, than to ultimately cause the death of an animal from weakness and loss of blood, after repeated shots, no one of which is in itself immediately fatal; and were it possible to carry it out in shooting the really large game, there could be no argument about the matter. Unfortunately this is impossible. Practice teaches us that no amount of experience or deadliness of aim suffices, even when large balls are used, to render the killing of such animals as elephants (I am speaking of the African species, which presents no certain mark in its forehead, as its East Indian *confrère* does) and rhinoceroses, and, in a lesser degree, hippopotami and buffaloes, by a single bullet, a moral certainty.

In my own experience I have found that the bullet which to-day has proved all but instantaneously fatal, has to-morrow, though seemingly entering at precisely the same spot, and at exactly the same angle, had no effect; and while this has been my own personal experience, not of once, but of many times, any hunter, white or black, will bear witness to the times without number where he has planted his bullet in the exact spot he desired without the slightest immediate result.

A hippopotamus (most of which are shot in the water) presents a small mark in the head, the penetration of which by ever so small a ball causes instant death, while a buffalo, when hit exactly in a well-known spot in the forehead, drops to the shot; and therefore, when the hippopotamus is in the water, and when the buffalo's forehead is turned to you, a small-bored weapon is of equal use with a larger one, but when these conditions are not attainable, as in nine cases out of ten they are not with the latter animal, the lighter gun becomes in comparison useless, as, like an over-hardened bullet, it will but pierce the bone, and not break it, while it produces no shock whatever to the system, and, though very possibly mortally wounding the animal, renders the chances exceedingly small that the hunter will get it, thus inflicting more pain, as death from such a tiny ball may not take place for a week, or even a month, afterwards. In the case of elephants and rhinoceros, there is, on the contrary, no place at which the entrance of a ball is certain to be at once fatal; and though there are spots in the ear and shoulder of the former, and in the shoulder of the latter, which not seldom prove so, yet it is utterly impossible to predicate as to when it will and when it will not.

As an instance of this, I may mention the case of a rhinoceros at which three shots were fired, all from the same angle, and all of which could have been outwardly covered by a crown-piece, the two first of which had no effect whatever, while the third killed it dead; and it all tends to prove that, as it is impossible under any circumstances to make sure of killing with one shot, resort must therefore be had to heavy missiles, which will sicken and weaken the animal, and will produce the same effect in an hour that smaller ones would take a week to accomplish.

On one occasion I happened to witness, and indeed to take an active part in, the capture of a young rhinoceros calf of the species I have already mentioned by the native name of kulumane, and as it afforded us an unusually good opportunity of studying the habits and characteristics of this hitherto unrecognised species, it is worth while to give an account of it, although, unfortunately, the little animal did not exist very long in captivity, dying a few days after we had caught it.

Its mother had been shot by one of the hunters on the previous day, and, true to the instinct so generally displayed in similar cases by the young of all rhinoceroses, it remained the whole night by the dead body, and when we visited the place next morning we found it still there. We had, in anticipation of its being so, provided ourselves with a number of strong rheims, or thongs cut from the hide of a buffalo, and at once set to work to catch it; and as the thicket in which its mother lay enabled us to surround it unperceived, we had but little difficulty in approaching near enough, and, after some trouble and confusion, in slipping a noose round one of its hind-legs, for although it continuously made short charges out at any one it saw, it would not go any distance from its mother's corpse, and made no attempt to escape. Ultimately we succeeded in securing another thong to the other leg, and ten or a dozen men having got hold of each, we attempted to drive it out, but, with pig-like obstinacy, it utterly refused to go in the desired direction, charging back on us, or going the wrong way, while it puffed and snorted, and now and then squealed with rage. At intervals it got jerked off its legs by the sudden tightening of the thong held by the men opposite to those it was charging, on which occasions it would lie where it fell, and refuse to move. After a time, however, it somewhat calmed down, exhausted by the violence of its efforts, and we hit upon a plan which enabled us to guide it towards camp. One man was sent in front of it as near as he dared to go, and was instructed to run in the proper direction the instant it noticed and charged him, and ultimately it settled down into a sober jog-trot, the man still running in front, and I and my European companion bringing up the rear, convulsed with laughter at the ludicrous appearance it presented as it trotted along, followed by its numerous attendants, all the while emitting loud snorts, and its hide glittering with the perspiration induced by such unusual exercise.

We had anticipated considerable difficulty in getting it across the somewhat broad river, on the opposite bank of which our camp was situated, but it took the water better than we had expected, and was soon tethered there in safety.

The bottom in which it was contained abundance of the rich grass which forms the chief food of *R. simus*, but it did not eat much of it, though, even on the first evening, it consumed a large quantity of the young shoots and tender leaves of the thorn branches provided for it, and seemed to be most fond of the hack, or waitabit thorn, turning over the other kinds with its snout and tasting them, and then passing them by to search for the former. On the second evening, however, I noticed it, after returning from water, commence to eat the surrounding grass; and though it did not show as great a relish for it as it did for the thorn-shoots, it ate it, both then and afterwards, in such large quantities as proved that it naturally forms a by no means inconsiderable portion of their food, and this is a more important point than it seems, as showing the individuality of the species; both of those which form the "black" subsisting almost entirely on thorn branches and roots, while *R. simus*, as I have said before, feeds chiefly, if not solely, on grass. It was also noticed to be remarkably partial to the leaves of the umganu tree, a water-loving species, which is found in the damp bottoms, and whose fruit, formed by the natives into an intoxicating drink, is so esteemed by the elephants that they annually come hundreds of miles in search of it to places where it is common. It used to be taken down to water twice a day, and very soon became tame enough to be led there by a couple of men without attempting to charge; in fact, before its death it would come to any one who brought it a bundle of thorn branches, and, unless irritated by seeing a dog, to which it had a great aversion, or by too much familiarity, would not attempt to hurt him. When annoyed it warned us of the fact, and of the advisability of getting beyond the limits of its tether, by its forcibly expelling the air through its closed lips, forming a noise resembling an emphatic sneeze, while at the same time it imparted a sudden stiffness to its neck, very similar to what may be observed in cattle when displeased with anything they see passing. This was all particularly interesting to us; for although the sound they make was one well known to every hunter as the precursor of a charge, the imminent danger it usually announced had prevented any of us from hitherto learning how it was made.

We ascribed its death, which occurred before long, to too sudden a change from its mother's milk, but, if a specimen were really wanted for this country, and there is not a single one as yet, I have no doubt that even this difficulty—a serious one in a land where cattle do not exist on account of the tsetse—might be got over by the sacrifice of the lives of a few cows, for, as the bite of this insect does not cause immediate death, although they would ultimately die, yet they might be brought down to the plains, and would probably live long enough to take the young rhinoceros on to the higher districts, where plenty of milk could be procured.

Although I have come across kulumane in greater or less numbers in all parts of South Africa, I have never found them so common as they were, and are even to this day, despite the hundreds that have been shot, in the valley of the Black Umfolosi. In many parts where they only occasionally occur, they are often mistaken, both by whites and blacks, for *R. simus* not yet attained to its full growth, but there their numbers are so large that it is impossible to feel a doubt of their being a distinct species, especially as both *R. simus* and *R. bicornis* are also represented, the former in considerable numbers. It is also noticeable that where the latter species is common the kulumane is rare, and *vice versa*, while *R. simus* seems to exist independently of the others. Different districts, however, appear to be more or less suitable for each distinct species; in the valley of the Black Um folosi the kulumane decidedly preponderates; in the great thorn district which is watered by the upper portion of the Umkusi the common white is more plentiful; in all the country lying between the Umkusi pass in the Bombo mountains to the Mbuluzi both the black species are found, *R. bicornis* being the most common, though both the other species are also represented, while on the great flats to the south known as Hlopekulu *R. simus* alone practically exists.

The best shooting that I had at kulumane was in this valley of the Black Umfolosi, a spot that at one time contained more variety and larger quantities of game in proportion to its size than any other that I have visited in Africa. My introduction to them took place before I had as yet killed any large game, and it was at one of them that I fired my first shot at anything larger than the small antelopes. Our party, which had but lately arrived, and which had hitherto been staying at a native village, started on that day to camp in the open, and as the absolute distance was not great, I did not go with the carriers, but, taking a native with me who was acquainted with the country, I kept on one side in search of game. The country presented the usual peculiarities of all thorn districts, stunted aloes and thorns clothing the stony ridges, and gradually increasing in numbers until on the flats the latter formed vast thickets, many of them all but impenetrable, while a few euphorbias grew in the hotter spots, and the water-courses, dry during winter, were lined with wild dates and bananas and tree-ferns, with here and there a wild fig-tree, or a white-stemmed umtombe towering above the rest. We were just in the act of entering one of these thorn thickets when the native who was guiding me, and who was in front, suddenly stooped down, glanced back to see if I was following, and then, making a motion to say he saw something, ran rapidly though cautiously forward, while I repeated his actions without an idea of what they meant, until he pulled up and pointed out a black mass in front of us, at the same time whispering "kulumane."

It was a troop of six or seven of those animals, standing huddled together, so that, though I could see their outlines, I could hardly distinguish one from another, but as it was evident by their stamping and general uneasiness that they suspected danger, I at once fired. As the bullet told—and it always does so loudly on these thick-skinned animals,—they trotted out, going across me and slightly separating, so that I could see them plainly and had a capital shot with my second barrel, bringing the one I fired at down on the spot; but it jumped up again, and the whole of them, either turned by the shot, or, more probably, only then discovering for the first time where we were, came thundering down straight at us, barely giving me time to follow the native's example and spring into a small tree, on either side of which they passed, enabling me from my elevated position to see where both balls had taken effect. The first had broken the fore-leg below the knee, while a white spot behind the shoulder marked the second, and I should undoubtedly have got the former, had I not allowed myself to be dissuaded from following them, as the great weight of a rhinoceros incapacitates it from travelling far on three legs, and a broken limb may always be accounted a fatal wound. The ball of the foot is also an extremely tender spot, and I remember seeing one that had already gone four or five miles with a bullet through the lungs completely disabled by a chance shot hitting it in the former place, making it squeal with pain, and stand on three legs, holding up the other, unable to place it to the ground.

Some time after this I was returning to camp one evening with fifteen hunters after having been engaged all day with a troop of buffalo that had taken refuge in the reeds. We were marching in native fashion, my gun-bearer leading, myself next, and the hunters and two or three water-bearers following us in Indian file, when four rhinoceroses made their appearance about two hundred yards off, trotting towards us along the very path that we were on. Of course, from the way we were walking, only two or three of the foremost could see them, but that did not prevent the others following our example as we sprang to leeward of the path, and lay down in the long grass. The great brutes trotted on, perfectly unsuspicious, and, with their usual blindness, taking no notice of the line of black heads that bordered the path, until I, having allowed the first three to pass me, opened fire on the last, and, staggering him with my first barrel, brought him on to his knees with the second.

The instant I had fired the whole line took it up, and the irregular volley that succeeded lasted for fully a minute. The rhinoceroses, severally wounded in half a dozen places, broke into a gallop, and seemed going to make their escape, when one, a yearling, suddenly halted and commenced squealing, and its mother, enraged by the sound, wheeled on the spot, and came charging down upon us. The scatter she caused was complete; no one had a breech-loader, and therefore no one was loaded but myself, so, while I made the best of my way to a tree, I kept my eye on her, and seeing her pressing one of the water-bearers whom she had singled out, I pulled up short and fired, attracting her attention to myself. I gave her the other barrel as she came on, puffing and snorting, and then made for a tree; but there was no necessity for doing so, as she broke down immediately afterwards on one of her fore-legs which had been pierced by a bullet, but had not hitherto given way, and which placed her completely at our mercy. Seeing this the hunters descended from the trees, and for some minutes there was a general ringing of iron ramrods on ill-fitting bullets, while I fired at, and tried to finish, the one I had at first brought to the ground, but, though I tried every spot I knew of, taking the most deliberate aim, it was not till the sixth bullet that it fairly fell, having hitherto been plunging about, trying to rise from its knees. A far greater number of shots were fired by the hunters at the cow and yearling before they killed them, and I have no doubt, counting misses and badly-aimed shots, that there were over fifty bullets expended altogether on the three head; yet I have seen three rhinoceroses killed with three single shots by some of these very men.

R. Keitloa is a species of which I have personally only killed one specimen, and, though I have seen twenty or thirty pair of horns that were either killed by my acquaintances or by my own men, I have but rarely met with it alive, and that chiefly far inland of the Portuguese settlement of Lorenço Marquis. It exists, however, more plentifully to the north than to the north-east or east, and has been met with by other travellers in considerable numbers, whose testimony would seem to point to the fact of its being savage and morose in disposition, one very noted sportsman (Andersson) going so far as to consider it more dangerous than *R. bicornis*. Such, however, is neither my own experience nor that of the other hunters, both European and native, whom I have consulted on the subject; all accounts going to prove that it bears no comparison whatever in this respect to the dreaded upetyane; and I should feel inclined to place it on a par in disposition with the kulumane.

The one that I killed I was fortunate enough to finish with a single shot, though under circumstances that with *R. bicornis* would certainly have insured a charge. The previous night had been a very disturbed one from the continued roaring of two lions which had taken up their abode in the same thicket in which we had camped, and which had so far prevented me from sleeping that had it not been for the necessity of hunting to procure food, I certainly should not have gone out that day. Soon after I had done so, however, we saw some eland running across us, and hoping that they might halt again before long, we started in chase, and had run perhaps a couple of miles when a flock of rhinoceros-birds rose out of a clump of bush just in front, and I saw the snout of a rhinoceros protruding from it.

The birds had alarmed it, and it was only by rushing in that I got a slanting shot at it as it trotted off through the open in full view, and as it took no notice, and I had not heard the crack of the ball, I fancied I had missed, and not only did not hurry myself to reload, but allowed the Kaffir who accompanied me to go after it alone, until I heard it squealing, sure proof that it was mortally wounded, and then a shot.

Hastening to the spot, I found it standing, screaming and swaying its body to and fro, while its nearly full-grown young one was quartering about trying to get our wind, and the native was observing the whole proceedings from the top of a tree, at the bottom of which was his gun. I at once fired at the young one, making it charge past and go straight off, and then I went up to its mother, which had now fallen, and found that it was an umkombe tovote. My ball had penetrated from close in behind the shoulder through the head of the heart. The native had missed it, and had so frightened a number of Amaswazi who happened to be in that direction by the whistling of the bullet, that they had taken refuge in trees, but from its body we cut out four old balls, which had seemingly been in it for years. Its horns, which were unusually good, measured twenty-four inches for the front one, twenty for the back, and this, as far as the difference in their length goes, has been the average of those I have seen, except in one pair (unique in my experience) where the hind one was slightly the longer.

Generally speaking, the habits of the different species are the same, slightly diversified by their peculiar characteristics. Leaving their lair about four o'clock in the afternoon, or later if the district is much disturbed by human beings, they graze towards water, or, if of the black species, browse on the thorn shoots in their way, reaching it soon before or after dark, distance sometimes deferring their arrival till a later hour, and if it is a mud-hole, they probably have a roll after drinking. They then start for their favourite feeding-ground, a rich grass bottom in the case of *R. simus*, the dense ukaku thickets in the case of the other three, keeping along the regular beaten paths in doing so, which they make all over the country, and which they make use of night after night. After generally, though not always, watering again about daylight, they retire to their sleeping-places sooner or later, according to what extent the country is free from human beings, reaching it at any rate before the heat of the day. This is always in an extremely sheltered and deeply shaded spot, and so heavily do they slumber, that a practised stalker could almost touch them with the muzzle of his gun, unless alarmed by the birds which accompany them in search of ticks. I do not, however, consider it a good plan to fire at a rhinoceros lying down, from the difficulty of judging exactly how your bullet will penetrate, and now, after many unavailing attempts, I always rouse them first—an easy thing to do, for on the breaking of a twig, or a cough, they will get up and stand, turning round and round, trying to discover what has disturbed them, and you can then aim where you like.

This, with me, totally depends on the angle at which they are—the upper part of the heart being the mark,—and it is therefore impossible to say more than that the best place is about the shoulder, behind or before, as the case may be. A ball entering the centre of the chest is often immediately fatal, and in all front shots there is a fair chance of cutting an important blood-vessel. In the flank, when it is running nearly stern on, and three inches above the tail when it is quite so, are both good marks, but it must always be borne in mind that, with the rhinoceros, as with the African elephant, there is no place that is perfectly certain to prove fatal. I have heard much about a spot in the head, between the ear and eye, or up the nostril, and I even know of two cases—not in Africa, however, but India—where the animal was killed by wounds in that part only; but in my own experience I have never seen or heard of a single bullet in the head being successful, except to stun, and from the extraordinary thickness of the skull-bones, and the peculiar position and smallness of the brain cavity, I do not see how serious damage could be caused, unless by chance.

As I have before said, sufficient anecdotes of the ferocity, chronic bad temper, and cunning of *R. bicornis* might be related of themselves to fill a volume. Their cunning is only equalled by their viciousness. In most, if not in all cases, they will at once charge on getting the wind of a human being, and if they cross his track, they will often follow it up like a dog, making none of the puffing sound natural to them when angry, till they absolutely see him. When wounded, and occasionally when much disturbed, their spoor consists of parallel straight lines, so that it is next to impossible to overtake them without being discovered, and giving them an opportunity of charging you from one side. They will wait with the utmost patience concealed in thick jungle, until you almost touch them, and then rush out at you. When they do catch an unfortunate being, they knock him down and knead him with their feet, returning again and again until nothing but a shapeless mass remains, uttering all the day their shrill squeal of rage. This I once saw myself.

Four of us, consisting of myself, three native hunters, and my gun-bearer, were on our way to join a native hunting party some twelve miles off, and just after crossing a small stream about half way we saw a flock of rhinoceros-birds hovering over an ukaku thicket, and evidently accompanying some game passing through it. The place was of no great size, so two of the hunters ran round to the further sides, while I and the remaining one went into it, and in a few seconds struck the spoor of an upetyane. I am thankful now to recollect that I at once suggested leaving the vicious brute alone, partly because it was such dangerous work, and its death would do us no good, partly on account of the time it would waste and the distance we had yet to go. However, the hunter wanted to go after it, and to have said more would have implied fear on my part, a thing one has to guard against when, being the only white man amongst natives far in the interior, one's comfort, and not impossibly one's life, depends upon one's prestige; and so we went on, and in scarcely five minutes I saw it, having already heard it snorting like a steam-engine, trotting along, tossing its head, and looking like mischief personified, having evidently got the wind of some of us, and being quite as anxious to find us as we it. It was about fifteen yards off, and I instantly let drive with both barrels into its shoulder, springing as I did so into the tree under which I was.

My unlucky companion, who was a little distance on one side, and had hitherto only heard it, came running towards the shots, and absolutely met it face to face; he at once fired and turned to run, but it was too late, and he was caught on the spot, thrown up with a single toss, which must probably have stunned him, and was then trampled out of all semblance to humanity by the bloodthirsty brute. Any description would be sickening; I could do nothing, for my gun-bearer had disappeared, seeking safety in some other spot, and I found that I had not a single cartridge left in the little pouch I carried; but after a minute I could stand the inaction no longer, and getting down from the tree unperceived, I stole away, and as soon as I was out of reach, began to shout to the others. Two of them soon came up, my gun-bearer and a hunter, one of them having hidden himself on finding the sort of animal we had to deal with; and I having got a supply of cartridges, we went back to the spot until we got sight of the brute, still trampling and squealing, when kneeling down, we fired at it together.

My nerves had been so much shaken, that I was unsteady and missed clean, not twenty yards off, but the ball from my companion's great elephant-gun sped more truly, and the brute fell on its knees, where, by dint of repeated, if not very well-aimed shots, I succeeded in keeping it until he had re-loaded, when we finished it off together.

Other instances of the same sort are not wanting, but that was the only one that ever occurred within my personal knowledge, though, during the time I was hunting, two of my men were killed by rhinoceroses—one by an upetyane, the other by a kulumane—and from what I heard of the details, they must have been very similar. I only know of a single instance of a person escaping with life. A lot of Kaffirs were crossing the Bombo flats, and a woman, carrying her baby on her back in the native fashion, joined the party for protection. During the journey they were charged by an upetyane. Everybody threw down their bundles, regardless of breaking calabashes and pots of fat, and climbed up trees, all except this woman, who, impeded by her burden, and terrified out of her wits, was overtaken and tossed. When she fell again, the rhinoceros came up, sniffed at her and the baby, and walked away, not attempting to do any further harm, and luckily she was only bruised. What had caused it to do this no one knew, and therefore ascribed it to witchcraft. Perhaps the resemblance of the baby's squalling to its own made it so unusually merciful.

One killed in Zululand, in 1871, destroyed no less than seven people before its death. It had been well known for some years as infesting a certain district, and had succeeded at different times in catching three native women while drawing water. Possibly its presence in the thicket adjoining the stream might have been accidental, although the Kaffirs appeared to think that it had stationed itself there with malice prepense. In August that year a son of the Zulu king died, and, as is customary, all the males of the country were sent to hunt in the bush, and by the act of shedding blood purify themselves and the nation from the defilement consequent on his death. One of the largest regiments, the Tulwane, numbering perhaps 2000 men, came across this brute, and he at once charged it, causing a general flight. This was, however, only momentary; they came back, and though merely armed with assagais, ultimately killed it, after a hard fight and the loss of four of their number, one of whom, if I mistake not, was an officer, besides several more who were placed *hors de combat*. There must have been over a thousand spears in it before it fell.

My first introduction to this animal was by no means a pleasant one. I was hunting as usual, and buffalo having been reported in the reeds which lined a small stream near our camp, I was skirting along them in hopes of finding their fresh spoor; and after going some miles I saw two rhinoceros-birds, which were coming from the same direction as I had, make a swoop, and settle a few hundred yards ahead. On reaching the place I could hear something breaking inside, and as the bank was high and there was a tall dead tree on it, I told my gun-bearer to climb up and have a look. He did so, and on coming down, reported two upetyane. I had long wished to kill one of those animals, as I had already killed all the other species, including a modified form of *R. Oswellii*, but it would have been foolish to have gone into the reeds after them; in such cover I should have had little chance of inflicting any damage, and less of coming out alive; so I climbed up the tree myself, hoping to be able to have a shot from there. I, however, found I could not, as only one was in sight, and it was in such a position that I could not depend on wounding it seriously. Breaking off, therefore, a dead branch, I threw it in, and in a few minutes they walked out on the opposite side, going slowly, and looking about uneasily to see whether the noise portended danger. I can still see the picture in which they formed a part. A great sea of reeds rustling and waving with every passing air, dotted with a few old trees, naked and dead, stretching out their white branches above them, and edged for the most part with dense evergreen bushes. Far away an immense flat, unbounded as far as the eye could reach, and covered with masses of dark jungle alternating with patches of the white sun-dried grass between, and here and there glimpses of a lagoon, half buried in reeds. Complete stillness, and no signs of life, except the two rhinoceroses as they walked quietly away, and two solitary human beings watching them.

In a few minutes more they were concealed by the intervening bushes, and I came down, and crossing over, took up their spoor and tried to follow it; finding great difficulty, however, in doing so, as their foot, being very small, hardly, indeed, larger than that of a buffalo bull, and very soft, leaves no impression but that made by the three toes, and on ground as hard and dry as it is in winter in Africa, even that is very slight. Few people would believe the fact that, except during the wet season, it is far easier to track a buffalo than an elephant or rhinoceros, despite their great weight and size; the mark made by the harder hoof being so much more clear and well defined. I had in consequence to go slowly until I reached the thicket, where it became easier, and after tracking them for some distance the spoor led us into an extremely thick mass of ukaku thorns, along an old rhinoceros path which wound through it. Here at last I overtook them, and caught a glimpse of one, and though the only part of its body that I could see was the fore shoulder, I at once fired. With a succession of tremendous snorts they instantly charged.

It would be quite impossible for me to describe what occurred. One saw me as I tried to get away, and chased me as I dodged through and in and out of the thick thorns, until at last I found myself alone, hardly knowing how I got there, standing breathless and bleeding, my clothes torn to ribbons, my cap gone, and scarcely a square inch of my body that had not its particular thorn. My bearer had disappeared—it had been much against his will our ever following them, and I did not see him again that day—but I was so thoroughly roused by the pain I was in, that after loading, as soon as I could find my gun, I did not lose a moment in getting on the spoor, which I was glad to find spotted with blood. They did not stand again for several miles, but ultimately went to a place that I knew well. It was a large patch of thorn by the river, and in the centre were several cactus-trees, round which the tangle was so thick, that except at one spot there was no entrance. Some years before a native hunter had been found dead in it, with a buffalo lying a few yards off unable to rise, and ever since the spot had been avoided. Just before reaching it the spoors had separated, an unusual, but for me fortunate, occurrence, one going on, the other making towards it, a drop of blood on the latter showing it to be that of the wounded one. I soon, however, got confused in the maze of tracks it had made in standing and walking about, and fancying it had thought of entering, but had changed its mind and gone after the other, I went up to the narrow opening, then only a few yards off, and where it had evidently passed in and out several times, and looked in. At first it was too dark to see, but as I got accustomed to the gloom, I decided that the place was empty, and was in the act of turning away, muttering, "It's gone on," when, with a loud grunt, it rushed out, just brushing past me as I shrunk on one side. I ran in and climbed up the nearest tree, hardly a second before it returned in search of me, puffing and snorting, and as it stood listening for some indication of my whereabouts, not three yards from the foot of the tree, I gave it both barrels in the shoulder, and before the smoke had cleared, it had forced its way out, clearing a path for itself, and I could hear it as it galloped away. Coming down, I loaded and again went in pursuit, finding it standing in the open, about fifty yards from the edge of the wood, from the concealment of which I again fired, making it charge, but I dodged behind a tree, and it passed through the smoke, and then stopped and walked back to its former position. Determining to get nearer, I stalked up behind a solitary thorn-tree to within fifteen paces, and then planted another ball, like the last, in the shoulder, bringing it down, but it struggled up in spite of my second barrel, and stood, only looking round at the noise I made in loading. It was beaten at last; though it took three more shots—nine in all—before it finally fell dead. Six of these were well placed about the shoulder, one was rather too far back, one in the head, and the last in the centre of the chest.

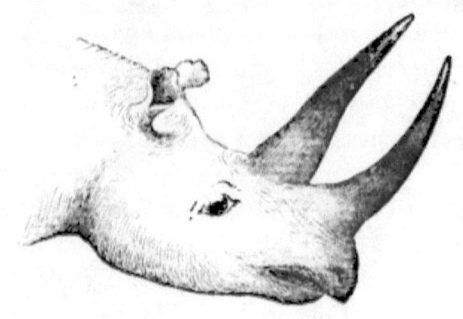

CHAPTER III.

ELAND.

"Who's that come, Unfusi?" I asked, sitting lazily, sketching Kaffirs' heads, under the shade of an umganu tree, on a hot summer afternoon in 1868.

"It's Umfana Wezulu," replied the boy addressed.

"Has he killed anything?"

"Yes, he's got a tail in his belt; I think it's an eland."

"Call him here then," I ordered, anxious to hear about it, for eland were scarce, even in those days, in the district between the Black and White Umfolosi rivers where I was hunting; and when he came I asked him where he had killed it, and how many he had seen. The spot he mentioned was a mountain, called, as is the case with so many hills in different languages, the "Big Hill," and was about fourteen miles off; and he said that he had seen five of them, two bulls and three cows, one of which latter he had killed. A question or two about why he had not shot a bull, and the direction he had left the others going in when he returned, elicited that he had fired at and missed the bulls at starting, and that he had positively run down the cow by sheer speed, and shot her when at a standstill. It was not by any means the first time that I had heard of such a thing being done, for it is a common expression of the natives, when speaking of a remarkably good runner, to say that he could run an eland down; but I had always looked upon it as a figure of speech, and was rather taken by surprise when a man whose running powers I had personally tested now told me that he had done so, and enforced his assertion by bringing home the animal's tail. On several occasions I had had bursts after buffalo when the same man was present, and had always distanced him, but he was one of those wiry, tall, thin-armed and thin-legged men, with no body to carry worth speaking of, who could run for an indefinite period, and would be as fresh at the end of ten miles as at the beginning. However, I fully made up my mind to have a try after the eland at the very first opportunity, and for several days I went out especially in search of them, though unsuccessfully, until at last I came across them in the following somewhat curious manner.

Originally I had left camp with a considerable following of hunters and attendants, and for some distance we had kept together on the fresh spoor of a herd of buffalo, but when we reached them, and they broke away without giving us a chance of a shot, all of the hunters disappeared in pursuit, while my own boys, water-bearers, meat-carriers, etc., probably thinking that I also had gone on, ran forward without me. I, however, had already had one or two long days after this same troop, and felt pretty sure that they would not stop again that day, and that those who were after them would, as they actually did, return empty-handed; and so, turning off, I made in the direction of the Big Hill, before mentioned. After going one or two miles I was so pestered with the unceasing attentions of a honey-bird—which would not be driven away with stones, and whose cry, recognised as it is by the game as denoting the human presence, was not a pleasant accompaniment to a hunter—that I turned and followed it, and descending at the end of half a mile into a partially dry watercourse, I saw it make a peculiar flutter, such as I had formerly seen it do when it took me to, and in that way pointed out, a big snake, and on cautiously coming forward prepared to see a leopard, or at the least a snake, I found a hunter in my employment lying fast asleep. He was a white boy of eighteen or nineteen years of age, white at least in blood and features, though a native in education, habits, manners, and ways, having been brought up among them on a Zulu mission station, and therefore preferring at all times their society as more congenial than that of his fellow-countrymen. I had found him idling at the station, and offered him the command of my hunters, and payment for whatever he might personally kill, thinking that, as there was nothing to do but to see that the powder was not stolen, and that the hides were taken care of, he could not possibly go wrong, and that it would be a pleasant change for him to have such capital shooting as a matter of business. Yet such was his sloth and want of energy, qualities conspicuous in all African-born whites, that during the four or five months he was in the game country he only killed one buffalo, and devoted his whole time to following the honey-birds, and devouring the honey they took him to, so that when this one showed him to me I half thought it must have recognised him as an old acquaintance and wished me to awake him. Not, however, being desirous of disturbing the slumbers of this dirt-begrimed "honey hunter," as the natives, from his never bringing anything else home, had learnt to call him, I went on across the watercourse, and was in the act of kneeling down to drink some of the lukewarm water it contained, when I caught a glimpse of a white-looking shadow some quarter of a mile off, which I soon made out to be an eland; and, as I thought I might get close to it by crawling up the stream channel, I started to try, and by dint of imitating the motion of a snake in some places, while in others I could use my hands and knees, I before long got opposite the spot on the bank which I had marked, and, on cautiously looking over, I could see one cow pretty plainly, and several others looming through the thorn-trees. When I say, see the cow plainly, there was only one part, her flank, that was really visible, the long grass concealing all below her belly, and her fore part being hidden by the trees; however, as she stood turned away from me she presented a most undeniable shot, and I put my bullet in at her last rib, perfectly certain that she would not go a hundred yards afterwards, and jumping up, I ran forward to try and get a chance at the others. They, however, were not in sight, only the cow I had fired at being so, and she, after a minute or so, pulled up, hung down her head, trembled a little, and then swaying her body slightly from side to side, she knelt down, and in a few seconds was dead. I did not, however, wait any longer than to see that she was down, being bent upon keeping, or rather getting, the others in sight, and went tearing on at full speed in the direction they had taken.

Luckily my somnolent *chargé des chasseurs* had been wakened by the shot, and as the elands went towards him, he was able to shout directions which enabled me, when they saw him, and sheered off from the report of his gun, to so gain on them that, as they emerged into the comparative open, I was barely twenty yards behind. Several times I half pulled up and tried to get a shot, but the numerous clumps of bush and groups of trees through which they were running rendered it very difficult, and as every time I made the attempt I lost a great deal of ground, I gave it up, and settled down to running steadily at about a hundred and fifty yards behind them. There were only three, two bulls and a cow, and I at once selected a great blue bull, old and fat, and nearly twice the size of the cow, as the one I should try and run into. He was leading, more as a matter of duty than pleasure I fancy, with the cow next him, and their ground-covering trot was keeping me doing all I could, and not gaining a yard, but rather, if anything, losing. I was, however, in very good condition, and as soon as I got steadied after a mile or so,

I found myself able to improve the pace, and making a strong burst, I got within ninety yards of them, but, on their looking round and seeing me, I had to keep myself at top speed for the next hour or more, barely holding my own. So far we had been running on an almost dead level, but now the ground suddenly changed to a broken stony ridge, leading to a still rougher hill, and though the stones were against me, the steepness was in my favour, and I gained so steadily, that I thought I could afford the delay of firing, and so, pulling up, I did the best my long run would allow, which was only to knock the dust up among their legs. The shot, however, made them swerve heavily, and I almost think that what I lost in distance I gained in wind, for we were on a steep part of the rise, and the extra exertion the fright gave them must have blown the fat old bull a good deal; indeed, as they slightly altered their course, I could see that his mouth was open, and his tongue hanging out. When they got to the top of the rise they again rather left me, as their long-reaching stride carried them down the opposite side, and the succeeding half-mile across the flat left me good for very little—the elands, except the bull, who was evidently rather blown, seemingly being no worse than when they started. I was going very heavily up the next rise, certainly not gaining, rather losing ground, and as we neared the top I felt that the table-like plain which forms the summit of the Big Hill would be too much for me, and I tried to pull up and fire, but I could not make up my mind to lose so much ground a second time, and before I could decide they were over the top, so, with my heart in my mouth,

"THE OLD FELLOW TAKING HIS OWN LINE"

and not another hundred yards of go left in me, I struggled up after them, until my eye fell on the flat, and found the eland, not two hundred yards away as I had expected, but standing about ten yards from the brow of the hill, the old bull blowing like a steam-engine. Of course I instantly fired, but was so unsteady that I missed clean, and they started off again, the cow and young bull going together, and the old fellow taking his own line. I gathered myself together for another effort, and after running several hundred yards I gave him another shot, again missing, as could be told by the flying dust beyond him, but it made him swerve round, during which I thought he was going to fall, and then he pulled up about sixty yards off, and stood and looked at me, his lowered head and laboured breathing proving that he was fairly done at last. I then sat down, and resting the gun on my knees, tried to steady the sight upon him, but finding it impossible, I had to give myself time.

Even breathless and tired as I was, with my eland still standing unwounded before me, I could not help admiring the extreme beauty of the picture. Although I was on the top of a mountain, it was a perfectly dead unbroken flat all around that I could see from my seat, covered with long waving grass white with seed, and among this stood the eland with nothing else in sight, save where, between him and the sun—which, low down, was pouring a flood of light over his head and horns—a black spot could be detected, ever growing larger and nearer, and which, had the poor brute seen and understood it, he would have regarded as the harbinger of his fate. Unconscious, however, of the descending vulture, as indeed he seemed to be of my presence, he stood motionless, save for his heaving flanks, a magnificent specimen of the largest antelope in the world. His bluish dun colour contrasted well with the black stripe that marked his back and withers, while his shape, of which a prize ox might have been proud, proved his age and condition. His immense hump, and the deep dewlap which hung below his knees, his great square quarters and straight back, and the enormous breadth of his chest and neck, on which his finely-shaped head almost seemed out of proportion, all combined to show that he possessed capabilities for putting on flesh found in no other antelope in Africa, and rarely equalled among any animals in the world.

As soon as I was steady enough I shot him, and he fell on the spot, the first and last eland that I ever fairly ran unwounded to a standstill; though, as I examined his immense carcase, unwieldy from fat, and set on such fine-boned slight-made legs, the marvel to me was that he should have run as well as he did. The distance we had come must, I judged, have been over eleven miles, a great part of which I had to retrace before reaching camp, and he had accomplished this in so short a time, that although personally in the very highest of training, I was completely done up, and felt the effects of it for several days after. Like all old eland bulls, his horns, though hard and thick enough, were short and ugly, and not to be compared to those of a cow or of a younger bull, and his proportions were nine feet two inches from the root of the tail to the horns, and six feet thick at the withers, making him the largest of all that I ever measured either before or afterwards.

There is only one species of eland, or elk, as the Dutch colonists, with their talent for giving absurd names, have erroneously called it, the *Antilope Oreas;* but there are two varieties, the common and the striped; the latter, found exclusively in South Africa, and gradually lessening in numbers, until in Central Africa it entirely gives way to the former, while there is a neutral ground inhabited by both, where, unless I am much mistaken, they interbreed.

Dr. Schweinfurth[1] thus describes the variety inhabiting the interior :—" All the elands that I saw had extremely short sleek hair of a bright yellow tan colour, verging on the flanks to a light bay ; the mane was black and erect, being about three inches long. In every district through which I travelled I observed their skin to be always marked in well-defined stripes, which are not, as some travellers have supposed, to be taken as indications of the youth of the animal. I have seen full-grown specimens that were marked on each side of the body with no less than fifteen parallel stripes, about as wide as one's finger, of a pure white, running from the black line of the back transversely down to the middle of the belly, which is often marked with a large black spot."

With this description no fault can be found, though as far as regards the stripes not being an indication of youth, I consider it a somewhat doubtful point. I have myself shot an eland without a vestige of a stripe, the young calf of which was striped, and I know several such cases. Personally I am inclined to agree with Dr. Schweinfurth

[1] *Heart of Africa,* p. 249.

so far that I believe that a calf that is striped at birth will to some extent retain the marks when grown up, though some people maintain the contrary, and point to the fact of the unstriped cows having calves with stripes, which, they say, will gradually die away as the animal grows older, and at last entirely disappear. My explanation of it is simply that the two varieties interbreed, and the result is a striped calf, while the irregularity, and often extreme faintness of the markings when the animal has attained its full size, would seem to favour some such theory.

The common kind exactly resembles the other, except in wanting the markings, and being, if anything, of a darker colour, as well as being decidedly their inferior in size; the great striped cows rivalling the young bulls of the other variety in their immense proportions. Their weight is wonderful, averaging between 800 lbs. and 1100 lbs., while the old blue bulls reach to 1400 lbs. or 1500 lbs.

On two different occasions, besides the one I have mentioned, I have had good days on foot with eland. The first time I accidentally, and quite unexpectedly, fell in with a great herd while I was chasing some gnu; one of which I had wounded but at once resigned on seeing the rarer game. I had not noticed them in time to attempt any concealment, but as, like all game when in large herds, they were slow to start, and kept pulling up in small parties of a dozen or more to look back, I had time to run in and fire four barrels before they closed into one mass and went away. Only one, a cow, fell, though one or two more were evidently hard hit, and one at least afterwards dropt behind. There were about one hundred and twenty, I calculated, exclusive of some thirty calves, which were considerably in their seniors' way, and the pace they went at was so slow as to enable me to keep within two hundred yards, and to fire occasional shots without losing ground. I had a native with me, luckily a long legged and winded one, and we ran very steadily together for about five miles, during which time I had finished off one of those already wounded, and brought down two others. We felt convinced that so large a herd, with their progress so much impeded by the calves, would soon run themselves out under this scorching sun, but as, in the meantime, they kept on, I tried to aim at several of the great bulls, which, distinguishable by their dark colour and superior size, trotted amongst the front ranks. My efforts were rewarded with only very moderate success, merely wounding one and causing him to lag behind, so, thinking that if I pushed him he would probably separate, I made a spurt and ran in within a hundred yards, when, pulling up, I fired another four barrels in succession. One of the foremost fell on the spot, and the wounded bull, accompanied by a cow, dropt astern, while the herd trotted on to the top of the next ridge, where they halted for a few minutes, and, on resuming their flight, left another bull standing, unable to go further. Unfortunately, my native had got himself badly spiked on one of those tremendous thorns, sometimes as much as nine inches long, which are scattered so dangerously on the ground; and as all these eland had to be finished off, and camp, fifteen miles distant, had to be reached, I was forced to leave the rest in peace.

As it was, I had killed seven head, two of which were great bulls; but if I had come across the herd early in the day, and had had a couple of strong-running gun-bearers with me, I have no hesitation in saying that, dependable upon my shooting, I could have got double. I never saw eland run so slowly or take so little notice of my shots; but the size of the herd, which, though by no means very large to see grazing together, was unusually so to run together, as they generally split up into smaller groups when disturbed, partly accounted for it, while the presence of the young calves had a great effect, though they seemed a good deal more "fit" than their fat-laden mothers.

The other occasion was once when camped by the river Sutu, I was asked to join two other white hunters who were going to visit a kraal on the outskirts of Swaziland, where some of their native hunters were stationed. I agreed, and we started after breakfast, commencing by wading across the river, which is here nearly a quarter of a mile broad and very picturesque, and then striking across the thorns in the direction of the next stream, the Umsundusi by name, where we were to sleep. No one had brought an extra gun-bearer except myself, there being only one man to each of the others, and he being occupied in carrying their respective sleeping gear both A. and H. were in consequence carrying their own guns. Suddenly, when we were about half way, a small herd of buffalo appeared running straight towards us—a not uncommon incident in much-disturbed districts; and while I made a rush for my gun, my companions both fired, seemingly without effect, and the herd had passed, so that I only had a stern shot, when I followed their example; as, indeed, I remarked aloud at the time, for the knowledge that my bullets could only have entered behind and driven forwards might have been of use, and a guide to the ownership of the animal, under the hunters' law of first wound, had any of them been, as they were, ultimately killed. Not that any thought of a dispute had crossed my mind, for it is but a fair tribute to the native hunters with whom I was accustomed to hunt to say that a less jealous, or more honest set, as far as regarded shooting, could not have been found, and that during all the years I hunted among them I never once had, or heard of, a serious dispute, even when—it being, from some circumstance, such as similar bullets or the like, quite impossible to assign an owner to the game—the matter had to be decided by one of the petty officers who are appointed for such purposes; though, even then, if any one claimed the first wound with a fair show of reason, although he might not be able to prove it, and no other evidence than his word could be adduced, in most cases his claim would be tacitly allowed. I mention this, as such a very different line of conduct was pursued by these white men on this and subsequent occasions, that I was much struck by the contrast.

Following the buffalo with my eye, I saw one of those I had fired at separate from the others, and after loading, which, as I had a muzzle-loader, delayed me some time, I ran after it, but before I could go very far on the spoor I heard a shot in front, and then met H. returning with his dogs, which had bayed it. He told me that it was one which he had wounded, though the native with him afterwards told mine that they only found one wound, and that that had broken the hind-leg, which his bullet could not have done, as the buffalo were facing him when he fired; besides which, a piece of the ball which they had found in the splintered bone retained some scratches I was accustomed to make on mine, although it was so flattened as not to be otherwise recognisable. We had not got far on our way back when we were met by a native of A.'s, asking us to hurry and help him to kill *his* buffalo, which had also separated; and, while complying, a few questions enabled us to discover, as we expected, that it was one of those we had all fired at, but which we two, intent upon the one already killed, had not noticed. A. *had*, however, and seeing it lie down in the open had fired two shots at its stern, which made it rise and betake itself to some thickets beyond, into which, particularly as he had but lately been caught and well bruised by an old bull, he did not care to follow it alone, and indeed, having had no practice at spooring, he probably could not have done so, had he attempted it.

On our arrival, both H. and A. went towards the spot at which it had entered, while I was still giving directions about bringing some of the meat of the one killed to where we intended to sleep, and as I was running forward to overtake them I heard a shot and saw the buffalo break to the left, giving me a stern shot, which did not do much towards stopping her. However, H.'s dogs were good, and they brought her to bay while I was loading, and H., who had fired, but was again ready, ran in and dropt her with a shot in the shoulder, while I, getting up as she fell, went up close, and on her trying to rise knocked her down again. As is so often the case, she would not die outright, though quite unable to rise, and received either two or three more bullets in the head before uttering her last moan. The instant, however, that this was the case, A. and H., to my great amusement, at once claimed her; though an examination of the wounds showed that she had received seven bullets, not including those fired to finish her on the ground, viz., two of A.'s, two of H.'s, and three of mine. The two of H.'s, though they had really killed her, could by no possibility give him any claim to her, as they were both fired after she had left the herd, and the point in dispute was, whose bullet had caused her to do so. A. had fired at her twice on the ground after she had separated, but he said he had missed her with the first shot, and that, therefore, as she had two of his bullet-marks, one of them must have been made when she was still with the troop, and that, as he had fired before me, she was his. There was no question but that I had struck her while she was with the troop, as there were three of my bullets in her, and A. had only fired twice since; but arguing was of no avail, and he finally took the tail. The natives, however, all said that *both* the buffaloes were undoubtedly mine, and so in all probability they were; but seeing that both H. and A. were very keen to claim anything we jointly fired at, and as I did not want the hides, I, though rather disgusted, thought it better to let the matter drop, and say no more about it.

It was darkening twilight when we reached the Umsundusi, but the two men who had been sent on with the meat had collected a good deal of firewood, and on such a lovely night in such a climate, little camp-making was necessary. A level place was found to leeward of a row of wild date-trees which bordered the stream; a few branches were arranged in an irregular semicircle; an armful or two of grass strewed over the inequalities of the surface, our mats stretched out, and a couple of fires kindled at their feet, and sufficient had been done both for our comfort and safety. It is wonderful, however, how soon a comfortable and waterproof hut can be run up when it is wanted, if one only knows how to do it; and if one has no tent, or, as is so very likely, it has gone astray, how to keep dry during the tremendous thunderstorms which so often come on during the night is no despicable knowledge, and, under two conditions, namely, the possibility of procuring three posts and the nearness of reeds—both of which are almost always the case with the African hunter—nothing can be simpler, and he may, after a very few minutes' work, defy all that the elements can do, unless the wind unfortunately changes after the fire has been made at the hut door, and the smoke persists in coming in and stifling him, as it once did to me.

As soon as the camping-ground is chosen, a couple of men should be sent out with a hatchet, one or two of which, tomahawk pattern, ought always to be carried, and told to cut two posts of eight or ten feet high, with a fork at one end. It does not much matter even if they are not, as they very likely will not be, perfectly straight, though the ridge-pole, which should be about the same length, is all the better for being so. In the meantime, send as many men as you can spare to cut reeds. You are

sure to be near water, and water in the tropics generally means reeds. Half a dozen large bundles will be sufficient, which can be cut in the same number of minutes. On their arrival build the hut in the following manner, and let the men, meanwhile, cut grass, of which there is certain to be plenty, at least during the wet season :—
Steady the two posts in the ground about seven feet or eight feet apart, and place the ridge-pole on the forks; then scrape a furrow an inch deep parallel to it, into which stand the reeds in layers, putting the larger crossways, and binding them together with the bark of monkey rope, or of almost any tropical thorn or creeper, which a boy will prepare in a couple of minutes. The reeds are then resting on the ground and ridge-pole, enclosing a space of at least seven feet long by three feet six inches or four feet broad at the bottom, rapidly narrowing to the top. On the side away from the wind leave room enough for a doorway, beside which the fire ought to be lighted. One or two bundles of grass put over the ridge-pole and the adjoining post will make the hut quite sufficiently waterproof for all ordinary weather, though, if there is any danger of a thunderstorm during the night, a small drain should be cut across the upper end, as a running stream of cold water down one's back is not pleasant.

When a hut is required in an uninhabited country for several days' use, a large well-finished one of the above description will be found most comfortable. During dry and hot weather the two ends can be left quite open, causing a draught of air to pass over you; while if it is winter and cold, an extra quantity of grass round the sides to keep the wind out, and a great fire as close as ever you like to your feet, ought to keep you pretty warm.

I have already spoken of our "mats," and as they are the most indispensable and characteristic article carried by the African traveller or hunter, it is worth while to describe them and their contents. The word "mat" includes bed, bedding, clothing, and everything not food, taken with one, and is a long rolled-up bundle, mats outwards, borne on the head of the "utibe" or "mat-bearer," the number of whom depends on the luxuriousness of the traveller and their own capabilities, as they are often mere boys of ten or twelve years of age. Personally, when actually hunting, and continually shifting my sleeping ground, I used one strong man for the purpose, with as light a bundle as I could manage with; and though sometimes we lost one another, yet, as a general rule, although he seldom knew in the morning where we should sleep at night, and was unable from his load to follow our hunting line, he usually managed to turn up about dark, attracted by the sound of our guns or seeing the smoke of our fires, and so generally enabled us to have a good night's rest—a thing that I attach much importance to, always feeling that though after my exertions I could be sure enough of actual slumber under any circumstances, yet that up to a certain point increased comfort implied greater real rest, and with me, better form for the next day's work.

The mats themselves, of which I had two, were formed of thick soft grass, woven by the Zulus, and measuring eleven or twelve feet long by three or four feet wide. One end was turned back for a couple of feet, and the sides sewed up so as to form a bag, into which a small air-cushion for use as a pillow, all the articles necessary for the toilet, a change of clothes, and a spare pair of shoes, were stuffed. The next and most important, as well as the heaviest article, was a waterproof blanket of Cording's, eight feet long by four feet wide, with four strong eyelet holes fitted with strings for pegs on each side, which, in packing, was spread over the mats. I found it a most useful thing, saving me from the effects of the damp ground, which one is equally subject to whether sleeping out or in native huts, while, when I happened to be camping out in the rain, with no other shelter available, I could turn it into a tent (by the help of a couple of forked sticks and a pole), which, with a little management, would keep me tolerably dry. On the top of this I placed a pair of sheets of the finest material consistent with strength, as it was often too hot to bear anything more over one, and a woollen blanket, of which I felt the need on raw, wet days, and even on fine ones during the half-hour which precedes dawn, completed the load.

This bed, while very portable, was also very comfortable, and nearly as soft as the mattress used by the young man of the present day. Between me and the ground were two soft mats, a thick waterproof blanket, and a sheet, rendering it almost unnecessary to level the inequalities with an armful of grass, as the mat-bearer, who, when there is only one, acts as cook and housemaid, generally does.

Next morning we resumed our march, skirting along the deep, still, reed-encircled pools of the Umsundusi,—a favourite resort of crocodiles, and seeing many water-antelopes and koodoos, both of which species are very common here. The guns kept skirmishing about on either side of the line of march, sometimes, guided by the honey-bird, robbing a bees' nest, but, more generally, unsuccessfully following some of the gnu which were feeding on the surrounding ridges. At last, when we were all together, a herd of sassabi were seen, and after a rapid and successful stalk we found ourselves within one hundred and twenty yards of where they were grazing, and were not long in sending six bullets in among them. The one I aimed at fell, my second barrel being a somewhat random affair, as also did another, but it recovered and went on, and A. wounded a third. H., however, at once claimed mine, suggesting that I had probably hit the one that had got away, and, as it was all a mere matter of assertion, the bullet having gone through the body, I tossed him for it, and he won, though, in my mind, there was not a shadow of a doubt on the subject, as I had never taken my eye off the animal, and all H. could say, when pressed, was that he fired in that direction.

Nothing more was killed, and late in the afternoon we found ourselves at our destination, where we were greeted with the intelligence that a large herd of elephants had passed two days previously, but as the country about was open, without any covers, and merely dotted over with scattered thorn-trees, there was no chance of their standing within thirty miles of us.

The next day, glad of the opportunity, I went out alone, and succeeded in bagging two doe sassabi, while A. killed one, and H. nothing. The sassabi (*Bubalus lunata*) is very rarely, if indeed ever, found to the southward of the river Sutu, though existing in considerable numbers in many spots to the north of it. The Dutch misnomer for them is Bastard Hartebeest, though I could never see any resemblance that could justify the name. Their average size may be taken as about five feet six inches long from the base of the horns to the root of the tail, and four feet in height at the withers, and their colour is a dark, purplish red, the hair coarse and almost black along the mane, becoming lighter towards the flanks, and the horns, which are small—being seldom over a foot in length—strongly resembling those of a young reed-buck ram. They are found in scattered thorns, generally in small groups of from two to ten head, and never enter covers. I do not consider them a difficult antelope to shoot for a good rifle shot, as standing chances at from one hundred and fifty yards to two hundred yards are easy to obtain, and they will often allow one to walk up to within that distance in full view before even attempting to take to flight, while, when wounded, I have found them unable to go far, and easy to finish, and their flesh may be classed with that of the best of the choicer antelopes.

It being their breeding season at this time (August), there was considerable difficulty in selecting a herd which had no calves, but after firing one or two unsuccessful shots at gnu and solitary sassabi bulls, I saw a herd of four, which consisted of two old cows, and two three-parts-grown calves, and as it therefore seemed as if they were barren this year, I determined to try them from where I was,—two hundred yards, and by good luck broke the foreleg of the nearest cow. They started off, but as soon as her lameness was noticeable, they pulled up again, and stood, allowing me to run up to within fifty yards and knock the other over dead. I then had to act the part of retriever, and ran the broken-legged one until she lay down, dead beat, and I cut her throat, during which time I might have killed the other two again and again with the greatest of ease, and indeed was rather tempted to do so, as they were very little, if anything, smaller than their mothers. However, I fired at nothing more, though the country was swarming with gnu, sassabi, zebra, and impalla, and one herd of the latter that I saw was the largest I ever came across, and must, I computed, have contained about nine hundred head.

The next day was the one to which I have gradually been coming—the one on which I found the eland. H. and I started early, and walked together so far, though we agreed that it would be better to separate before we came to the game. Before doing so, however, I made a successful shot at a bull sassabi that had been feeding on the ridge where we were, and which, after watching us suspiciously for some time, was just jumping away when I fired from about one hundred and twenty yards distance. There was no immediate effect, and he whisked his tail and galloped off, apparently in the best of health, till, after a few hundred yards, he suddenly pulled up, and after a short stagger fell not to rise again, the ball having struck him in the centre of his chest and gone through and through him.

Luckily for me, H., who was hide-hunting, thought it worth while to send one of his men to report the beast's death in camp, so that I was enabled to proceed at once, and to keep both my men with me. Going on, I saw a troop of zebra, and after a long crawl I got a capital shot, and hit one hard, but in the confusion of tracks we lost it. Next I fired a couple of barrels at some gnu, which, disturbed by H. firing, came galloping across me, but they were some way off, and nothing but a very deadly wound will make one of these tough brutes even show he has been hit. The country seemed literally crammed with game, troops of gnu, zebra, impalla, and sassabi feeding in every direction; indeed, there was far too much for my purposes, as the herds being so near together, the alarm spread all the more rapidly, and everything seemed conscious of some approaching danger. Towards afternoon, on nearing a spot where there was a little water, round which the game was feeding in countless numbers, I saw a herd of eland, and tried all I knew to stalk them. The ground was, however, so open that the gnu, which had been suspiciously turning in my direction for several minutes, at last took to flight, and communicating the alarm to the various species of game in sight, they all joined into an immense drove, nothing short of one thousand strong, upon which I jumped up and ran on in hopes of a shot; but although I could easily have killed either gnu or zebra, some of which passed me within twenty yards, I was forced to fire at two hundred and fifty yards at the eland, as I found that I could get no nearer, and that, led by the fleeter kinds, they were fast leaving me.

I then pulled up, as I saw I was driving the game away from home, and concealing myself in the long grass, I sent a boy round to try and head them, and turn them my way. This he did not succeed in doing, but instead of returning, he made signs for me to come on, and on doing so, and reaching the top of the rise over which the eland had disappeared, I was surprised to find one standing within a few yards of me, and as it turned its head round to watch me, I could tell that it was unable to go further, and must be the one that I had fired at. With game that is not likely to turn upon one there must be always a certain amount of pity felt, increased, in cases like the present, when the animal, one of the most beautiful in the world, is standing close to you sick to death, though giving no outward sign of having received a mortal wound, and watching your movements with the great beseeching eyes that are characteristic of the antelope and deer tribes, and one hastens, in sorrow, to put an end to its pain. The uncomfortable feeling, however, vanishes as you approach and admire the splendid head your victim carries, and little pain mingles with the pleasure with which you give orders as to how it should be severed, so as to set the horns off to the best advantage, and, at the same time, not to over-burden your men.

I had been under the impression that it was a young bull, but after its death I found that it was a cow of the striped variety, but so large, that we found it no easy task to break her up, and were very glad to see some Swazis appear, who were trapping wild cats, and who not only helped us, but prevented any of the meat being wasted. When we had finished, and the men had made up their loads of skin, horns, and tit-bits, we started homewards; but as they had seen another herd of eland not far from where the first came from, I went by myself in the direction pointed out, leaving the burdened natives to take the more direct road.

I found them on the spot described—a bare open—and on seeing me they at once broke away at a trot, but in a few seconds pulled up again to have another look and allowed me to get within one hundred and fifty yards of where they were standing. I fired at the nearest, a cow, for there was not a bull among them, and hit her hard, causing her to run alone for some little distance, though she ultimately rejoined the rest. I then gave chase as fast as I could, and owing to the slow pace of the wounded one, which they would not desert, another five minutes took me within easy shot, when finding a large heifer between me and my cow, I fired at the former, smashing the leg high up, upon which she broke into a gallop and went on with my dog at her heels, while the cow, utterly done, pulled up and stood within a few yards of me. I now discovered that I had left my big bullet-pouch with the Kaffirs, and that my small one contained nothing but the bullet which had killed the last eland, and which I had cut out. This I managed to ram down with considerable difficulty, and then went after the heifer, it being evident that the cow could not make its escape, and guided by the dog's barking I soon reached the troop, which were evidently waiting for the wounded one and which absolutely allowed me to come within twenty yards before they made off. Unfortunately the heifer was standing so that I could not see her, and I had to run on after them, waiting for an opportunity.

In all my life I never saw so many magnificent chances as crowded themselves into that quarter of an hour. The wounded one several times halted, and the rest, in waiting for her, allowed me to come within a few paces before they would start, and if I had only had bullets I might have killed half of them. I could not, however, get a satisfactory chance at her; but at last, as she lagged a little behind, I got a broadside shot and fired. My disgust may be imagined at seeing the bullet, my last one, strike up the dust on the other side of her. Of course I thought I had missed, and was agreeably surprised when she suddenly came to a standstill and then fell down, the ball having passed through her. She was not dead though unable to rise, and I had to wait so long, firing powder to guide them, until the men came up with my pouch, that when they at last arrived it was too late to go back after the cow; indeed, it was getting dark already, and there were eight miles to go to camp through the pathless thorn jungle. I was afterwards sorry that I had not slept out and got her in the morning, as I should have been sure to find her, my men having seen her as they passed standing a few yards from where I left her; and the hyenas are such cowards that they would not touch her while alive, though no doubt they ultimately had her.

I got home a little after dark, having run all the way, but the men lost themselves and did not arrive until three hours later; I found that H. had killed a zebra, and that A. had had a chance at some gemsbok, but had missed them.

Next day we returned to the Sutu, though I should have much liked another day after these eland; but the unhealthy season was rapidly coming on, and though I did not intend to leave the country myself for some months, both my companions, in common with all the other European hunters, wished to do so, and were consequently anxious to return. We had a long and tiring day's walking, and on the way a buffalo was shot, whose ownership was of course disputed, and H. killed a young gnu,—our bag for five days thus being three buffalo, two eland, five sassabi, one zebra, and one gnu, besides what went away mortally wounded, of which to my gun alone there were at least two head.

More eland are killed from horseback than on foot; for as it is utterly out of the question to make a practice of running them down, and as they generally inhabit the treeless flats, where they cannot, except by chance, be stalked, while the uncertainty of their movements and their keeping out of cover, renders it impossible to find them like other large animals by the aid of their spoor, some more certain method is needed than the chance meetings which occur to the hunter when in pursuit of other game, more especially as their hide is held in great repute among the Dutch colonists, who make trek-tows for their waggons and rheims for their oxen from it, even preferring it to that of a buffalo. The demand thus induced has so diminished their numbers as to have restricted this noble antelope to a few favoured localities, even in which it is becoming more scarce every day, while not many years ago it formed a component part of almost every landscape in the southern and eastern portions of Africa.

Unlike the elephant and buffalo, it, in common with the rhinoceros, has not so much been driven further inland as exterminated, and many a story I have heard of how a whole herd, numbering perhaps a hundred, of these beautiful and peaceful animals has been killed, bull and calf, by the improvident hunters and their natives, the latter of whom notably have the bump of destruction largely developed, while one-half of the hides thus obtained would rot for want of carriage. Unfortunately, they are also slow breeders, rarely, if ever, producing calves on two consecutive years, and not always each alternate year. July and August are the months, but one rarely sees a third part of a herd with calves running. It is the only time that they are in any way dangerous, and then only to dogs, the cows especially impaling them on their long straight horns in defence of their young. I had once two of my dogs killed in that manner; they were trained and accustomed to run into a herd of buffalo and seize hold of the smallest, which was not uncommonly a good-sized beast, and to keep it stationary and bellowing for help until released by some of the old ones coming to its assistance, and thus afford a shot to the hunter if he was up in time; and one day coming across a herd of eland with young calves, they both dashed in, but before they could catch a single one they were mobbed by the cows, and in a few seconds gored to death.

I have personally ridden down eland on several occasions, though, as they are the slowest antelope in Africa, it is no great feat to do so. Sometimes a young cow in low condition will give one a real gallop, there being much the same difference between it and a corpulent old bull as between a wild young Highland two-year-old, able with ease to clear a five-barred gate, and a stall-fed ox fit for Smithfield.

One of the longest chases I ever had was after such a cow. I had been out after oryx, had ridden a wiry old cow to a standstill after a good deal of very hard galloping on nasty stony ground, and had killed her so far from camp that there was no hope of getting her meat in till next day, though at the time our people were half-starving. As it would do no good to continue hunting at such a distance from camp as she had taken me, and as my horse seemed dull and tired beyond what his work accounted for, I was walking him towards home, and had already come several miles, when I saw in front a solitary eland cow feeding with some gnu and zebra, and I at once determined to try and drive her campwards, and ultimately kill her within reach of our men. To spare my horse, however, in the first instance, I dismounted, and getting into the hollow of a dry watercourse, led him until we were opposite to where the antelopes were grazing, and then mounting, I walked across the flat towards them. In a second they all raised their heads and ceased feeding, and after a long stare, always more prolonged at a horseman than at a solitary human being, they started away, the zebra leading, followed by the eland, and the gnu, with their wild plunging gallop, bringing up the rear, the whole going as I had foreseen straight up wind, and consequently in the direction in which my camp lay.

I rode quietly enough after them, just at such a canter as would not push my horse though continued for hours, but which would keep me at the same time in sight of the chase; and for about four miles we went along in the steadiest fashion, without alteration or hindrance, till the gnu, tired of such monotony, gave their tails an extra swish, and stretching themselves out till their bellies almost touched the ground, tore away at right angles to their former course. The zebra, with whom the eland was, seeing this, hesitated, then wheeled and pulled up facing me, like a dismounted regiment of cavalry, and ultimately, as I came on, galloped after their late followers. It was now necessary for me to exert myself, and anticipating no difficulty in heading an eland, I went off at full speed to prevent its going far in the wrong direction. The gnu, which had already made some way, wheeled still more as they saw me alter my course, and seemed bent upon retracing their steps, even if, as did not appear unlikely, they should come into collision with me in so doing. However, I was watching the zebra, not them; and as I noticed that they also displayed an inclination to break back, I rode straight at them, the gnu meanwhile cutting across me, not twenty yards in front. It required fast galloping to accomplish my purpose, but a couple of shots helped to turn them; and the moment I saw them going up wind again I rode hard right in behind them, and kept them going, so that they shouldn't have time to think about again changing their course. This, however, was only successful for a short time, and before we had gone far they broke back in spite of me, it taking all my time and all my riding to drive out the eland from among them; and though I succeeded in that, I could not turn her head in the required direction till after going at full speed for nearly a mile, which distressed my already tired horse so much that only careful nursing enabled me to keep up with the ground-covering trot of this young and active cow, who seemed to be going quite at her ease. I could, of course, have shot her, but, as I was still seven or eight miles from camp, it would hardly have helped our men had I done so, and so long as she headed right I was very content to see her going.

A few minutes after this I got one of the most sudden and complete falls I ever had. My horse came down with a tremendous crash in a gaping ant-eater or hyena hole, the mouth of which was covered over with the long bent-down grass, and shot me half a dozen yards over its head on to an ant-heap, from which I picked myself up, more astonished than hurt; and finding that neither my horse's legs nor my gun were the worse, I jumped on again, glad to have escaped so easily, and in three minutes after it happened was again at full speed after the eland, which, however, had got concealed by the scattered thorns, and might easily have made its escape if it had altered its course, but keeping the line, I again caught a glimpse of it a quarter of an hour afterwards, although so far ahead that had it not still been making towards camp I should have given it up. I suppose she must have slackened her speed, for I gained very rapidly, and soon resumed my original position about one hundred and fifty yards behind her, and on doing so I noticed that she was very much blown, and would, I feared, give in before we should reach camp.

Hardly had I done so, however, when she suddenly freshened up, redoubled her pace, broke off from the wind, and then changed her trot to the lumbering gallop natural to them when much pressed. As all my endeavours to turn her were fruitless, I was tempted to shoot her, but while glancing in the direction of camp, wondering how far off it was, I saw the cause of her strange behaviour and how sensible it was, for out of the waving grass, not a hundred yards distant, had risen the majestic body and great floating mane of a large male lion, which, evidently disgusted at our conduct, was standing watching us. Of course I didn't try to turn the cow any more, for some time at least, although I very nearly left her to tackle the lion, but the thought of the starving natives on seeing an eland decided me, and I stuck to the latter. After a little I gradually brought her round, now very tired, as indeed both I and my horse were, and she trotted quietly and slowly in front of me until she got the wind of the camp and swerved, upon seeing which I rode in alongside, and dropped her dead with a ball in the shoulder, and before many hours were over there was but little left, even of her great carcase.

This eland had gone some fifteen miles from start to finish, and though I could easily have ridden her to a standstill at any time during the last five, and indeed had to ride slowly so as not to over-press and knock her up, yet when I killed her I had no reason to think that she could not have kept up the same pace for an indefinite period. From which I conclude that at its own pace an eland could probably tire out a horse confined to the same, though that might be, according to the age, sex, and condition of the animal, one that a foot-runner could keep up with, or, as in this case, one that required fast galloping to equal.

It is rare, for all the numbers that are killed from horseback, to hear of any very large bag made in that way on a single day, the average of the foot-hunters, considering the number of days on which they find eland, being considerably higher. This is probably owing to the herd being never so pushed by the latter as to force them to break up all over the country, thereby enabling shot after shot to be fired among them, many of which, though fired at random, or, at the best, family shots, take fatal effect, though, no doubt, leaving a far larger proportion of wounded; on the other hand, on horseback, one gallops into them, scatters them in all directions, kills the one that is singled out, and then goes after another, and by the time it also is ridden down and killed, it is very likely that there is not another in sight, and quite possibly no other chance can be obtained the whole day.

Once in 1868, a friend of mine had taken his waggon into a part of Swaziland which abounded with eland for the sole purpose of filling it with their hides, for which, at the time, there was a very large demand, and on hearing from him of his having done so, I joined him with two horses to assist in shooting them. The country, though treeless, was anything but flat, and we soon found great difficulty in killing more than one or two apiece during the day, though we not unusually saw more than one herd in that time, and after talking it over in camp, and seeing that it was our over haste that forced them to break up too soon, we decided to act differently next day, and try to get enough to complete the load and enable us at once to leave for the colonies, which good fortune and a very exceptionally favourable disposition of the ground made us succeed in.

We were "outspanned," as the Dutch expression for halting with waggons goes, on a great open hollow, bounded on all sides by hills, which, though rideable in most places, were not only very hard upon the cattle, but in some parts too steep for anything, though the eland did not seem to care at what angle they went so long as it was down hill. A waggon encampment, though here losing the fine effect of great fires gleaming among the recesses of dark jungle which the bush country affords, is always more or less picturesque, and on this night, as I saw it on going outside after bringing our conversation about circumventing the elands to a close, it seemed to me especially so. There was just enough moonlight to make the tent of the waggon, and the smaller one I inhabited close by, show snow-white against the dark sky, and to enable one to see the outlines of the oxen which were fastened to their yokes, some lying, others standing, in a long line extending twenty yards from the waggon itself, and to note their immensely wide-spreading horns breaking the sky-line, while from the small and neglected fires enough smoke rose on the quiet air to denote their existence, and the direction of what breath of wind might be stirring, and round them, more from force of habit than for protection from cold or wild beasts, lay all the natives, with two or three great yellow Boer hounds belonging to my friend, while the occasional stamp of a horse's foot betrayed where the outlines of their legs might be traced beneath the waggon which otherwise concealed them.

I did not even go into my tent that night, but sitting under the waggon out of the reach of the dew, smoking and enjoying the refreshing coolness, I fell asleep where I was, and did not awake till the grey dawn of morning was struggling for mastery with the light given by the setting moon. It was chilly, and I was cold and stiff, but the natives were already up, and I was almost immediately able to get a cup of hot coffee,—a luxury that no one in Africa, rich or poor, would dream of dispensing with at daybreak ; and after seeing the horses carefully groomed and lightly fed, we had our own breakfast, which, as may be guessed, consisted of elands' tongues and coffee, and then, saddling all our four horses, and selecting the two lightest boys as after-riders, we started for, as we hoped, and as it turned out, a final day.

We made our way towards the foot of a conical hill which commanded an extensive view, and for the top of which a native look-out had started even before I had awoke, and who now came down to us and described the positions and respective numbers of three herds of eland that he had seen, and among which we had to choose one to go after. Fortunately the largest herd was also in the most favourable spot for our purpose ; it was about a mile up a broad glen with practically perpendicular sides, which extended without a break for some three miles, a pass which led to a flat beyond then occurring, while the main glen, after narrowing considerably, and with a steady rise, held on its way for some distance, until terminated by a forest-covered ridge that bridged it over, while beyond it was again continued. Its formation was no doubt of prior date to the small stream which, rising in numerous springs in the table-land above, came down the dividing spur, and which had perhaps deepened the valley it had found in existence. It was naturally a spot much favoured by the elands, the small rills trickling over the steep sides combining with the heat and moisture to cause the grass not only to sprout earlier, but to retain its spring-like hue even during the dry season ; and as it was not by any means the first time that we had found them there, we were in consequence aware that, unless headed, they would as they always had escape comparatively unharmed through the opening already mentioned. It was therefore necessary to send to the waggon for men, as at least two would be wanted to guard that pass, and we also thought that if a man could be placed at each end of the bush, where they must necessarily otherwise break, they might perhaps be turned back again to us in the valley.

All this took time, and before we got away, the sun, in more general use among hunters than watches, marked eleven o'clock. However, we felt that the time had not been wasted, and trotted along under the cheering influences of fresh air and bright sunshine, until we came in sight of the great herd, numbering upwards of two hundred, which was scattered, chiefly at rest, though some were still grazing, over the whole of the bottom of the glen. On those feeding perceiving us, and giving the alarm by their anxious gaze, the others began to rise, first singly or in pairs, doing so leisurely and stretching themselves before turning to watch us, but soon in groups of half a dozen or more, until the ground seemed alive with them, every eye being turned on our movements. We were still walking, as we had done the moment we saw them, so as not to give the alarm too quickly, and now took the opportunity of giving the after-riders their last instructions, which were simply to ride steadily in the rear of the herd so long as they kept heading for the top of the glen, and, while assisting us as circumstances allowed, to keep their horses fresh and ready for us when we wanted them; our own tactics being that one should ride on each flank, firing when near enough, and that we should not attempt to do anything more than follow stragglers, or any so severely wounded as to leave the rest, when the after-riders would slowly accompany the herd in our places, until, on nearing the top of the glen, we should urge our horses to their utmost, and, galloping through the herd, attempt to force some, at all events, to retrace their steps, when they would be easily killed.

Before long, the various groups began to trot up to each other, though after a junction, they would again turn to stare, until, when we were still a quarter of a mile off, they had formed themselves into one compact body, and soon afterwards went away at their accustomed pace; and we, for the first time galloping our horses, soon took up our respective positions on either flank, and about sixty yards behind, while our boys kept between us. Before starting we had tossed for sides, as shooting from horseback, at no time very easy work, is rendered all the more difficult if one has to do so from the left-hand side, as whoever was on that flank would have to do. I lost the choice, and in consequence the first half-dozen shots I fired—for both of us commenced as soon as we got close enough—were clean misses; however, as I had plenty of cartridges and a light rifle, I kept on until the fall of a young bull showed that I got the range. R. had already made some wounded drop out, and though I was too busy to look after him much, I could hear occasional shots some way behind. There were several very fine old bulls, and I did my best to kill one without going too near and making the herd scatter, but I fired five shots at him before he gave way, two of which struck him, while another hit a cow just beyond him in the stern, making it rear up and climb on to those in front. As soon as I saw that he had separated, I wheeled my horse sharp round, the cruelly severe curb in general use for this work giving me great command over it, and in a few strides I laid it alongside of him, and almost putting the muzzle of the rifle to the beast's shoulder, I dropt him, shot through and through. I then turned to the cow I had wounded, and which had gone off in another direction, and although I overtook her in about ten minutes, it took me so long to finish her, that by the time she fell, I found that the others were far ahead and out of sight, though I could still hear R.'s rifle cracking at intervals.

Of course I followed at full speed, but two falls I got from concealed holes stopped me a good bit, and they were past the opening into the plain and well up the valley before I even got into sight again. On my way I passed two eland that R. had wounded; but as they seemed quite done up I rode on, desirous of getting up in time for another shot before they reached the head of the glen; but, while I was still several hundred yards behind, I saw R. ride right into them, and the great herd, separating into fifty parts, made for every point where egress seemed possible, not a single one however turning back. I rammed the spurs in savagely, but my horse was tired, and before I could come within certain range, all had made their escape; and despite the shouting of the men stationed in front, trotted unmoved close past them.

The instant I reached my after-rider I exchanged horses with him, and telling him to keep me in sight, I started away in pursuit. But, now that the chase was a stern one, and the ground favoured the antelopes, I no longer rode with a slack rein, so that, though I made the most of my time consistently with sparing my horse, some time elapsed before I caught sight of some of the game heading down the gentle but stone-covered declivity which extended for five or six miles, and ended in the commencement of the thorn country.

So long as the herd had been together it had been difficult to pick out the finest animals, but now that they were scattered, and therefore in full view, and I had little chance of securing more than one, it became advisable to take some pains in selecting it. Fortune, however, favoured me; for on pulling up and scanning each group, I saw that among those furthest to the left was an enormously large bull, his withers standing nearly two feet above the back of the one next him; so without further hesitation I started at the angle that I judged would bring me to them.

I did not ride fast, for the ground was covered with large irregular stones, over which, however, the elands, big bull and all, went at an astonishingly fast pace. Half an hour's steady galloping brought me within twenty yards of them, and then jumping off, I let fly at him, and heard the soft thud of the ball as it entered without meeting with a bone. My horse, unfortunately, though in other respects good, was rather gun-shy, and generally plunged back at the report, and so a slight delay occurred before I could remount it; but as the few cows in the herd swerved when I fired, and the bull kept straight on, I was in time to ride in between them and cut him off. The inconvenience arising from my horse refusing to allow me to remount him when I got off to fire made me wish to either ride the eland to a stand-still, or get alongside before I gave him another shot; but the old fellow, although his laborious breathing said plainly enough that he would not keep it up long, was going at a slashing trot, seemingly in no wise inconvenienced by the numerous stones that hampered my animal so much, nor any the worse for my bullet, and it was some considerable time before I overhauled him; but at last, wheeling half round to enable me to fire with the greater certainty, I put another ball into his short ribs. The smoke in my face and the tremendous shy my horse gave prevented my seeing what was going to happen, and it was not until the brute came down with a crash under me, hurling me actually against the eland's body, that I understood that an accidental collision had occurred, for an eland never charges. Luckily, on picking myself up I found that neither I nor my rifle were much the worse, and on seeing that the eland was standing within thirty yards, I at once reloaded. He was evidently sorely distressed, open-mouthed and tongue protruding, and with heaving flanks that told of the difficulty the lungs had in performing their office, and which proved to me that there might be some foundation in fact for the stories I had heard of fat old bulls, like this one, dropping dead without a scratch, merely from over-running.

My next shot finished him, and after he had rolled over, or rather subsided, for his short legs hardly raised his body an extra foot from the ground, I turned to my horse, and was sorry to find that in falling he had cut himself rather severely, and was so lame that there was nothing for it but to make for the waggon; and a long weary journey I had of it, my after rider having carefully taken himself off, leaving me to go some fifteen miles dragging a leg-weary and lame horse across a country which at the best I knew but imperfectly, and with only about an hour of daylight remaining. However, a fine moonlight night came to my help, and I reached camp between ten and eleven o'clock, after a sixteen hours' absence.

I found that R. had made the very unusually large bag of nine eland, five bulls and four cows, thus making up our total to thirteen head. Several of his, he said, were very large animals; but my bull turned out to be a third larger than any of them; and the inhabitants of a neighbouring village afterwards told us that he was a well-known animal, celebrated for his unusual size, as well as for the skill with which he had hitherto evaded all attempts on his safety; always feeding on the highest and most inaccessible positions, where danger from above was impossible, and from below would be easily seen, always accompanied by half a dozen wary old cows, all of which acted as sentinels when he slept, and, when he descended into the thorn country, invariably having a body-guard of gnu, whose wonderful instinct and power of scent, added to their naturally suspicious nature, render them the most difficult antelopes of all to approach.

The next day was devoted to skinning and cutting up the meat ready for curing, and as soon as ever the hot sun had sufficiently dried the extended hides, and the 'biltongue,' or sun-dried meat, began to show that it would keep, we started on our homeward journey with a waggon laden as full as it would hold, with the hides, horns, and meat of the elands.

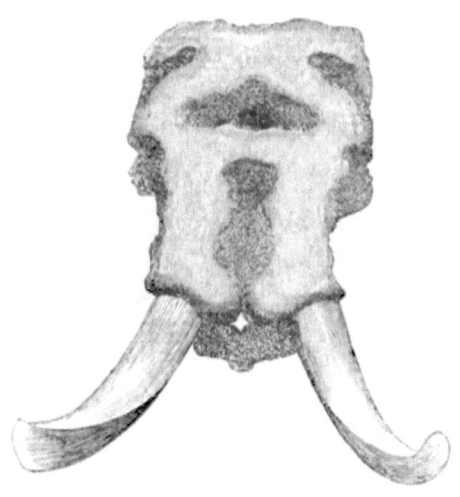

CHAPTER IV.

ELEPHANT.

LATE one afternoon I was descending a gentle slope, waist-deep in grass, and dotted over with thorn scrub, through which I could catch glimpses in front of a mass of reeds, upwards of a mile broad, and extending far out of sight on either side; their great height so diminished by the distance, that they looked, with their broad green leaves, more like fields of sedge-grass of only a foot or two in length. It was summer, and though the sun was low, and was shining directly in my face so as to almost blind me, the heat had scarcely diminished, and all animate nature was still hiding itself in the deep shade of the flat-crowned mimosas and other trees that afforded an equal protection.

No wind stirred the leaves, and except the startled whirr of the great locusts that rose at my feet, there was not a sound in the air.

I had got separated from the other hunters while following a large herd of buffalo, and had not seen any of them for more than half an hour, and was now going in the direction I thought they had taken in hopes of crossing the spoor, and thus finding them; for the chase had taken us so many miles away from our camp, that I did not know the country, and could only guess from the glimpses of these great reed-fields, of which I had often before heard, that I must be somewhere near the junction of the Black and White Umfolosi rivers.

As I got down and nearer them their immense extent struck me more and more forcibly, and it was with a feeling of curiosity that, after looking in vain for some signs of the rest of my party, I waded through the long tangled grass that fringed them, and entered into the cool aisles formed by their bare stems, while overhead, though to me it had seemed perfectly calm outside, there was a subdued murmur, pleasant to hear, rising from the overhanging leaves that all but shut out the sky.

I had come down hoping to find water, having had none that day, and before going many yards I found some in the great deep footprint made by an elephant at some former period, when the ground was soft after wet weather; it was very drinkable, though perhaps not very inviting-looking, especially to any one unaccustomed to thankfully drink anything sufficiently liquid to be swallowed, without knowing, or, at any rate, without caring to investigate, what its component parts might be.

Having satisfied my thirst, I turned to go out, though not exactly on my former footsteps, and had almost reached the edge when I came across the track of an elephant evidently of quite a recent date, and turning along it out of curiosity I found unmistakable evidences of its having been there within the last few minutes. This led me on, though I certainly did not intend to follow the animal up into the reeds; I should not have cared to have done so by myself, for I knew by hearsay that these elephants were proverbially rogues, and always showed the strongest antipathy to human beings, but at the same time I could not exactly bring myself not to go a few yards upon a track so undoubtedly recent as this, and there was a sort of feeling that if I did chance to find it standing close by, and happened to kill it, what a great thing it would be, for many a time old elephant-hunters had told me that they would not dare to fire at one of these, and there were camp-fire stories innumerable of how men had followed them in, in spite of warning, and nothing more had ever been heard of them, save, perhaps, the report of their guns, or the wild savage trumpeting of an infuriated elephant. Indeed, the dread in which the spot and its denizens were held among the whole hunting community was amply proved by the fact, that, although it was a matter of perfect certainty that these reeds concealed large quantities of ivory, elephants having lived and died in them long before the memory of living man, or the traditions of their forefathers, no one had ever dared to search for it.

So I followed the great footprint; further and further among the gloomy avenues and cave-like passages formed by the great thick stems, many of which were almost as large as a bamboo. It was agreeably cool, but too silent and sombre after the bright sunlight outside to be otherwise pleasant, and it certainly was with a feeling, if not a sigh, of relief, that I turned to come back. There was no difficulty in this, as I had the elephant's tracks to guide me, though I should have been puzzled to do so without them, for every reed precisely resembled its neighbour, every formation they assumed had its counterpart on every side, and there was no shadow, no indication of there even being a sun, all around being black, gloomy, and still.

A tropical twilight is but brief; the sun is hardly set before the long shadows of evening set in, and in a very few minutes more the stars are shining, and it is night. It had been late when I came into the reeds, and I had penetrated far farther into them than I had intended, so that before I had got half-way back it was already almost dark. I hurried on, anxious to get out, although the elephant's spoor, my only guide, was momentarily becoming more indistinct, and then, all on a sudden, I missed it entirely. No doubt I must have been a little flurried, though at the time I did not think so, and tried my best to hit it off again by going back on my own trail; but I must have gone wrong, as I could not find it, and it soon became so dark that it was impossible to see any marks whatever on the ground. I did my best under the circumstances; I stopped for a minute to consider, and then, thinking that I knew the right direction, I tried to keep straight on in it, guiding myself in doing so by a slight breeze of wind that had risen with the declining day, but after a few steps I found myself blundering into mud-holes, and at last, in the utter darkness, I walked into a pool of stagnant water, out of which it was with great difficulty that I extricated myself. I had seen several of these long slimy lagoons as I came in, into which huge iguanas plunged with a sullen splash as I passed, and which from the marks on the mud I could tell were the abode of crocodiles, but while there was light it had been easy to skirt them, though now they seemed to be on all sides of me, and whichever way I turned I found myself in danger of sinking into them.

However, I wandered on, still believing that I could not be far from the edge, and that it would not be long before I gained it, and unwilling to even admit to my mind the possibility of having to pass the night alone in such a spot, while, if I had only known it, I was plunging further and further in among these pathless reeds; often above my knees in mud, with my body all sore from the sharp points of the reeds with which I was continually coming in contact, I still kept on, until I suddenly found them become thin, while beyond was a glimmer of light that raised my hopes of getting out, attaining to almost certainty, as I stepped out into an open covered with long grass. Alas! it was but a delusion, but an oasis in the desert. I walked across it; it was quite a hundred yards broad, and on the opposite side found reeds again, and then skirting all round it with a like result I saw that it must be one of those bare places which I had heard existed here, and whose presence enabled the elephants and hippopotami to feed without leaving their stronghold.

It was here, where I could see the stars, that I first discovered that I had been going exactly in the wrong direction, and that, as I had been wandering about for upwards of an hour, there was no saying how far I might have penetrated into the heart of the reeds; it was at any rate quite plain that I could not hope to find my way out that night, and that if I again risked myself among the unknown mud-swamps and lagoons that intervened I should probably have to watch till daylight to protect myself from the crocodiles which during the hours of darkness wander about in search of food, and the knowledge of whose vicinity would effectually prevent sleep, although perhaps when outside I might scout the idea of their attacking a living human being on dry land.

There was a great island-like patch of reeds nearly in the centre of this open, and I determined to take up my quarters there, as nothing could then come near me without my seeing it. The spot was dry too, and by no means an uncomfortable lair, and I set about making my position as bearable as I could, thankful that I had at any rate escaped from the noisome, fever-producing pools of stagnant water that had hitherto surrounded me. I had a flint and steel, tobacco and pipe; so, after hunting round and round the edge of the reeds for such dry stems as I could find, and carrying several successive bundles of them to my temporary camp, I collected from amongst the long grass enough that was sufficiently withered to serve as tinder, and, lighting my pipe, I knocked the glowing ashes into it, and soon blew it up into a flame, which, as I heaped the dry stems over it, after clearing the ground in the vicinity to prevent any danger of a general conflagration, soon became a roaring, crackling fire; and as I spent nearly another hour in collecting more fuel among the reeds, I soon had enough embers to retain life for several hours, and to enable me to produce a blaze with the untouched supply of fuel that I kept in reserve, should I wish to do so during the night. Food of course I had none, but smoking served as a substitute, and there was something weird in sitting there alone in the heart of these ill-famed reeds, which could only be compared to the feelings of the midnight watcher in a ghost-haunted house,—not altogether unpleasant, but wholly strange and flesh-creeping.

It was long, therefore, before drowsiness crept over me; every now and again I could hear a distant crackle that told that some of the inhabitants of the place were abroad on their nightly wanderings, while an occasional nearer rustle spoke of the movements of the cane-rat or the iguana. Lions, I had heard, formed their lairs here, but I knew it would be on the edge, and that they would go outside to hunt, so I did not fear their disturbing me; indeed, unless it was a water-antelope, nothing smaller than an elephant or hippopotamus was likely to be seen so far inside. Even when I did ultimately lie down, it was long before I could sleep, but at last tired nature got the better of my excited imagination, and I passed away into the land of dreams, waking, however, at such frequent intervals as proved that my rest was but broken and disturbed. It must have been long past midnight from the position of the Southern Cross, when at one of those waking moments my ear caught the sound of breaking reeds, evidently caused by the passage of some large animal close by, and on sitting up and examining the ground in the direction from which it seemed to come, I could distinguish the loom of something so large that it could only be an elephant passing along the edge of the open. It was not it, however, which I had heard, but its companions which were out of sight, and which I could still hear crashing through the reeds. I watched it for several minutes as it moved slowly forward, by which time it was opposite to and nearly directly to leeward of me, when suddenly one of those beyond trumpeted shrilly, and the whole herd broke out and came towards me. They had got my wind. Luckily, however, they did not keep straight below me, but a little on one side, and one huge animal, which, as I could not see those appendages, was probably a tuskless cow, came and stood within ten yards of me, its great ears standing out like sails, and its trunk raised to catch any taint in the wind. I hesitated a moment about firing, and then, the temptation overcoming my prudence, I covered the shoulder, as it was too dark to make sure of the ear, and pulled the trigger, producing a headlong charge and a deafening trumpeting that at one time seemed to be right overhead. I had sprung away to leeward as I fired, while the elephants charged upwind, so that, except for the second when the cow charged the smoke, I was never in any danger, but fearing lest they should turn and catch me in the open, I crawled vigorously away till I reached the edge of the reeds, and then ensconced myself in the thickest patch I could find.

That they were a vicious lot was evident from the way they quartered the ground to windward in search of me, screaming loudly with rage, but luckily they kept in that direction, and, though one did come down to where they had first got my wind, he failed to strike it again and rejoined the others, and they then soon all disappeared in the reeds, though I could hear them trumpeting in the distance for some time afterwards.

Once satisfied that they had gone, I did not remain very long in my concealment, and returning, I coaxed the embers into a blaze, and soon had enough fire to scare them if they returned; but I did not feel inclined to sleep any more, and sat and smoked, with intervals of dozing, or going to get more fuel, till daybreak, which took place about five o'clock, when, as soon as there was sufficient light to enable me to see distinctly among the dark reeds, I started once more to try to find my way out, having first assured myself of my true course and how I ought to keep the wind to maintain it. The lagoons were almost as much trouble as they had been the previous evening; often I had to go along their edge, seeking in vain for a crossing, sometimes, after wasting half an hour in so doing, only to be brought to a standstill by some marsh, and have to retrace my steps and look in the contrary direction. A considerable time had passed in this manner, during which I had probably not made more than two hundred yards in a straight line, when the wind died away, and, excepting the very occasional glimpses I could catch of the sky, I had nothing left to guide me, save this, that I had noticed that the reeds mostly inclined, at least as far as their tops were concerned, in the same direction as I wished to go in, which I accounted for by the action of the prevailing south-west wind, and which was sufficient to prevent my going far wrong. The ground became easier too after this, and before long I struck a well-worn game-path, such as elephants make, and which I determined to follow, as I believed it to be used by them when going to and returning from the outside. I had not been on it for five minutes before I heard the heavy tread of some wild animal approaching, and at once stepped to the side and concealed myself in the reeds. A few seconds sufficed to bring its head into sight, and I was somewhat disappointed, though perhaps at the same time rather relieved, to find that it was a hippopotamus instead of an elephant that I had to deal with. As it got opposite to me I broke a reed, causing it to stop and look round inquiringly. I had never fired at one before out of the water, and had expected that it would have afforded me a certain mark when it turned its face towards me, but I saw at once that at this angle the ball would almost certainly glance, so, waiting till it gave me the opportunity, I aimed at the eye, and could tell, despite the pall of smoke that hung over it, that it had fallen. Stealing, therefore, a little on one side to enable me to see clearly, I put another bullet into its shoulder, having seen so many rhinoceroses only stunned with similar wounds that I half expected it, like them, to rise again. I saw, however, a second afterwards, that I had fired into a dead carcase, and whipping out my knife, I severed its pig-like tail, glad to have killed something in these famous reeds, even though it was not an elephant, and also by no means despising the supply of food which I had thus secured.

Although I had not yet by any means effected my escape, twenty-four hours' abstinence from food rendered my going further impossible before I had satisfied my hunger, and so a repetition of the evening's fire-kindling took place; and when, by heaping on bundle after bundle of reed stems, I had secured sufficient heat, I cut two long stripes from the ribs of the animal, and stuck them up to roast before the embers. I had hardly sat down after doing so, with the purpose of turning the ashes over and keeping their hottest side towards the meat, when I heard the report of a gun, followed at a short interval by another, and I recognised by its peculiar deadened, dull sound that it had been fired as a signal, with the barrels close to the ground. Of course, I joyfully and immediately answered with two shots, and then by heaping a lot of the green reeds on to a portion of the fire, so as to create a great smoke, which I knew they would at once see, and in about ten minutes I heard a shrill whistle, which, as being more likely to strike the ear, is often used by the natives in preference to shouting; and after some little time having elapsed, owing to the difficult nature of the ground that intervened, five of my hunters walked up, and, standing in a body leaning on their guns, looked first at me and then at the hippopotamus, as if they had discovered some new species of animal. Of course, I had an idea of what their astonishment meant, and I was laughing before I asked, "Well, did you never see a hippopotamus before?" to which was only deigned the usual ejaculatory exclamation of surprise, "Wau." There was more intended than mere surprise at finding me alive and in such good case after a night spent in these reeds. There was also the feeling of a nurse whose charge has been missing some time, when she discovers it in safety, and seemingly unconscious of its danger, in some position of great peril—half of thankfulness at the relief, half of anger at its daring.

The simile is not overdrawn. As I have before mentioned, respectable native hunters, of some standing, who have accompanied their master from the colonies, feel themselves responsible for his safety, and will often beg him not to run into some danger for which they personally do not care.

This mute exhibition of astonishment soon, however, gave way to curiosity, and, as it appeared that they had heard my shot at the elephant during the night, and its subsequent screaming, I had to give a full account of my adventures; but I was unable to persuade any of them to accompany me in going back to see what the effect of my shot had been, and, after breaking up the hippopotamus, we made the best of our way outside, and reached our camp the same evening.

I have already, when speaking of the hard work attendant on buffalo-shooting, mentioned that it cannot in that respect compare with elephant-shooting. This is caused by the immense distances the latter travel when once disturbed, or when moving from one part of the country to another, thirty or forty miles on a stretch being nothing uncommon. I think I went through more fatigue on one occasion when following a solitary bull than in all my hunting experience. I was staying at the time —summer—in some Amaswazi villages, having been fairly driven from the plains below by the ravages the fever was making among my people. One evening some of the Bombo people, who are nearly related to and intermarry with the Amaswazi, arrived on some marriage business, and soon after one of my hunters came into my hut to say that they reported having crossed fresh elephant spoor on their way. On sending for them, and cross-questioning them, I found that they had seen but one track, but that it, from certain indications they had noticed, was certainly not more than a couple of hours old. The news was received with great pleasure, as every one was tired of our forced inaction, and preparations were at once made to start at daylight.

The morning broke dull and heavy, and though there was as yet no wind, the scud flying from the south-west showed that a gale might be expected from that wet quarter, and I therefore fortunately told my servant to roll my blanket up and give it to one of the men, as we knew from the distance that we should be obliged to sleep out at least one night. There were eight or ten miles to go in the first instance before we reached the flat, and the path down which we had to travel could not have been rougher or more disagreeable, covered as it was with innumerable sharp-edged stones, which cut into the naked feet of the Kaffirs, and made me wince, even through my shoes. There were six of us in all—three hunters, two carriers, and myself,—the guns being placed in cases made of leopard or antelope skin, which, so long at least as they were not wanted for use, would keep them dry.

Once on the plain the walking became easy, and for another fifteen miles we slanted across it, beginning to look out for the spoor towards the end. I had told the men at first to try and shoot something for food, but it was not until the spoor was found that anything showed itself, and then unfortunately I allowed a duiker, which stood within a few yards of me, to go away, not as yet knowing when the elephant had passed, or how far off it might be. In truth, at that moment it was fully forty miles away from the spot where we were standing, and, though we did not know it at the time, that was to be our last opportunity of obtaining food for upwards of twenty-four hours. On examining the footprints of the animal, the great size of which showed that they were those of an old bull, we found that they had been made by it on the day previous, and we then followed them till near nightfall. It was evidently on a journey and bent upon reaching some particular place, keeping straight on in a bee-line without feeding or halting, and we had very little doubt but that we should find it in one of the great reed bottoms on the banks of the river Sutu. We stopped to camp rather earlier than usual, to enable us to try and get some meat, but we all returned at dark empty-handed to make the most of a duiker's shoulder, which, among so many hungry men, any one of whom could easily have finished it, was not more than a mouthful apiece.

To make things worse it came on a bad night, as indeed it had threatened all day, with a strong gale blowing, and sufficiently heavy showers to wet me through, and then towards midnight, as I was sitting by the fire with the blanket over my head, miserably attempting to smoke, a lion began to roar about a mile off. He was answered by another from an equal distance on the opposite side of us, and then, alternately roaring, they came nearer and nearer, until their voices sounded so close out of the darkness, that we were forced to rouse up and mend our fire, and coax it, despite the rain, into a decent flame. The lions, having once discovered us, were in no hurry to go away; and emboldened by the darkness and the badness of the night, kept marching round us, growling and roaring; once, when I threw a flaming brand at them, coming so close that we took up our guns. Fortunately, as I believe no gun except my own would have gone off, they confined themselves to this; but between them and the wind and rain we passed a nearly sleepless night, and looked miserable enough as we got up at dawn and resumed the spoor, close to which we had slept.

The rain, which continued, had not obliterated it, as the ground had been soft when the animal passed and it had received a couple of days' baking since, but we rather feared that it would do so, and therefore hurried on. Towards noon, however, it partially cleared, and when we caught sight of the Sutu the rain had ceased. The elephant all this time had kept steadily on, hardly pausing to strip a tempting tree or two of their branches as it passed, but before reaching the river it had entered a thorn thicket, and seemed to have stood about and fed, as many of the trees were stripped, and several of the smaller rooted up.

We reached the edge of the reeds late in the afternoon, and found that, as we had expected, he had gone into them; so, time being of the greatest value, I decided to divide our forces, and, late as it was, to follow him up at once. One hunter and a carrier was despatched to hunt for food, as, whether they disturbed the elephant or not, we could not go much further without eating; one I sent up outside the reeds to search for any spoor that might indicate that it had left them, while I undertook the task of following it through the reeds. The spoor was now,

I judged, that of the previous morning, probably of about the time at which we had started, and the animal having travelled all night, and most likely all the day before, was, I expected, standing somewhere within this great reed field. A fine broad path he made for himself through it as he broke his way down to the water to quench his thirst, and then, going down stream for a mile, he crossed. This was not a very pleasant nor an easy thing for me to do. An elephant, of course, crosses where it likes, despising all considerations of depth or crocodiles; but I had to think of both, and not remembering from my former knowledge of the place that there was any ford here, I went on some distance until I came to one, and then crossing, proceeded to look for the spoor. It was easy enough to find, leading, as I had expected, into another reed field of great extent, containing the thickest and tallest reeds I ever saw, and forming a cover in which I knew elephants generally stood when in this part of the country. I had hardly followed it in when another track, also of an elephant, crossed the one I was on, and being above it, was plainly one of a later date, so, leaving the other, I followed it for some distance, discovering before long that not only was it the same elephant, but that it had been here that very morning, and was, I did not doubt, standing not far off.

Unfortunately it now began to get dark, and having acquired a wholesome dread of getting lost in the reeds, and not wanting to get separated from the others, I was forced to turn and go back. I soon found the hunter, and we proceeded to make a camp and light a fire, but it was not until we had quite given them up and supposed that they had not been able to find their way back, that the others returned, bringing, to our great satisfaction, an impalla doe with them. I should be sorry now to say what we did, or what we did not eat that night, though I don't think there was much of the impalla left after breakfast next day, except two or three junks of roasted meat which the carriers took with them. So much did we enjoy our dinner that little attention was paid to the rain, which had recommenced; and even when we lay down, I personally, and I believe all of us, slept so soundly that it was not until morning that we awoke shivering to find ourselves lying in pools of water. Fortunately it was daybreak, and though it was still raining it looked more like clearing than it had done for some days, and by the time we had crossed the river and reached the reeds where I had left the track in the evening the sun was shining, and a white mist was rising which concealed the whole of the river bottom.

Our first object was to ascertain whether the elephant was still in these reeds, and to make sure of this we skirted outside them, carefully examining the ground, lest the rain should conceal the marks. About half way down we found them leading out, their faintness indicating that he had passed early in the night, but as he might have returned, we kept on to where a precipice rising out of the river bounded the reeds, and seeing no further traces, we returned and followed him, by no means pleased at his having left the cover where we had made so sure of finding him. There were two causes assignable for his having done so: either he had only been resting on his way to the Pongolo, for there was nothing now to hold him before we reached that river, or he had come across my spoor and that had started him off. His own was faint enough to give us some trouble, and consisted chiefly of a series of smudges, such as might have been made by a very broad cart-wheel hopping over the ground, but there was no real difficulty, and we followed him rapidly across the broad undulating flats that intervened between us and the Nkwavuma, where it was possible that he might halt in the reeds, though they were not sufficiently extensive for him to remain in. This was reached about mid-day, and we found that the elephant had not even paused, but crossing it high up, was heading for the upper part of the Pongolo, and we foresaw from its line that we should have to sleep far away from water, though after the late rains we did not fear thirst.

It was wonderful the amount of game we saw about here, and the quantity of fresh buffalo spoor that covered the ground, though scarcely two months before we had been forced to shift our camp from this very spot on account of its scarcity. We kept steadily on, however, until dusk, when we again camped for the third night. There was hardly anything to eat, and the little water we found was filthy lukewarm stuff, barely drinkable, but we were so tired that we soon forgot our hunger in sleep. Fortunately, one of the men awaking at dawn saw a duiker feeding close by and shot it, so that when we were awoke by the report we were gladdened by the sight of him returning with it.

This delayed us a good deal, the hunter's rule being to eat as much as he can whenever he has the chance, as he never knows when he may get another meal, and so the sun was high before we started, and it was noon before we crossed the Pongolo. The first thing that struck our eyes as we emerged from the ford was another spoor of the elephant on its way to drink, evidently of that morning's date, and before we had got through the broad bottom of waist-high grass that here separates the jungle from the river, we met two native hunters from the Bombo whom I knew, who told us that they had seen the elephant the previous day from the mountain and had come down after it. It was, they said, now standing in the jungle, and they had tracked it in so far, but had hesitated—or more probably, feared—to go further.

Our preparations were soon made; two men, one of mine and one of those from the Bombo, were told off to guard two fords in the river, where it was likely to pass if disturbed, the two carriers being sent round to watch from the rising ground on the other side of the jungle, while the two remaining hunters and I, after waiting long enough for the others to get into position, followed it in. It certainly had not been idle since its arrival, and from the havoc among the cactus-bushes and the trees one might have thought that a whole herd had passed.

The Bombo Kaffir and I kept the spoor, while my hunter was supposed to be keeping parallel to us, but had really, anxious to inflict the first wound, and so secure for himself the valuable pay for shooting a good tusker, gone on, and had struck the spoor before us. In consequence of this we had hardly heard the rumble that betokened the animal being in our immediate vicinity before a shot was fired, followed by the crashing of a heavy body through the thickets, and shrill trumpeting. The native who was with me halted and listened for a few seconds, and then saying "Come on," darted like lightning through the prickly cactus, and dodging in and out through the thick bush, arrived in a few minutes on the outside, and then ran at full speed along the edge, until, as we neared the end of the jungle and came opposite to a small break in it, he sprang behind a bush and knelt down.

Follow your leader's example, and ask the reason for what he does afterwards, is a good hunting rule, and one that, though at first I had half suspected that the man was running away, I complied with now. My reward was not long in coming; we had not been behind the bush for more than a minute when the branches before us opened, and the great quadruped, making little more noise than the smallest antelope would have done, walked out into the open, at last giving me an opportunity of seeing that he was indeed worth the trouble we had taken, and that his tusks, both in size and shape, were first-class. He was not ten yards from us, and we both instantly fired, bringing him down on the spot, but so momentarily that I had barely time to get my second barrel in before he disappeared among the bushes. Leaving the hunter loading, I rushed off by myself to try to cut it off should it break cover at this end of the jungle, but quick as I was, it was too late, and I only arrived in time to see him going away across the open about eighty yards from me, at which distance I fired both barrels at his stern.

As there was no use in following him up in a hurry, I

sat down and waited for the men to come up, more especially with the object of pitching into the hunter who had stolen a march upon me and frightened the elephant, for which, indeed, he did not care much, as he had earned five head of cattle as payment by first wounding it, and so securing it when killed as his own, and when they joined us we started in pursuit. It was bleeding a good deal, and was evidently hard hit, and in about half an hour we saw it about two hundred yards ahead, slowly walking away with lowered trunk through the thorn-dotted jungle.

I had some difficulty in restraining the others, who wanted to run in at once when we saw him, but forcing them to keep in Indian file headed by myself, we stole forward, taking advantage of anything that would conceal us until we got within seventy yards, when, as the ground before us was bare, we ran in, each one taking his own line and making as little noise as possible. At last he caught sight of the outermost, and the change from his attitude of sickness and dejection to that of furious anger was instantaneous.

I think this was the first time that he had seen any of his enemies, and the moment that he did so, cocking his huge ears till they looked like studding-sails, and elevating his trunk over his head, he charged straight back, trumpeting loudly. The man he singled out fired nervously, missing, and took to his heels; the other three hunters fired simultaneously, and followed his example, while I, being so near that I feared to draw his attention to me if I ran, knelt down behind a shrub large enough to conceal me, and as he passed in pursuit fired right and left into his shoulder. There was luckily a strong breeze blowing, and the smoke was instantaneously carried away, causing the elephant as he wheeled to catch sight of a small thorn-tree through it, and charge that, almost coming on his knees as he rooted it up, while I crouched flat under my bush hardly five yards from the infuriated brute. After accomplishing this, he went a little distance off and stood, throwing vast volumes of water over his body, among which I thought I could detect signs of blood, and I took advantage of the opportunity to thrust fresh cartridges in. The men also were reloading, as I could tell by the ring of the iron ramrods, and in a few minutes they came into view, scattered so as to distract his attention, and slowly approached, when, not seeing me, they began to shout my name out. Of course, I wasn't going to answer, but the noise so enraged the elephant that he charged them again; and after having put them to flight, pulled up before he had gone far, close to me, and in such a position that I could fire without moving. I selected the ear this time, and aiming carefully, I brought him to his knees, when, jumping up and firing the other barrel into his body, I put a hundred yards between us before I halted. He soon regained his legs, but as he was evidently unable to do further mischief, we all walked up to within thirty yards, and after several more shots—I using one of the hunter's six-bored guns instead of my own of ten to the pound,—during which he never ceased screaming with rage and pain, his huge body began to sway backwards and forwards in his efforts to keep his legs, and then, after tottering for a second, he came to the ground with a crash, completely smashing a small tree against which he fell.

"HE WENT A LITTLE DISTANCE OFF AND STOOD"

Some explanation may be needed of why the hunter who had first wounded it, and who really played a very insignificant part in its death, should have claimed the tail, and received payment for killing it, just the same as if no one but himself had been present. When large bodies of men are employed in shooting large game, it has been found necessary, in order to avoid continual disputes, that they should do so under a recognised hunting law; and as it would be utterly impossible in the case of a number of men firing at different times at the same animal to say which of them had inflicted the death-wound, it has been found to be the best plan to draw a hard and fast line, and to say that an animal belongs to the man who first wounds it, however slightly. It is necessary for his claim to be allowed, that he should follow it up, and though he may have merely scratched it, so long as blood is drawn, and may find it dead, killed by others, it belongs to him if he reaches the spot where it has fallen.

When we were shooting much in the reeds it was found advisable, from men first wounding the buffaloes while driving them in, and then waiting to claim them till the more plucky ones went in after them and killed them, while they remained outside, to make the rule that in such cases the animal belonged to the man who ultimately killed it; but this is the only exception to the hunting law of first wound. It is sometimes even carried so far that should a hunter wound an animal late in the day, and after following it, return without killing it, he has only to mention the fact in camp, saying that he intends to go after it next day, and the animal, though killed by another or found dead, remains his. In this manner much game really killed by one is not counted to one, and much that is killed by others, and first wounded by you, belongs to you ; but as the hunters are paid according to what they kill, the invariable application of the rule renders it possible for great numbers of men to shoot together, and to finish off without jealousy each other's game,—a thing that would be impossible under any other regulations.

On two different occasions at this same spot where we found this bull, I was lucky enough to kill an elephant with a single bullet. They are rare in this part of the country, only frequenting it during the deadly summer months, when there are no hunters left to take advantage of the opportunity, and it was during a season most of which I passed on the Bombo mountains instead of going out to the colonies, that I had these chances.

The first occurred one day when, having come down to try and get some meat, I was walking along the bank of the river when an exclamation from the native who accompanied me made me look about, and then catch sight of a herd of elephants going down through the open on the other side towards a ford. I was not very far from the spot on this side where, if they crossed, they would come out, and though I feared that they were only going to drink and would keep the breadth of the river between us, I crouched under the sparse reeds which grew along the bank and ran forward to it, arriving there a second before the first of the line entered the water. It was a tuskless cow, and she walked in some distance, the others spreading out like a fan behind her, and then they all commenced to drink, standing in a line facing me, and when their thirst was quenched squirting the water over their bodies. They were mostly cows amongst which I only saw one bull with good tusks, and thinking that they would go back after drinking I covered it in readiness to fire, but the first movement was made by their former leader, who, throwing her proboscis high in the air, walked forward, each of the others falling into line as its turn came with the regularity of well-drilled soldiers. I have since been told by hunters and natives that what I saw was unusual, and that elephants, when crossing a river, defer drinking until they have almost reached the side they are going to; but as I only saw them crossing on one other occasion, and that was under a heavy fire from upwards of a dozen hunters, I do not personally know if they are right.

There was a little air blowing up the river, and as the great fig-tree under which I was standing, and which I looked to for shelter if any of them charged, was some ten yards to windward of the path they would take on coming out, I climbed up it, so that the tainted air should pass over them, and in two or three minutes more the foremost walked up the bank. It was a beautiful sight to see them as they marched past, and I had full leisure to enjoy it, as there were twenty-three of them, and my big tusker brought up the rear. One by one they slowly filed past, quietly and steadily, making their way for the jungle above. Perhaps, properly speaking, I should not have disturbed them, but having marked them into the cover, should have sent my native to call my men, and keeping guard on them myself, should have awaited their arrival to make a combined attack, but the snowy whiteness and the immense size of the tusks of the last bull so struck me, that I had not the heart to let such a chance pass without trying to get them. He was, as I have said, the last, and as he mounted the bank, and while his hind-quarters were still concealed by it, I aimed at the shoulder and fired. The smoke hung heavily, but through it I could indistinctly see the commotion I had caused, while their shrill trumpeting struck my ear. As it cleared I saw that the herd was in full flight, all but the tuskless cow, which was charging down, looking the picture of rage personified; and glad of a chance to punish one of these brutes, through whose savage temper so much valuable ivory is lost, I aimed at her trunk which was twisted over her head and pulled the trigger. As the ball entered that tender part of the body she squealed with pain, and wheeling sharply, went after the others, and I jumping down ran after them, loading as I did so. Just as I reached the verge of the jungle I came upon the bull I had fired at, and was just going to fire again, when he moved a little and the native with me called out,— "Don't fire; it can't get away; its shoulder's broken; let's go after the others;" and seeing that such was the case, we plunged into the jungle at full speed, regardless of the thorns that pierced us, and followed the broad track of the herd. This pace we continued until, having passed out into the open, we reached an upper ford, where we found that they had crossed back, and though we followed them for the remainder of the day we never set eyes on them again; and as we saw from passing their downward spoor that they were making straight back from whence they had come, we turned towards dusk, and reached the banks of the Pongolo early in the night. It was, of course, useless to attempt to follow the wounded elephant before daylight, and there being nothing to eat we quenched our thirst and lay down as soon as we had kindled a fire.

Day had scarcely broken before we left our sleeping-place, and crossing the river, made the best of our way to where we had left the elephant; but as we approached the spot the light of several smouldering fires in an old deserted camp of ours hard by caught our eyes through the grey dawn, and on going up we found that they had been made by some of our own party, who, having heard from some one, probably some one who had happened to be looking down from the mountain at the time I fired and had heard the elephants trumpeting, what was going on, had come down, and on following the spoor had found my disabled animal painfully hobbling after the others, and had finished it off, as indeed was very plainly to be seen by the amount of meat about, and the hundreds of vultures that covered the great fig-trees which lined the river. Hardly had I arrived before a long line of Bombo natives made their appearance, in accordance with the colonial proverb that where the carcase is there will vultures and natives appear as if by magic, some carrying pots of native beer, which is always grateful to those who, living on the produce of their guns, rarely taste vegetable food.

I need not enter into the disgusting details of how the animal was broken up, and how the blood-smeared naked savages fought and squabbled over its flesh; but, enormous as the carcase was, little was left save bones for the vultures to pick after all had departed, staggering under the loads which they carried on their heads in bundles made of green branches.

On the other occasion to which I have alluded as killing an elephant with a single bullet a troop of them had been heard in this same bush from the top of the mountain, and word having been sent to me, I went down that evening with my hunters, and sleeping at a ford about three miles lower down, started after them next morning. On arriving at the spot, and while examining the numerous tracks in search of the latest, we heard the peculiar rumbling noise that they involuntarily make, and without troubling ourselves further about the spoor, we entered the bush, each going his own way.

In a few minutes after doing so I came across a track which, from certain indications, could not, I knew, be more than ten minutes old at the outside, and before I had gone far I heard the branches breaking in front of me in such a way as proved that the animal was still feeding. Every now and then from different parts all round me came that peculiar rumble, proving that the herd was scattered, and that I was right in the middle of it, so, stealing along this narrow path among the cactus, I crept forward foot by foot; quite certain that I should see one of them in a minute, and noting as I passed the evidences of their enormous strength in the uprooted trees and broken branches lying in every direction. At last I caught sight of the great black hind-quarters of one, my attention being drawn to it by the violent shaking of the bushes, and as I could not fire at it with any hope of success in its present position, I at first crouched down, intending to wait till it turned, but when it moved forward and

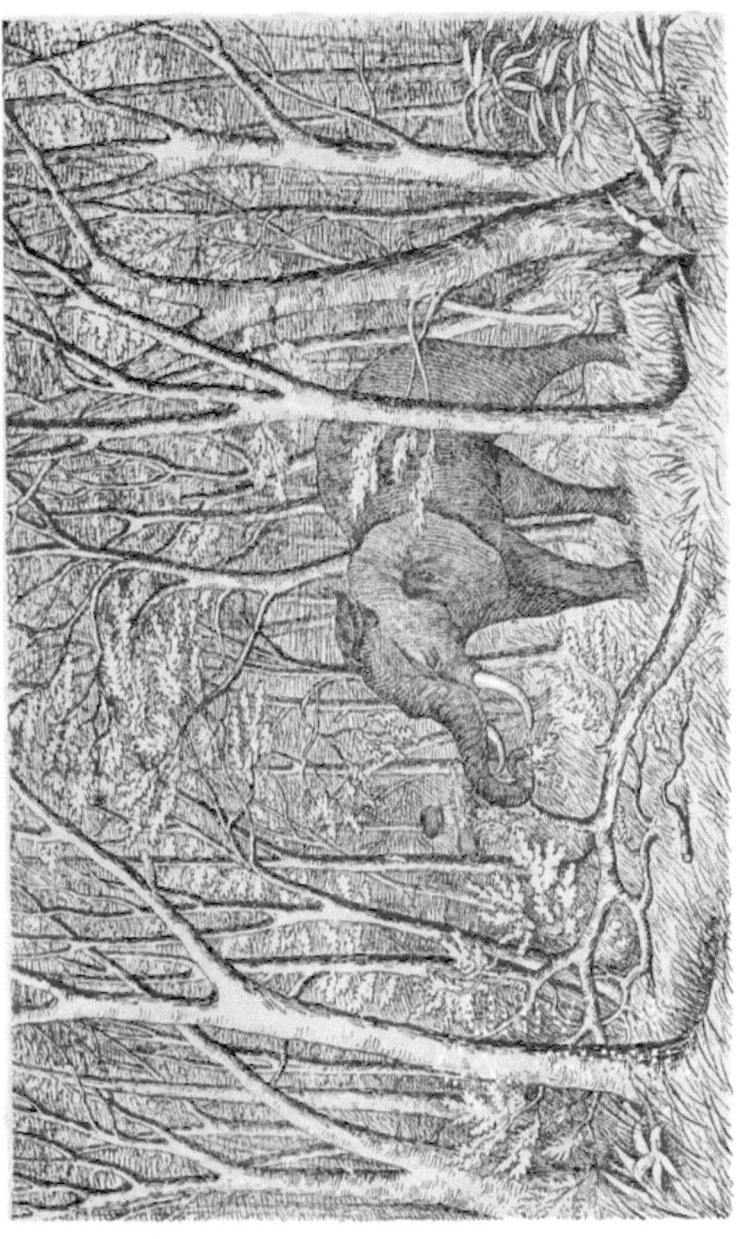

'ITS TRUNK COILED ROUND THE BRANCHES OF A TREE

became concealed by the intervening branches I stole after it again, in a state of nervous excitement lest any of the other hunters should fire in the meantime and spoil my shot. I had only taken a few steps, with my eyes fixed on the spot where I had last seen it, when that curious rumble sounded again, seemingly right over my head, and looking sharply round, as I started nervously, I saw one that I had overlooked standing partially concealed in the bushes not many yards off, its trunk coiled round the branches of a tree which it had uprooted, and was now feeding on, and as far as I could make out, its tusks seemed so small that had I seen my way out of it, I would gladly have let it alone; but I was equally afraid to move forward or back lest it should hear me, and seeing no other alternative, I raised my gun, and waiting till a flap of the ear enabled me to see the exact spot, I pulled the trigger and rushed right in behind it, almost touching its hind-legs as I passed, and jumping into a mass of cactus, despite the pain, I crouched down.

The shot, followed, as it was, by two more from the others, seemed to awake the whole forest; elephants were trumpeting in every direction, their position being indicated by the chattering monkeys, while I could hear the one which I had been following at first crashing down towards me, and in another second saw it, evidently trying to get the wind and puzzled at the noise. It was a cow with moderate tusks, and as she stood about ten yards off swaying her trunk about I fired at her shoulder, making her scream and dash through the jungle, breaking everything before her.

The herd seemed fairly roused, and were angrily trumpeting all round me, so, feeling pretty sure that they would drive us all out as soon as they got our wind, and not relishing the tones of one who was coming up from leeward of me, I got out of my prickly bed, and went up to the spot where the bull had been standing. He, I found, was quite dead; but I had hardly time to secure his tail before the one that I had already heard came charging up, having evidently scented me, and as I rushed down wind I must have passed within a couple of yards of it, though luckily it did not see me. Finding it so warm inside, and feeling pretty sure that I should find all the hunters there already, I made for the open, another of the elephants, which had been standing to leeward, giving me a smart chase for a couple of minutes on my way; but I got below the wind, and was soon clear of the bush, and found, as I had expected, the others already outside.

They were delighted at seeing a tail in my belt, no one else having got one, though one man thought that he had broken the hind-leg of a cow, but had been driven away by the others before he could make sure, and if he was right, as ultimately it turned out that he was, the animal was as good as dead. They said that those they had seen seemed very vicious and had charged them savagely, and we imagined that they must be a troop that we had heard of as remarkable for their bad temper, and which had the previous year killed a Dutch hunter.

They were still trumpeting at intervals, but apparently from the same spot, and we did not think that there was any fear of their moving before nightfall, when they would certainly change their quarters. After resting for half an hour we again went in, though now, as the elephants were in such a bad temper and on the look-out, we had to be careful, and the hunters wanted one of their number to accompany me; but as I have always found that a companion in such cover is only in the way, and, indeed, from impeding one's movements, renders the danger all the greater when a charge does take place, I objected to his coming and went in alone. I made my way up to where the elephant had fallen without seeing anything, and striking the spoor of the cow I had wounded, I went after her. It was no easy task. Her track was broad enough, but she had rushed through the densest masses of cactus, knocked over trees, and gone straight ahead through everything, and it was often difficult to get past. After her first blind rush she had turned up wind, and at last, moderating her pace, had again taken to the usual paths.

In ten minutes, expecting every second of the time to be charged, I saw a dark loom through the bushes, which I took to be her, and getting on a little, I made out her head and shoulder. This was enough, and I fired. The instant I did so the whole bush, hitherto so silent and still, seemed to become alive with screaming, charging elephants, and, fairly stupified by the infernal din, I did what perhaps was the wisest thing after all—namely, to crawl under the hollow formed by a fallen tree close to me, and lie still. Not a second afterwards an elephant passed over its other end, almost deafening me with its shrill trumpeting, while I could hear others all round me. An elephant in a rage is a magnificent sight when one is in safety; but a solitary individual in the middle of a dozen of them, all perfectly furious, and making the most frightful noise, is a little liable to get, as I did, perfectly stupid and unable to run or think. I was not equal to anything but to hide and lie still, and I ascribe it to the effect of the noise.

After a time the herd seemed to join and retire further back to windward, and as soon as I recovered my senses, feeling certain that among the din I had heard the heavy thud of a falling elephant, I went up to the spot where the cow had been standing, and found that although she had gone I had been right, and that she had fallen to the shot; and the few steps I took on her track disclosed so much blood upon it that I felt justified in thinking that she could not get away. I did not, however, I must own, care about following the herd, with which no doubt she would be, at this particular moment while they were still so excited and roused by the smell of blood, and hoping they might move and leave her by herself, I was just turning to go out, when I heard a shot lower down. This made the elephants trumpet again, and one of them charged down towards me, making me, as I objected to its getting my wind, take to my heels. After going some hundred and fifty yards I heard another shot close by, and on going towards it I walked right up to an elephant without seeing it, standing in a clump of thick trees which concealed it from me. I was quite close to it, and it swung its trunk round and tried to seize me, but I dodged and saw on looking over my shoulder that it was disabled and could not move, and therefore concluded that it must be the cow they had spoken of as having a broken leg. Whistling, therefore, to the men, I soon found them and told them that as the cow could not possibly get away, they need not waste time and bullets upon it now while there were fresh ones close by. Not one of them, however, would consent to meddle with the herd in its present humour, saying that it was as much as a man's life was worth to attempt it, and I quite agreed that it would be advisable to at least give them a rest before doing anything more.

It was consequently late in the afternoon when we next took up their spoor, I, as before, following my wounded cow. The whole bush about was much broken and strewed with branches which the elephants had broken off in their rage, and which, blocking up the usual paths, rendered my progress very slow. Some of the hunters, therefore, who, not having to follow the spoor, were able to pick their path and get forward more rapidly than I could, reached the herd while I was still some distance off, and I heard two shots, and then the usual commotion and noise among the elephants. They did not, however, this time merely confine themselves to charging about the spot where they could smell the smoke, but came down wind in a body, screaming loudly, and evidently determined to drive us out of the bush. I caught a glimpse of one man bolting as hard as he could, followed by an elephant, whose outstretched trunk was not ten feet behind him, and seemed as if it would grasp him every second. I let drive at it as it passed, but my shot served to bring the main body down upon me, and as I had to provide for my own safety, I could not see its effect; the brutes, with their usual sagacity, were coming back on their own spoor, and charged so viciously and pertinaciously, that it was only by leaving our former tracks, and striking out an entirely new line across the bush, that I succeeded in throwing them off. As soon as I could see the light on the outside, I thought I would not, if possible, go out with a loaded gun, and as I could hear the elephants breaking close by, I got behind a bush and waited.

Nothing came for some time, but at last I saw one down a glade about thirty yards off, crossing on its way back, and I instantly fired, and rushed out into the open down the bank and through the long grass until I reached the shelter of a great fig-tree. Then, on turning, I saw that the brute had followed me out, and had just wheeled and was making for the cover, and I had time to fire at it again, though I fancy that I must have missed, as it took no notice of it. Before long the others made their appearance from the different spots at which they had emerged, and as it was evident that we could at present make nothing of the herd, we decided to go and finish off the broken-legged cow, which was accordingly done, and then, after partially breaking it up and obtaining sufficient meat for our temporary wants, we went to our old camp and slept there.

At least five of the elephants were wounded, and some of them severely; one in particular, besides my cow, having fallen to the last shots. At daylight, therefore, we got upon their spoor, and found, as we had expected, that they had taken advantage of the darkness to shift their quarters, and from the blood-tracks we saw that the wounded had kept with them. I was not very well that morning, and went back up the mountain when we discovered that the elephants had gone, but the men followed them up till nightfall, and though they said that one of them was not with the others, but lagging behind at a considerable distance, as only a severely wounded one would have done, they were unable to overtake it, and returned the following day.

The natural history and habits of the elephant are too well known to require any mention here. The species found in Africa differs, as is well known, very considerably from its Asiatic brother, but as far as concerns the hunter the different formation of the head is the only important point. In India and Ceylon the forehead presents a certain mark, while in Africa it is quite impervious. I have fired without making the slightest impression point-blank from ten yards' distance with a gun of six bore at the exact spot that, in the Asiatic species, would be instantly fatal, and the experiment has been as fruitlessly tried dozens of times within my knowledge.

Elephants would appear to exist all over Africa, and not thirty years ago were as plentiful in our southern colonies—where they are almost now extinct—as they still are in some parts of the interior. The greed for ivory has done its work, and at the present day they are only to be found in one jungle in the Eastern Province of the Cape Colony, where they are preserved; in Kaffraria and Natal, where they were common twenty years ago, they are extinct, and even in Zululand there is but one spot where they still exist. They frequent, as I have mentioned, the country from the Pongolo northward, during the summer season, retiring to their fastnesses in the interior at the approach of winter. The general time of their arrival is simultaneous with the ripening of the fruit of the unganu-tree, of which they are passionately fond, and doubtless come in search of. This fruit is capable of being made into a strong intoxicating drink, and the elephants after eating it become quite tipsy, staggering about, playing huge antics, screaming so as to be heard miles off, and not seldom having tremendous fights. Native hunters fear to approach them when in this state; but on the principle that it is safer to quarrel with a drunken man than a sober one, I consider that, so long as you possess sufficient nerve not to become flustered by their trumpeting, or by the exhibitions of strength displayed upon the trees and upon one another, you have far more chance at such a time of killing several, as they are not so likely to take to flight at the first shot and perhaps make their next halt thirty miles off.

In all this country, however, you are lucky if you come across them twice or thrice in a season; and the nearest place on the south-east coast where elephants can be found in great numbers is close to the Limpopo, and belongs to a noted chief called Umsila ka Sotyongane. This, however, is an undertaking of no small magnitude. From the Bombo mountains, if you go by land, you have to go a week's journey through the fever-stricken country of Nozingile, chief of the Amatonga, to the Portuguese settlement of Lorenço Marquis, the most unhealthy place on that deadly coast; but this might be avoided by going by sea, though if, as is generally the case, one desires to take hunters and natives from Natal with one, as they are so much more trustworthy than the natives of the east coast, considerable difficulty will be experienced in overcoming their repugnance to a sea voyage. From Lorenço Marquis, a fortnight's journey inland through the low swampy districts inhabited by the Amatonga tribes in dependence upon Umzila, will bring you to Manjobo's, his commander-in-chief, who rules over a vast tract of table-land abounding in every kind of game except elephant; indeed, during the whole journey there is splendid shooting. After leaving here it will take about three weeks more to reach the king's, though the absolute distance is not very great; a fortnight of which is spent in passing through an uninhabited country, where delays are inevitable from having to provide game for the large party of at least a hundred men, which it is necessary to take.

Once on the ground you find yourself in a healthy country, too elevated for much fever, heavily wooded, and much broken; and here, after leave has been obtained from the king by a valuable present—valuable at least to him, and from the distance it has to be carried,—you will have as fine elephant-shooting as can probably be found in any part of the world. With a good staff of hunters two hundred are sometimes killed in two or three months. Uzmila, however, is fully aware of the value of his property, and will only grant permission for a limited time to shoot in, or for a certain number to be killed. Men on foot—elephants, in my opinion, should always be shot on foot; there can be no excitement if one can gallop away whenever they get angry and begin to charge, and here, as horses would not live, there is no alternative —have been known to kill ten and twelve, and rumour says even more, in a single day, and to my personal knowledge eight have been brought to bag; and those who would consider such shooting sufficient reward for the long and dangerous journey may depend upon finding it. At least they could have done so in 1872, and if the king strictly adheres to his present policy of preservation, there is little doubt that the shooting will not deteriorate much for several years to come.

The immense size and great value of this game renders its pursuit most exciting, though it is by no means so dangerous as most writers on African shooting would lead us to believe. I have before spoken of the different shades of danger encountered from the larger varieties of South African animals. At the head of the list stands the upetyane (*Rhin. bicornis*), because as a general rule it charges without provocation; the lion may be placed next, as it also occasionally does so, and escape from its clutches is rare; after these come the buffalo, on account of the sudden and vicious nature of its charge, which is difficult to evade, and therefore often has serious results; and lastly I would place the elephant, for although a rogue is more to be dreaded than a solitary buffalo bull, though they are not so dangerous in Africa as in India, it is, generally speaking, far easier to escape a common specimen of the former than of the latter. An elephant will abandon pursuit even when it can see you, which an enraged buffalo would never do; and while nothing can be more common than to be chased in the bare open by them, it is exceedingly rare for any one to be caught.

There are two great points to be borne in mind so long as you are in jungle: firstly, always to run down wind; and secondly, to make continual short tacks while doing so. If you can get below the wind, and remain quiet, you will very likely, if loaded, get a splendid chance at the elephant that is looking for you. It will rarely continue its charge for any length of time, but sometimes the whole herd will combine, as in the instance already related, and drive every hunter out of the bush, quartering about till they strike each individual's wind, and following it up until he is reached and turned out, after which they will retire back into the jungle, and stand ready there to repeat the attack if they are again followed. When receiving a charge in the open, it is advisable to run up-hill if possible; or, should the animal be above you, run down until you are almost overtaken—as you soon will be—then double, and run back again. Its great weight and impetus prevent its turning quickly, and once above it you have very little to fear, especially if the hill be steep and your wind good; indeed, in such a case it will very soon abandon the chase.

Rogue elephants are rare; indeed, it seems to me that it is necessary for the full formation of that amiable animal's character that it should inhabit a well-populated district where continual opportunities are afforded it of attacking defenceless people, of breaking into their fields, and in general of losing its natural respect for human beings; and as such conditions seldom exist in Africa, from the elephant chiefly inhabiting districts devoid of population from their unhealthiness, the rogue, properly so called, is seldom met with, though the solitary bull, the same animal in an earlier stage, is common enough. The most dangerous elephants are undoubtedly the tuskless cows, and the dread inspired by them is so great that the best native hunters often fear to approach a herd accompanied by one of these brutes. I am sure that if the statistics of the accidents that occur in elephant-hunting could be learned, the greater proportion of them would be found to be caused by these females.

I have said nothing about shooting elephants from horseback, partly because I have a prejudice against it, partly because I have never seen it done. There is, however, no doubt that in many districts more may be killed in that way than in any other, though it labours under the very serious disadvantage of almost certain death to the horses employed, as well from the "sickness" which is so fatal in some parts, as the tsetse fly found in others.

It may be interesting to give some account of this disease, commonly known in South Africa as the "horse sickness," and which bears a curious affinity to the "tsetse" in that, though existing separately, they are always worst when found together. It is next to impossible to say what it is caused by, for while there are theories innumerable, two people can hardly be found to agree on the matter. As regards locality, it is most common on the coast lands, or on such in the interior as bear a similar character. As with tsetse, though found on the plains or hills bordering a low-lying country, it is most virulent in the thorn districts, and it also presents a similar resemblance in that though almost dormant during winter, in many places being quite so, it is bad during the whole of summer and worst in autumn. Certain conditions have been discovered by experience to be nearly certain to produce it, among which exposure to the night air during that time of the year has been found most fatal. At the same time, the animal is in comparative safety so long as it is being ridden, and it is only when it is turned out to graze or to stand about that much danger is incurred. So the question arises, Why is the night air fatal only under one set of circumstances, and not so in another, although it must equally be breathed in either case? In some districts the grass is considered to be the cause, as in them, unless the horse has actually been grazing, it never dies, while in others, its merely being tied up outside during the night is almost sure to prove fatal. It is curious, however, that whatever the seeming cause, the symptoms remain the same, merely differing in their greater or less intensity, congestion of the lungs appearing to be the immediate cause of death. No treatment avails, unless exceptionally, and then it is doubtful whether the horse would not have recovered in any case. Prevention, possible enough to the colonist, is utterly impossible to the hunter, the very use to which he puts his horse necessarily bringing it into the most deadly districts; the night air, the dew, and something eaten in living or freshly cut grass are among the surest producing causes, and it is palpable that the hunter's horse must of necessity be exposed to every one of them.

Perhaps one of the greatest attractions of watching water-holes by night in an elephant country is to see these enormous denizens of the forest approach, marching up in single file, terrifying all the smaller animals by their heavy tread, and wading into the deepest spot, stand there for hours, occasionally cooling themselves by throwing water over their bodies. They come vast distances to water, and if there only happens to be one spot containing it in the neighbourhood, and they entertain any suspicion of its being watched, they are able to go several days without a fresh supply. It is usually the largest animals who act as leaders on these occasions, and their sagacity often induces them first to go to leeward of the spot before approaching it, and therefore, after the first few nights, the watcher is seldom successful.

There are but two spots in these large animals where a bullet may be expected to be fatal; namely, behind the ear in the head, and behind the flap of the ear in the shoulder and breast. When a limb is broken the animal is practically *hors de combat*, though, owing to the porous nature of the bones, and the absence of marrow, a bullet will only pierce, not smash them, but when thus perforated they will give way when used to support its great weight. In this point they resemble the rhinoceros and hippopotamus. A case which was related to me by my late friend Mr. Leslie illustrates that in many things elephant-shooting resembles that of other large game, especially in the uncertainty of a bullet, however well aimed, killing, and in the peculiar tenacity of life they display. On the same day he shot two elephants in Zululand, one falling to a single ball, while the other took either thirty-five or thirty-seven, I forget which, to say nothing of some hundreds of spears, before it was killed, the last ten or so of them being fired at the animal standing like a rock in the open, not thirty yards off, never flinching or even shuddering when the balls struck it, until at last it fell down stone dead.

I cannot leave this subject without adding my protest against the wanton and wasteful wholesale destruction of these animals that has now been going on for so many years. It is utterly impossible that it can last much longer, as any one who glances at the statistics of the export of ivory from the east coast must at once see. Slowly, but surely, this most useful animal is being extirpated, merely for the purpose of supplying Europe with ivory ornaments and billiard-balls, and before many years are over the inhabitants of Africa will grieve, when it is too late, at the short-sighted policy which has allowed them, for the purposes of immediate gain, to kill down the only animal capable of becoming a beast of burden through the tsetse-infected districts of that continent; the only animal that the traveller could place reliance on as enabling him to dispense with the costly and troublesome retinue of natives he is, in default of some such aid, forced to take with him, and which from the ease and comfort it would afford in travelling would enable him, whether in the interests of commerce or science, to pass with comparative immunity through the fever regions. Of course it is out of our power to prohibit its destruction by the independent tribes of the interior, but surely something might be done by the imposition of such a duty on ivory as would render the profits on its sale and export so small as to practically stop the trade in it. Difficulties there no doubt are, especially in connexion with the Portuguese settlements and other outlets without our territory, but if the subject were as strongly taken up as its importance deserves, they might be overcome, and the thanks of succeeding generations earned by the preservation of this valuable animal.

CHAPTER V.

LIONS.

We had been camped high up on the Pongolo river for some weeks, but the game having shifted their quarters in consequence of being so much disturbed, I determined to move lower down and follow it. So one morning, all our moveables being safely secured on the heads of the long line of carriers who performed the duties of beasts of burden in that tsetse-infected country, and all the available hunters being ordered out on the flank to look for meat, after being told that they would find us at nightfall somewhere on the river-bank, I started in front, accompanied by a couple of servants, to find a suitable place for a new camp. The requisites for this were various: a sufficient nearness to the river to render fetching water easy and safe during the hours of darkness, with enough elevation in the ground to raise us above the fatal miasma which nightly steals forth from the lower bottoms, while at the same time a close and ample supply of firewood was a necessity; and even all these would be worthless unless plenty of fresh spoor proved that we had again overtaken the game.

After going several miles, our followers, numbering some thirty men, who had hitherto marched steadily behind in Indian file, humming the air of a hunting-song, which occasionally broke forth into words, began to feel the overpowering heat of the mid-day sun, and to grumble at the distance, pointing to the numerous tracks of rhinoceros, buffalo, eland, and other large animals, as a proof that we had come far enough for the principal object of our search, and that nothing remained but to discover a camping-ground.

This, however, did not seem likely to prove an easy task. We were passing through a low thorn jungle which bordered the river for half a mile or so, and extended to the rank bottom of reeds and tambuti grass through which it ran, while the whole country in front and to our left was one vast plain, covered with scattered mimosa and other thorn-trees deepening here and there into impenetrable thickets, the black shadows of which looked cool and comfortable in the blinding glare of the sun; while on their edges a quick eye could distinguish the dark outline of various kinds of antelope, standing motionless, waiting till the lessening heat should permit them to come out and graze. The soil itself was so soft and spongy that we sank to the ankles at every step,—a sure sign, in such a land, of certain fever and probable death to any one rash or ignorant enough to form his camp there.

Disregarding, therefore, the grumbling of the men, I kept on, until my perseverance was at length rewarded by finding a spot seemingly created for the express purpose for which I sought it. Rising out of the river-bottom was a small level ridge of some three hundred yards long, descending abruptly by perpendicular banks into the dry water-course which ran along its other side. On this ridge, among other smaller ones, and within a few yards of each other, were two immense trees, one a wild fig, the other a flat-topped mimosa.

I saw at a glance that they would answer capitally, the former for the general camp, the other for myself and my own attendants; while on examining more closely I saw that there were several old native paths leading down to the river; and in descending to drink I found that it either was or had been a ford, as the paths were continued on the opposite bank, though they did not seem to have been in use for a considerable time. Concluding, therefore, that the water during the rains had altered the bottom, as I knew it often did, and had rendered it impassable, I thought no more of the matter, and, returning, ordered the men to off load and to make a camp, which, after a very considerable period spent in solacing themselves with the inevitable snuff, they proceeded to do.

There were, as I have said, some thirty hands, ten of whom were small boys, mat-bearers, as indeed many of their seniors were; these at once departed to bring in firewood and to fetch water, the elder men dividing themselves into two parties; one to cut reeds for me and grass for their own and their absent masters' beds, the other to cut great branches of thorn, with which to form a rude but strong fence round three parts of the fig-tree. My own camp was easily made. The flat circular top of the mimosa served as a roof, which we could afterwards make rain-proof by spreading wet buffalo hides over it, and a fence of reeds was put all round, which was further strengthened from the attacks of prowling wolves, or other wild animals, by an outer ring of thorn branches. An entrance was left facing the fires of the larger camp, beside which the boys told off for that duty made a great pile of wood to replenish the guard fire which would be lighted there during the long night. Inside, after the ground had been scraped and all inequalities removed, several armfuls of grass were strewn, over which we spread our mats and blankets.

It took some time to do all this, and the men were still dragging in great logs and trunks of fallen trees, which had proved too much for the strength of the boys, when the hunters began to arrive. The first half-dozen came in quietly enough, put their guns down, and took off the belt which supported their bandolier and powder-horn, without saying a word, unless to ask for water. No one questioned them, for it was evident by their silence that they had been unsuccessful. Next a solitary voice was heard chanting a hunting song, which, as soon as its owner was near enough for the camp boys to distinguish which division of it he was a member of, was joined in by all those who belonged to the same, until he had got fairly inside, and had detached the two buffalo tails that announced what kind of game it was, the death of which he was thus celebrating.

This singing of the hunting-song—"ukuhuba," as it is called—is a native custom almost invariably followed when the hunter has killed any large game; and the chant, though somewhat monotonous, is pleasant, and, to those accustomed to it, very inspiring. It is often sung when a body of hunters are starting together in the morning, and I have seen lame or otherwise disabled men almost crying at not being able to go out when they heard it. It bears a strong resemblance to the war-song, which, when sung by a large body of men, so excites their wild natures that it is unsafe for a stranger or European to go near them for a time.

Several more men dropped in by twos and threes, some with and some without the tails of slaughtered game as trophies, but still eight, and those the best of the hunters, had not returned; and the twilight was darkening before we heard their song, which they were singing so loudly that it was evident their success had been great. As they marched up in Indian file, headed by my principal hunter Umdumela, we could see that the last man was carrying something.

It was too dark to see what, but I concluded that it was the tit-bits of some animal they had killed; but when, instead of turning into their own camp, they kept on to mine, still chanting, while their leader shouted to those already arrived to turn out and join them, I at once knew that something unusual had happened, and was not much surprised when the wet skin of a lion was thrown down at my feet, and all the hunters and camp boys, having turned out in obedience to their officer's orders, formed a semicircle in front of me, and commenced to dance and sing the great hunting-song, only used on occasions such as these. I know what was expected of me, having seen many lions killed; so, after allowing them to dance—*i.e.* to emphasize the measure by stamping in unison with their feet, and marking time by the motions of their arms—for several minutes, I sent my boy for my gun, and, holding the barrels perpendicularly for the sake of the general safety, I fired them both off. This was at once taken up by the hunters, who had all brought their guns out in readiness, and who fired one after another, in capital time, until the last shot was spent.

When I thought there had been enough of it, I asked who had been the successful man, and a fine, tall grey-bearded old hunter came forward. "You, Atozake!" I said, in some surprise; for he had but lately joined me, and, from an incident that had just occurred, I had fancied him rather the reverse of plucky.

He and a comparatively young hunter had very severely wounded a solitary buffalo bull, and it had taken refuge in a patch of thorn-thicket so dense that nothing could be seen a yard distant in it, and there, though within a few yards of the animal, and hearing it coughing, as only a buffalo shot through the lungs will cough, they had left it, and returned to receive the openly-expressed jeers of their companions.

"Yes, sir, me. Now that the old man who was afraid

has killed the 'chief,' what will the boys who laughed at him say?" was the reply.

"Not much, I suppose; but you'd like to have the claws, I fancy. Well, you shall have them; but don't get me into trouble in Zululand by wearing them there on our way home. Now tell me how you killed it, and let the rest of the men go to their own camp." A suppressed murmur of thanks for my giving one of their number the much-prized claws, worn as a necklace, and in Zululand belonging exclusively to royalty, and we were alone. "Now, how was it?"

"You know, sir," he replied, "that I reported last night that I had wounded a cow (buffalo), but that it was too dark to follow it up; so this morning I took up the spoor, and found it lying dead, having fallen just outside the jungle it had been making for, and by the carcase there were three full-grown lions feeding. Two of them, lionesses, ran away as soon as they saw me, but the third, a male, walked coolly and slowly after them, turning round his great head every moment to watch me.

"There was a thorn-tree between us, and when I got pretty close to it I thought I would try and make him go a little faster, so I knelt down and fired at his stern. His hind-quarters dropped, and he began to roar, but as I stood under the tree loading, ready to climb up, he partially recovered, dragged himself to a small bush not far off, and lay down under it. Then I fired again, but it was too far for me to make sure, and the bullet struck the ground close by him, only producing a snarl and an angry dash of his paws. I reloaded, and this time ran on to a small mimosa not a hundred yards from him. I ran quick, for I was afraid of his charging, and it was lucky I did so, for I barely had time to climb up before he reached the spot, roaring terrifically; though when he saw that I was out of reach he turned back to his bush, and I then came down, and walking out as far as I dared, took a quick aim from my knees and pulled the trigger, but the gun missed fire. As soon almost as he saw me kneeling he charged again, and I had to run back to the shelter of the tree until he returned to his old position, growling horribly.

"Mahlatine now came up, having heard my firing, but when he saw that it was a lion, he climbed to the top of the tree, and would neither come down nor give me his gun, so I walked out and tried mine again, but with a like result, both as regards the gun and the lion. As I was making for the tree a thought struck me, and as I got under it I shouted to Mahlatine, 'Shove down the stock of your gun to help me up, I shall be caught,' and as he lowered it, I loosed it from his hand with a sudden wrench, and turned to look for the lion. He had not come far out this time, disgusted with his former ineffectual attempts to overtake me, and was already limping back, so, resting the gun on a lower branch, I fired and struck him, making him roar with pain and rage, and, when he saw the smoke, charge towards it. I saw that he was too much maimed to catch me, and stood where I was, with the second barrel ready when the time came, and at thirty yards off I shot him in the chest and rolled him over, only sufficient life remaining for a few mighty struggles before he breathed his last."

Dismissing Atozake with the commendation that his

pluck deserved, and prophesying that Mahlatine would not hear the last of it for some time to come, I had my dinner, and then crossed over to one of the camp-fires where a knot of old hunters were spinning yarns, and sat there and listened, asking an occasional question on some point of natural history, till it got late—late at least for us, who rose with the morning star—and going inside, was about to lie down, when a rush of all the dogs, barking violently, made me come out again. No one took much notice, thinking that it was some prowling wolf that had ventured nearer than usual, till a voice was heard out of the darkness, exclaiming, "O my lords, the dogs will eat us up." "Who's that?" was instantly shouted by a score of voices; and, unless I had interfered, a long conversation would probably have taken place before the dogs, savage brutes that they were, would have been called off. When at last they were kicked and beaten into comparative silence, three lanky, half-starved-looking lads made their appearance, evidently by their looks mat-bearers, who told us that they belonged to a native officer of the chief Nozingile, who had been sent to the Zulu king, and was now on his way back. They had lost themselves, they said, and had seen the glare of our fires, and thinking it was the jungle burning had come to it to sleep.

An hour or two after this all was still, save the deep bell-like notes of the toads rising from the damp river-bottom, and the sharper tones of the tree frogs mingling with the harsh and grating accents of the cicadæ, while above all could be heard the heavy snoring of the wearied hunters. The heat was excessive; and, unable to sleep, I had been sitting for some time on my mat smoking and looking at the magnificent constellations of the southern hemisphere, among which the Southern Cross stood out pre-eminent in all its beauty, when my eye fell upon my favourite gun, which had been placed against the fence within reach of my hand, and I noticed that the boy whose duty it was to do so had omitted to oil it, and to wrap something round the nipples to keep off the dew— always very heavy during this season of the year. Taking it up, I found the bandolier in which he kept his gear, and carefully cleaned and oiled it, with that affection that so old and trusty a companion deserved. I was still in the act of hunting for a piece of rag to tie round the nipples before returning it to its former position, and had moved down towards the entrance to secure the assistance of what light the now smouldering fires afforded, and had thus brought the fig-tree and those sheltered beneath it into full view, when the terrified yelp of a dog struck my ear, and, raising my eyes, I saw a tawny yellow mass bound into the opposite camp, and, uttering a muffled roar like distant thunder, seize the nearest human being and carry him off shrieking in the direction it had come from.

It had all occurred in far less time than I take to describe it, and I had had neither time nor presence of mind sufficient to do anything; but now, as it passed the outermost fire on its way towards the reeds, I raised the gun, covered the shoulder, and fired, causing it to drop the man, and, with a tremendous roar that seemed to shake the ground, to spring upwards—how many feet I should not like to say, for fear of correction from the stay-at-home naturalists,—and as it did so I put the second barrel in. It fell to the ground and struggled there, still roaring in the most fear-inspiring manner, and in its agony tearing up great clods and tufts of grass with those terrible claws. Seizing another gun, I fired again right and left as quick as I could, and then catching up a little small-bore rifle, I emptied it also, thus expending my whole battery.

Shouting to the hunters to fire, I hurriedly commenced loading, glancing meanwhile to see what had become of the men. There was a cluster of some dozen round the trunk of the fig-tree, impeding each other in their eagerness to place themselves in safety, while its branches were as crowded as it appeared possible they could be. My reiterated cries of "Fire" were at last responded to by a solitary shot from some hunter, who, not completely overcome by terror, had taken his gun up with him, and the lion, who had never ceased his furious struggles, nor ceased to roar, answered it by regaining his legs, and tottering towards the tree. The men around it rushed frantically away into the darkness; but as I watched, while I rammed my bullet home, I could distinguish the dark outlines of two figures crouching at its roots, with the dying flicker of the fires gleaming on their gun-barrels. The lion staggered on, weak but vindictive, and seemed to me to have almost reached them, when two flashes of red light blazed out, and he fell without a movement, shot simultaneously through the heart and brain, while the two hunters, uncertain of the effect of their bullets, bounded away in opposite directions.

As soon as I could see that the brute was really dead, I went to look after the man who had been seized, and who was still lying moaning where he had been dropped, and, on examination, I found that it was one of the boys who had come into camp that evening. They were, as I have said, Amatonga; and as there is no love lost between them and the Zulus, of whom and of neighbouring kindred tribes my men were principally composed, they had been compelled to sleep by themselves, on the outside of the rest, and thus this unfortunate lad had become the man-eater's prey. We carried him into camp, and examined his injuries. The lion had merely bitten him; had not used its claws at all; but what a bite it was! It had held him by the neck and shoulder, and literally crushed the whole of the side of the chest in, and had probably damaged the spinal cord, for he never recovered consciousness, and breathed his last a few hours after.

This sad event prevented any of the excitement and rejoicing that the death of such an animal would have generally occasioned, and the men, though mostly unable to sleep, conversed quietly and in whispers during the remainder of the night. Death, however, is so common in a country where fever reigns, and in a profession which, like that of a hunter, entails the risk of almost hourly meeting it, that the next day brought no change in the usual employment of the day; and I, accompanied by one hunter and my water-bearer, started at daylight to hunt. We soon saw from the spoors that the buffalo had been for some time on the ground in large numbers, and scarcely a mile from camp we crossed the fresh track of a herd, which, after drinking at the river, had struck across the plain for the cooler knolls beyond.

Two hours' hard walking brought them into sight, lying scattered under some trees on the ridge above us, where what little breeze might blow during the mid-day heat would reach them. It seemed possible, by crawling through the waist-high grass, to reach the nearest unseen, and as I like to have my shot to myself, I told the hunter to crawl on and get within range of the next troop, and then to wait until I fired, when he would either have a chance at them when they stood up, or at those disturbed by me, which would probably try to join the others; and, to give him ample time to get into position, I remained where I was for some minutes. On commencing my stalk I crawled through the grass for a quarter of an hour or so, sometimes, when the ground seemed bare, wriggling forward like a snake, but usually on my hands and knees; and the buffalo, though I could not see them, and dared not raise my head to look, could not have been more than forty yards off, when I came upon the great footprints of a lion.

The instinct of a hunter to read whatever the ground can tell him made me follow the trail for several yards, deeply pondering over the "sign" as it came under my notice, and then to abruptly turn off at right angles, and make for the higher ground. I had discovered three things. Firstly, that the lion had been there within the last few minutes; this I knew by seeing a blade of green grass that his huge paw had crushed, with the wet sap upon it, as it could never have been under that blazing sun had a longer time elapsed. Secondly, that he also was stalking the buffalo; this could be seen by the deep impress of his fore-paws, showing that he had been crouching, and therefore throwing more weight upon them, and also from the fact of the buffalo remaining undisturbed, as they must have seen him had he been walking erect. And, putting these two together, I drew the further conclusion that he was at that moment close to me, possibly within two or three yards, and that I had better get above and scan the ground before I did anything else. I had to go a little back to gain the shelter of a projecting rock, but I did so as quickly as possible, and, once there, I cautiously raised my head and peered over. The two buffalo that were in sight were lying down, and I could just distinguish the flapping of their ears as they lazily drove the flies away, evidently perfectly unsuspicious. For some minutes I could see nothing of the lion, till an unnatural movement of the grass attracted my attention, and there, sure enough, was his majesty, with his head between his paws, stealing up, foot by foot, to within springing distance; and, as my eye glanced back along the broad trail he had left, I saw three other heads laid flat—the wife and family of the stalker—watching his movements with hungry eyes. It was too interesting a sight for me to have disturbed it; indeed, it was too late, even if I had wished to, for almost immediately the lion gained his distance, crouched himself flat, until he seemed sinking into the ground, and with a low and probably irrepressible growl, launched himself at the nearest buffalo. It was a large, full-grown cow, not impossibly experienced in attacks of this sort, on the back of which he lighted, and though taken at a disadvantage, she struggled up, despite his weight and his savage teeth tearing at her neck and shoulder, seeking to crush the spine; and, probably unintentionally, she staggered under the tree, the lower branches of which threw him off, though his fore-feet still retained their hold, and I could see his head buried in her back. How much longer, and with what termination, the fight would have lasted it is hard to say, though that it would ultimately have ended in the lion's favour, even if his family had had to lend their assistance, is more than probable; but the appearance of my hunter on the scene put a summary end to it. He had heard the growl of the lion as it sprang, and the bellowing of the cow told him what it meant; so he had quietly approached to a tree not twenty yards from where the combat was taking place, and seeing that he could fire at the lion with perfect impunity, the tree by him being a tall one, he was only too glad of such an easy opportunity of distinguishing himself, and not noticing that three other lions were within fifteen feet of him, he took a cool aim, and shot it through the back, splintering the bone, and causing instant death.

I had not noticed him till I heard the shot, but when I looked up he was energetically swarming up the tree, having become aware of his dangerous proximity; while the three lions, equally frightened, were scampering away as fast as they could. I could hardly fire for laughing, but I sent a bullet after one of them, which made them mend their pace; and then, seeing that the buffalo was still standing there, I gave her the other barrel in the shoulder, making her plunge forward, half-falling, and then recovering, gallop away. Before skinning the lion, we followed the cow up, as I was convinced that she was too much hurt to go far; and finding her in a clump of bush, in an excessively bad temper, as even an unwounded buffalo is sure to be when harassed by lions, we finished her off with a couple of balls as she charged out at us.

It was not for several days after this that we became aware that we had to do with another man-eater, though this time of a different description. One morning before sunrise we saw from camp two water-antelopes come down on the opposite bank to drink, and taking my little rifle, I killed one from our side. Hitherto no one had crossed, but a couple of the best swimmers now went down to examine the ford, and, to our astonishment, reported it good, and comparatively shallow; so a party of carriers crossed, cut up the antelope, tied it up in bundles or branches, and placing it on their heads, returned. The last man—and he was a few minutes behind the rest—was followed by a native cur, round the neck of which a great strip of meat had been hung, after the native custom, for its future use.

When they were in the middle of the stream I heard some shouting, and on being told that a crocodile could be seen swimming down towards them, I hurried to the bank with a gun. The brute was quite visible, carrying part of his head and nose above water, and several of us fired without hitting it. There could be no doubt of his vicious inclinations; the only question was, whether it would be the dog or the man that would suffer; but, aware of his intense liking for the former, I fancied he would not pass his favourite morsel when it was so much nearer and handier to him. Suddenly he sank, and, knowing that now was the dangerous time, I called to the man to keep still, stand his bundle in front of him, and, facing up stream, to hold his assagai ready for instant use.

Luckily my warning was not needed; a howl and a splash, and the dog had saved its master's life by the sacrifice of its own.

After this the brute never left us till its death, and became the torment of our lives. If we bathed, there it was with its ugly head as close in as it dared to come, watching us; if the boys went to draw water, they were afraid to go in where it was deep, and consequently cool, and brought us lukewarm stuff instead. Two of our dogs disappeared, both placed to the crocodile's account, as they were known to be fond of lying in the stream, cooling their bodies during the great heat. We could not cross there, and were obliged in consequence to go round some three miles every time we wanted to do so; and some Bombo Kaffirs, who had come to us, bringing beer and Indian corn for the hunters in exchange for meat, said that the ford had become disused, as I had noticed the day we arrived, on its account, and after two men had been taken by it.

The amount of lead that was wasted on the quarter of an inch of head that it showed us was a serious loss in such an out-of-the-way place, where every bullet ought to tell, and its death was determined upon. Once we armed ourselves with spears, and wading through the shallows, surrounded the hole in which we knew that he lay; but, having got so far, a panic seized us, and everybody splashed out as quickly as possible. At last I told one of the hunters to watch for it all day until he killed it, as we knew it always came up for an hour or two underneath a bush on the opposite side, but at the first suspicious indication would sink again, and only reappear in midstream, where he offered such a small and misleading mark that no one (and we had some pretty good shots) could hit him. This scheme was successful, for, on the very next day the brute came up directly underneath the man's ambush, offering him a shot at three yards' distance, and received a bullet through the skull. The camp-boys hauled it out amid great rejoicings, and we found that it was a female, and measured twelve feet nine inches; and though we continually saw crocodiles sunning themselves on the sand-banks, both just above and below, none ever infested the ford again in our time.

The public must feel some difficulty in forming a true estimate of the prowess of the African lion, from the number of conflicting statements made by different travellers and hunters. The truth appears to be that, while each one has formed an opinion from the behaviour of the particular animals they chanced to meet with, the fact that every single lion differs from another in temper and disposition has been allowed to drop out of sight. That some lions will make a point of attacking every human being they see, without the slightest provocation, admits of no doubt, while it is at least equally certain that there are others that can hardly be forced to retaliate, and which, even when wounded, will always rather run than fight.

Generally speaking, however, and subject to the above exceptions, I have found that the lion of South and Eastern Africa rarely goes out of its way to attack people, and will in point of fact shun a conflict when avoidable. There is nearly always some explanation of its behaviour when it acts otherwise: either the hunter has approached so near before being discovered that the animal is afraid to turn tail, and, urged by its very fears, makes a charge; or it may be half-famished, and having got hold of some prey, either of your killing or its own, will not quit it without a contest; or, if a lioness with cubs, will fight in defence of their supposed danger.

In the above cases, utter immobility and coolness will often avert an attack, for if the animal, judging by your behaviour, imagines that you do not want to hurt it, it will, after trying you for several minutes, and even making one or two sham charges, often walk away and allow you to do the same; but merely raising the arm, much less pointing a gun at it, is sure to make it come on. Several instances of this have occurred within my knowledge. A large native hunting-party had gone out, and were scattered over the thorns, and one of my gun-bearers who had accompanied it suddenly found himself face to face with a full-grown male lion, without a yard between them. He had presence of mind sufficient to stand perfectly still, without even attempting to take one of the spears he carried in his left hand into the other, and after a couple of minutes the brute walked away, turning its head round every second to watch him.

This could not be attributed to the efficacy of the human eye, as the man afterwards told me that he had not dared to raise his from the ground. The lion before going far met another native, who raised his spear, as if to throw it; on which it instantly sprang upon him, and inflicted such wounds that he died within half an hour. I have no doubt that if this man also had stood still, he would have been perfectly safe.

On another occasion a hunter of mine was following the trail of a herd of buffalo through some dense thickets, alone, and armed with only a single barrel. Suddenly a male lion rose out of one of them, and, sitting on its hindquarters, snarled at him; he had hardly seen it when another, about three-quarters grown, showed itself within a few yards on one side, while from behind he could hear the low rumbling growl of a third. Partly turning, so as to watch them all, he saw that the latter was a lioness, and that three cubs not much larger than cats were following her. He had, unawares, got into the centre of a lion family. Unfortunately, one of the cubs saw him, and without exhibiting the least fear, ran up to him; upon which its mother, in terror for her offspring, rushed up, and, as he afterwards described it, fairly danced round and round him, springing to within a yard of him, sideways, backwards, and in every way but on him. Luckily he was a man of iron nerve, and bred from the cradle in scenes like these; he therefore remained quiet, taking no more notice of the frantic rage of the lioness than if she had not existed, for, as he said, "it was a hundred to one that I did not kill the mother, and, if I had, the other two would soon have avenged her." It ended by their ultimately retiring into the thicket, and watching him as he cleared out, but there can be no doubt that any hesitation, nervousness, or involuntary movement on his part would have been fatal.

There are many instances of lions having evidently attacked a human being from no other reason but surprise and fear at suddenly finding themselves so close to him, and, as in most cases when they come to close quarters, the result has generally been fatal. An old hunter once told me that while stalking a sleeping herd of buffalo he came across unmistakable signs of there being a lion in the vicinity, and being a man who took care of himself, he at once climbed up a tree, from which elevation he discovered the animal, a female, crouched on the edge of a clump of bush, watching the buffalo, and, no doubt, wondering how she could get unperceived across the bare space that intervened. Hoping that in her impatience she might rouse the herd and enable him to get a shot, he remained where he was until startled by hearing the report of a gun, followed by a roar, and then by the shrieks of a man. Concluding, as he said, that he could render no assistance to the unfortunate being, though doubtless urged by his own fears, he did not descend until there had been silence for some minutes, when, taking every precaution, he stole forward and found the man, who was a hunter whom he knew, lying dead, dreadfully mangled, within a yard of the spot where the lioness had been crouched. From his former elevation he had seen that the shot fired had severely wounded a buffalo at which it had been aimed, and as the body had not been carried off, no other cause could be assigned for the attack but anger, probably mingled with fear, at finding a human being so near.

The result of such unexpected encounters is not always so tragical. I remember meeting one of my hunters, a thin, tall, wiry man, and a good runner, going at full speed, quite regardless of the thick thorns he was passing through, and which had already striped his black skin with white lines, tinged with red. There was no

doubt that he was running away, and as I knew him to
be a plucky fellow, I first glanced to see if anything was
after him, before shouting to him. On seeing me he
pulled up, and then I noticed that not only was he so
breathless as to be unable to speak, but that he was perfectly naked, his scanty dress having got torn off during
his flight. When, however, he recovered himself, he
accounted for his alarm in the following words:—" After
leaving camp this morning I went up with Mahazula
to the Daka bush, but we had not been many minutes
inside before I missed him from behind, for ever since
you gave that boy a gun he is always wanting to steal
away by himself (he had been his mat-bearer, but, having
learned to shoot, I had given him a gun, which was a
constant source of jealousy and quarrel between him and
his master); however, I kept on, as there were several
buffalo spoors of yesterday evening, and I was momentarily expecting to come across those of to-day, when I
heard something moving quietly through the bushes, and
from the sound, which was approaching me, I fancied it
was a small antelope, probably disturbed by Mahazula,
and as there is no meat in camp, I kept quiet, thinking
that I would shoot it if it came near enough. You know
how thick the Daka is, and I was in the very thickest of
it, where those tremendous cactus bushes prevent your
seeing a yard in any direction, and the sound kept
coming nearer and nearer till the animal was evidently
within two yards of me; a silence of a few seconds
followed, then a rustle, and you may imagine my dismay
when, instead of a duiker, the enormous head of a lion
came out so close that I could have touched it with my

hand. As our eyes met he opened his great red mouth to its fullest extent, showing me every one of his immense snowy fangs. I don't know why he did so." I suggested 'to yawn.' "No, not that; I thought to eat me, but perhaps it was only to express his astonishment by a roar; any way I had no time to think about it then, and, on the impulse of the moment, I thrust the gun-barrel right in, pulled the trigger, and ran away as hard as I could, and, if I hadn't met you, I don't know when I should have stopped, for I was so frightened that I only thought of running, though I must have passed plenty of trees where I should have been safe enough."

After a great deal of hesitation on his part I persuaded him to return—he was nearly a mile already from the spot—and show me where it had happened, and after a most cautious search in the jungle, for a wounded lion in such cover is not an animal to be trifled with, he whispered to me that we were not more than a few yards from where he had been standing, and there being a tree handy we both climbed up so as to overlook and examine the ground, and there, lying in its thorny-cactus bed, a whole bush of which it had smashed in its last agonies, we saw the tawny body of a male lion. A shout or two to make sure that it was indeed dead, and we approached it, finding that the ball, entering at the roof of the mouth, had passed through the brain, and that death must have been almost momentary.

My hunter, changing at once from the extreme of fear to that of joy, immediately performed a solo dance round the carcase, as oblivious from the one cause as he had before been from the other of the innumerable poisonous cactus thorns which pricked his naked legs and feet. A curious sight it was in the deep gloom of the jungle, where the scorching sun overhead could only penetrate with an occasional beam, to see this naked savage dancing round the mighty body, holding his clubbed gun aloft, and chanting wild songs, interrupted with long strings of the "strong names" of his ancestral spirits who had brought him through the danger,—a sight to be remembered, and one only to be seen by those who penetrate the wilds of Africa.

An instance of a lion, not a man-eater, attacking a human being through hunger, occurred to me personally, and as the story also affords a remarkable instance of their hunting in concert it may be worth relating, though it did not end in the death of the animal. I was returning from the river Pongolo to my camp on the Nkwavuma, and my carriers being heavily laden it was determined to sleep at some water-holes half way, and as but one hunter accompanied me, and we had to find food for some thirty or forty men, we were forced to hunt the whole distance. The country between the rivers is mostly open flats, though in places there are some of the very worst patches of ukaku I ever saw; the trees growing almost as close together as reeds, and not a single one reaching above six feet from the ground, while the tangle of thorns is so great that, except by following the paths, often *cul-de-sacs*, which the game has formed, all progress would be utterly impossible.

Black rhinoceros in the thorns, and large herds of gnu and zebra on the flats, are the principal animals, at least during the winter season, when most of the water-holes are dry and the buffalo are congregated on the banks of the larger rivers. The gnu and zebra were, as usual, almost unapproachable, and, despite a few long shots that we fired at them, afternoon had come without our having got anything, but at last, as we were crossing one of the long wave-like undulations that constitute what in Africa is termed a flat, we noticed a herd lying down about half a mile off, the larger loom of which made us imagine that they must be buffalo and not gnu.

This, on nearer approach, we found to be the case, and my wise old companion, Umdumela,—than whom a better hunter, or a quieter, pluckier man never existed, nathless that he was somewhat of a miser, and beguiled our expeditions by orations on the sin and wickedness of not giving him higher wages,—saying that here, where stalking was impossible, I, in my European clothes, would have the best chance of getting near them, told me to walk straight up, and when they rose, to run in. These tactics were not altogether successful at first, but ultimately, after a good deal of running, I got within one hundred and twenty yards, and fired right and left, wounding, as the spoor showed, two. One of these separated at the first cover, from which, however, she broke on getting our wind, affording Umdumela a good chance, which was wasted through his gun missing fire, and after a hard run of two miles across the flat we saw her go into an extensive ukaku thicket beyond. This time we went round and entered at the top, so as to make sure of the wind, feeling certain of coming across her or her spoor, and the better to do this we separated, going down parallel paths.

I had not gone far when I saw something, a lioness I

thought, flash across me some ten yards ahead, and simultaneously I heard the imitation of the whistle of one of the commonest bush-birds, which is used by hunters to call one another in cover. In obedience to this signal, I retraced my steps, as that was the only way in which I could reach Umdumela, and found him standing pouring fresh powder into the nipple of his gun, and was told in a whisper that a lioness was lying a few paces in front. I told him that I had seen one jump away just before he whistled, and on looking beyond we saw that the spot where it had been was empty, while a little distance further on we not only found its spoor but that of the buffalo, causing us to examine the ground carefully to discover what had been going on. The track of the lioness led up from below past the spot where the buffalo had been lying until it reached the place where Umdumela saw her. The buffalo had evidently risen in a great hurry, and, as we had not heard it, must have done so previous to our arrival, and then returned on its tracks at a gallop, while on following its spoor we found that the lioness, even in her flight from us, had not resigned the chase, as was shown by her heavy footprints occurring at intervals until we reached the outside.

The ground on which we found ourselves after emerging from the thicket had no doubt been the bottom through which a river of some size had run at a former period, though the sole remnant of it was a chain of water-holes occurring at intervals, and extending for several miles parallel to the mountain; great white-stemmed wild figs, and other trees usually only found near running water attested this, while the immensely high tambuti grass, in places above our heads, proved the fertilization which the ancient periodical inundations had carried with them.

There could be no hesitation or difficulty in following the broad track left by so large an animal as a buffalo through this rank vegetation, and we walked rapidly on in Indian file, the hunter leading, I next, and the two bearers in our rear, until we reached what had evidently been the bed of the river, here about forty yards wide, and which was lined with such perpendicular banks, of twelve or fifteen feet in height, that we at once saw that the buffalo could not have gone down, and on examining the spoor we found that it was a lion the trail of which we had been latterly following, that of the buffalo having no doubt turned off on one side or the other.

However, as Umdumela said, the lion was evidently after the buffalo, and if we found the one we should find the other; so we did not turn back, but, separating, went along the banks, searching for an easy descent. Umdumela had got down, and I had just seen a place where I could follow his example, when the little boy who was my water-bearer that day—the merest child of ten years old, though the equal in endurance of many a man of more than double his age in civilized countries—exclaimed, "There's the buffalo!" and there indeed was that much-suffering animal hobbling away, evidently quite dead-beat, its broken fore-shoulder showing painfully, and the mere fact of its having lain down in the open being, in itself, sufficient proof that it could not go much farther; it was about sixty yards off, and I fired right and left, bringing it to a standstill with the second barrel. The noise of the shots was still ringing in my ears, when I heard a most ominous growl, apparently proceeding from the dry stream-bed, answered instantly by the majestic form of a male lion rising from among the shorter grass on the opposite bank, his mane erect and waving in the breeze, and his face turned to me, while he showed his great teeth, and growled savagely.

The first thing was to reload. I had a muzzle-loader, and while I was pouring the powder into the second barrel I saw Umdumela's head reappear on the spot where he had got down; the lion, which had hitherto been only uttering savage growls and menacing me by threatening to charge, though without really altering its position, saw him as soon as I did, and evidently looking upon him in the light of a reinforcement, seemed determined to bring matters to a conclusion before it could arrive, and at once charged down to the edge of the bank, roaring terrifically, as if to at once intimidate us and to encourage the lioness, which, except by a low and unpleasant growling, had not so far shown herself, though the trembling grass betrayed where she lay. Umdumela walked steadily forward, and I loaded as rapidly as possible, while the lion moved backwards and forwards, uncertain whether to spring down or not, still making as much noise as he could, when, to my considerable astonishment, I heard the old hunter, who was now within a few yards of me, address the king of beasts in his own language as follows: "I say, what do you want with us? Hook it, clear out of this; do you really think that buffalo belongs to you? You want to bag the game we wound—eh? What an absurd idea! I advise you not to question our right to the country;

don't rouse us too much, we're quarrelsome too. Get out, you dog! be off with you!"[1]

As he finished this tirade he joined me, and said, "That brute won't go while the lioness remains quiet, so when you're loaded I'll fire at her, and you watch him. Even if he does charge, he could hardly scale this bank in face of your two barrels, and he'll be too angry to think of going round." I put the caps on, and turned to look at my companions; the little boy, frightened enough, though he would not show it, was keeping in very close to me; the other two, inseparable companions, and men both noted, one as a hunter, the other as a spoorer, for a cool disregard of the commonest rules of safety, and for having the most illimitable confidence and belief in themselves, merely had their eyes fixed on my nipples, and as soon as they saw that they were capped, the one sat down to take a steadier shot at the rustling grass which concealed the lioness, and the other, shading his eyes with his hand, very likely because, as it would have been an insulting thing to do to another native, he thought it would show his contempt for the blustering of the lions, stood watching the effect of the bullet. I do not think that she was struck, though she answered with a loud snarling growl, and bounding away, half concealed by the grass, totally disappeared from sight as it became longer. I, however, had no time to watch her, for, as the shot sounded, the male sprang forward to the very edge, and I, momentarily

---

[1] I have not put the original in the text, as not one man in a thousand in this country would be any the wiser, but as my translation is a free one, I give it here word for word, for the benefit of Zulu scholars:—" Menabo, ufunani nati na. Hamba, suka kuleli: eyako, yini, leyo'nyamazane etyaywa ngati na. Um-hlolo wezwe! Ungalingoti 'kubanga izwe nati, ungasiqali, ngiyakutyela, nati sinenkane. Suka innja; mayihambe-bo.".

expecting him to jump down, and tempted by the magnificent mark his great broad chest displayed, knelt down and aimed at it, making him, as the bullet struck, lose his balance and fall over the bank. I reserved my second barrel, expecting nothing but a savage and vindictive charge, and my surprise was great on seeing the brute, looking not more than half his former size, pick himself up and follow the path the lioness had taken as fast as his legs would carry him. It was all done so quickly that I never thought of firing again before he was nearly a hundred yards off, and as he took no notice of my shot, I conclude I missed him.

Before going further we crossed over, and put an end to the buffalo that had caused us this commotion; but I wanted to see more of this brute that had proved himself so great a coward, and we followed his track, all dotted with blood-spots, until it entered a dense and almost impenetrable mass of evergreen bushes lining the old water-course, in which he had no doubt taken refuge, but in which it would also have been utter madness to seek him, and where we therefore left him in peace to die of his wound, as he certainly ultimately would, though it is only fair to mention that Umdumela was quite ready to go in had I not refused to do so.

As I have said, some lions make a point of attacking every human being they meet, without provocation or apparent cause, but these, as a general rule, are maneaters, no instance of their otherwise doing so having come within my personal knowledge, and only one, well authenticated, having been told me by native hunters. The man who first related the story to me, and who was an eye-witness of it, was then living in Natal, having retired upon his earnings; but some time afterwards, when passing by the place where he described it as having occurred, I found it corroborated in every particular by the natives of the district.

Three hunters had started together from the colony for the Amatonga country to shoot ivory for their European employer, and after having been absent for nearly eighteen months, were on their way back, and instead of as usual taking the coast road and passing through Somkeli's country, they made for the Pongolo Pass, having heard of some disturbances in Zululand which made them doubt their being able to get through it safely. On the day on which they left the last Amatonga kraals the people there strongly warned them not to pass by a certain reed-margined lagoon which otherwise lay in their most direct route to the pass, saying it was frequented by a savage lion which had already killed, though it had not eaten, two passers-by, and had on several occasions given vindictive chase to others. However, as lions at that date and in that part were very numerous, hunting in troops of even thirty individuals, and these hunters had been meeting them with mutual respect and forbearance on nearly every day of the eighteen months of their expedition, they thought very little of the warning and took that very path.

They had reached the lagoon and were passing within five or six yards of the edge, when, without further warning than a slight rustle, a lion sprang upon the foremost, crushing him to the ground. His terrified comrades, throwing away the chance of shooting the brute while it was still upon its first victim and its eyes probably closed, rushed to the nearest trees for safety, but, once there, feeling ashamed of their cowardly desertion of an old companion, they descended, and walking forward together were just on the point of firing, when, with a roar that almost deprived them of the power to run, the lion charged, caught the hindmost, and after shaking him for a second or two, gave chase to the other, who, however, had profited by the time to remove himself, by a bare foot or so, out of reach of the spring the enraged animal gave as it saw that one had so far escaped. It then returned to its last victim, not yet dead, took him up in its mouth, dropped him, tossed him from paw to paw as a cat does a mouse, and at last, as if wearied at so much unaccustomed gentleness, it allowed its savage nature to gain the mastery, and with one crunch of its powerful jaw put him out of his pain.

It next came back under the tree where the sole survivor of this fearful tragedy was, and looking up at him in a complacent manner, evidently aware that though it might not be able to reach him at present it could at least keep him a prisoner during its pleasure, quietly stretched itself on the ground, and after licking its great paws for a few minutes seemed to be asleep. The tree—one of the larger mimosas—in which the wretched man was thus confined, had two principal stems separating from the main one about six feet from the ground, into the fork of which he had thrown his gun when he climbed up, and after the lapse of a quarter of an hour without any sign of consciousness on the part of the lion, he could not help his thoughts reverting to it, and to how easily the brute might be shot if he could once obtain possession of it, and after another ten minutes, to see whether the animal would make any movement, he determined to try and reach it. Silently and quietly he moved down, foot by foot, until only such a distance intervened between him and his prize as could be overcome by stooping; but while in the act of doing so a gentle, and without doubt a perfectly involuntary, vibration of the brute's tail warned him that he was observed. He had presence of mind enough to know that any hurried movement would precipitate its spring, while he was equally aware that no time was to be lost; so, abandoning the gun, he quietly straightened himself, feeling with his upraised hand for a branch to trust to, while his eyes never left the lion's body. He was not a second too soon, for as his hand found and grasped the support it sought, his treacherous adversary bounded upwards, not in time to catch him indeed, but so nearly that he could feel the rush of the displaced air.

The disappointed brute roared furiously with rage at this second defeat, but wasting no further time where it saw it was useless, stalked away, took up the body of the man it had last killed, and having carried it to the other, lay down beside them both. A few minutes afterwards it was saluted with a six-to-the-pound bullet in its ribs, making it roar as only a wounded lion can, and charge up to the tree in hot haste. Of course, such a large-bored elephant-gun was only a single-barrel, and before it could be again loaded the savage beast had disappeared in the reeds, though, one is thankful to think, carrying its death-wound as a reward for its unprovoked attack.

"SILENTLY AND QUIETLY HE MOVED DOWN."

We now come to a part of the subject about which alone volumes might be written. I refer to the man-eaters. These, in Africa, are always lions, unless we except crocodiles, for, despite what Mr. Layard has written to the contrary, man-eating leopards do not exist, except as exceptions which prove the rule, and no such exceptional case has ever come within my knowledge, either in my own experience, or from hearsay. Hyenas have also, in a considerable number of cases, been known to attack and kill infants, children, and now and then to disfigure sleeping men, but I know of no well-authenticated instance of any but the so-called king of beasts making human beings his sole or chief source of food.

A great deal has been written about their craving for such food after having once tasted human blood, but I am inclined to class this idea with such fallacies as the power of the human eye, etc. Lions have doubtless some slight instinctive fear of human beings which urges them to let them alone so long as they are able to provide themselves with their usual food, and it is only in cases when they have become unable from wounds or sickness to catch game that they do otherwise. It is easy to be understood that, having once discovered that the difficulty and danger of thus earning their living is so very slight, they do not relinquish the habit even after having recovered from the illness which first induced it.

In two cases I have been an accessory to the death of well-known man-eaters, one of which had almost depopulated a district, and had killed between thirty and forty individuals; while the other, though inhabiting a country devoid of a resident population, and teeming with game, had become notorious from attacking hunters' camps. The district in which the former committed his depredations was in the north-east corner of Zululand, where a number of refugee Amaswazi had been located, and when I arrived they had been continued for nearly a year, so that many villages had been entirely deserted, and all had more or less suffered; for the brute did not confine himself to any one in particular, nor come at any regular intervals, but so timed his visits that no one was sure of his or her life from day to day. No fastenings were of any use against him, as his immense strength enabled him to force an entrance if he could not find one ready made, while the outer ring-fence of interwoven thorns supported by strong posts which guards all native villages, and is often of great height, offered no obstacle to his powers of jumping, a single bound being always sufficient to land him inside.

He usually confined himself to killing a single individual, and would claw one out from under the blanket or skin under which, with covered heads, they cowered with terror on his arrival, but on the two or three occasions on which he had met with opposition, and when he had been wounded with assagais, he had killed every soul in the hut, and so dreadfully mangled them that their bodies almost defied recognition.

I was staying at these villages for some weeks, first at one and then at another, as they suited the position of the game, or where I happened to find myself at dusk; but, although I several times heard of the lion having attacked one either just before or just after I had been there, I never happened to meet it, and the ignorant natives became anxious for my presence, saying that their enemy feared to go where I was.

This, however, was not destined to last. One sultry evening I arrived late at the outermost village, having been forced to leave the spoor of a herd of elephants from want of ammunition, and being very tired, I determined to sleep at it, sending on two of my men to fetch some from the place which I had made my headquarters. Tired as I was with my exertions on an unusually hot day, I soon fell asleep in the hut that had been given up to our use; but, as the heat was stifling, I was not at all surprised at being awoke towards midnight by a heavy thunderstorm, which crashed round us for half an hour or more. At last the hush came that always accompanies the tremendous rain which follows, and seems to quench, such storms, broken only by the heavy splashing of the big drops, and the gurgle of the water which flooded the ground, and I should soon have been asleep again had not a drop come splash into my face through the ill-thatched roof, almost immediately followed by a small stream, of which it had been the advanced guard. This necessitated my looking out for a drier spot, when suddenly, out of the quiet of the descending rain, came such a confused clamour of shrieks and cries, of yelling and moaning, that until I heard the voice of the lion, I was utterly unable to account for it. This lasted for full half a minute, and then came such a blood-curdling yell of mingled pain and despair as I hope I may never hear again, and which haunted my dreams for many a month after.

My men, and among them two old hunters, each of whom had killed several lions, shrunk crouching back to the further end of the hut, returning no answer to my words when I told them to come out with me and face the brute, though, as I opened the hut-entrance and looked out on the pitch darkness, it was evident how useless any such attempt would be. The death-yell we had heard was followed by silence for some time, during which the brute was probably departing with its victim, and the natives were still afraid of its return, and then the usual noisy lamentations for the dead broke forth, and were continued without intermission until daylight, though I was so tired that, without expecting it, I fell asleep again, and did not awake any more that night.

There was little to tell when morning did break. The brute had hit upon the most crowded hut of all, the one in which the people who had given place to us were sleeping in addition to its regular owners, and had picked out a young married woman, taking her from among several, and without injuring any one else; as they said, "A man does not stab more than one of his herd of cattle when he is hungry."

Previous to this, on my first arrival, the head man of the district had come and asked me whether I would assist him to destroy this brute, as, if so, he would turn out with all his people, and would beat up the country until it was found; and in point of fact we had already done this, on the occasion of the chief's uncle having been carried off, but the ground was then dry and hard, and our best spoorers failed to hit off the track. To-day, however, as the rain had ceased a few minutes after its departure, there could be no doubt about finding it, and as soon as I awoke I sent off to the chief to ask him to come with his men, saying that, whether he had arrived or not, I should take up the spoor at nine o'clock.

I did not at the time know that the woman who had formed the last victim was his relation, but when my messenger came back and told me so, adding that the chief was fearfully angry, it did not surprise me to hear that runners had been sent out already, and that he had threatened to drive out of the country any one old enough to carry a spear who remained behind, and that if I would wait until the sun had reached a certain part of the heavens (about ten o'clock), he would then join me.

I had already had breakfast when this news came, and to save time I took a hunter and a spoorer with me and followed the lion. About two hundred yards off we found the spot where he had made his disgusting meal, and then the track led right away towards a stream nearly a mile distant, where he had quenched his thirst. Keeping steadily on, he passed through several covers quite strong enough to have held him, and through which we had to pass with the utmost caution, until, at length, he came out on to the open and headed in a direction that we knew could lead nowhere but to the Umbeka bush, the thickest jungle for miles round, and as this was still nearly four miles off, I sent one man back to tell the people where to come to, and kept on with the hunter.

On reaching the jungle, which covered the entire side of a hill, and was stony and broken to the last degree, besides having its under brush formed of impenetrable cactus, we did not of course attempt to enter, but, separating, we walked round it, the upper and more rugged portion falling to my share, carefully examining every inch of the ground to see whether by any chance he had again left it; however, no vestige of his spoor could be seen, and by the time we got back to our starting-point, the whole of Tekwane's people were in sight.

The chief himself was with them, though he had no intention of taking any active part in the proceedings, and when we started retired with some of his old men to a place of safety, and a council of how to proceed was formed on the spot. My idea had been that the guns should guard the more likely passes, while the people, numbering near five hundred, should beat out the jungle. To this, however, the objection was offered that from the well-known thickness of the place, and the universal terror of the lion, the men would not attempt to beat it unless they were led by myself and my hunters. Such being the case, it was decided that spies should be placed in the tree-tops and other commanding positions, while the great body of the people were to enter at the top and drive it down, but knowing, as I did, how very dangerous the affair would become if the lion was wounded in such cover, in many parts of which one could not have seen it a yard off, I especially ordered my men not to fire unless they felt sure of killing or disabling the brute on the spot, and advised that every one, advancing in as unbroken a line as possible, and going slowly and making all the noise possible, should try and make it slink off before them, and enable us in the end to get a fair chance at it in the open.

Half an hour was spent in waiting for the spies to take up their positions, and then, the whole body, chanting a hunting-song so loudly that it could have been heard miles off, and must undoubtedly have broken the slumbers of the lion, marched up to the top, and spreading out, so as to take in all but the outskirts, where it was improbable that it would be, they entered the jungle, shouting at top of their voices, partly, no doubt, in obedience to my wishes, but quite as much to keep their own courage up. In this fashion, and amid cries of "Get up!" "Get out, you dog!" "Where's the dog?" to which they trusted a good deal as likely to intimidate the lion, we passed right through to the other side, and though the ground had been beaten quite as well as it was possible for anything smaller than elephants to do, no vestige of the animal had been seen.

Hardly, however, had the men begun to cluster out upon the open, before there was a shouting from the extreme left, which, when passed on by the innumerable stragglers, soon resolved itself into the lion having been seen there. Of course there was a general rush in the direction, which I accompanied until I met a man who had come from the spot, and who said the brute had just showed itself, and turned back. On hearing this, I stopped those nearest to me and sent them to collect every one they could find, and in a few minutes two-thirds of the people had come round me. I then divided them into two bodies; the larger, led by all my hunters, except one, who remained with me, I sent back to enter the jungle on the other side and to beat through it, shouting and firing their guns, the other I took myself down to a stream which, at four or five hundred yards distance, faced the spot where the lion had shown himself, and made them lie down in the bushes which lined it. About fifty men I stationed round the jungle, telling them never to cease making a noise, and I also removed the spies from in front of us.

It took a long time to do this, a longer for the men to begin to beat, and we waited for an hour by the stream-bank before anything happened. I had left my place and gone to drink, and as I turned to come back, a stir and rustle among the bushes where the men lay concealed made me think something must be in sight, and as I got back the man next me said, "There he is," and I soon caught sight of him standing under the shade of a solitary tree outside of the jungle, with his head turned in the direction of the beaters, evidently uncertain whether to await them where he was, or take to flight; but at last, doubtless considering that this was a different phase of the human character from the one he was accustomed to meet with during his midnight maraudings, he turned tail, and coming towards us in long easy bounds, was soon within a hundred yards of those concealed furthest down. Most fortunately I had told every one not to show themselves on any account before I did so myself, and so the brute, unsuspicious of danger, made for a ford near to which the hunter who had come down with me had stationed himself. At sixty yards off he fired and rolled the brute over like a rabbit, it performing a complete somersault before it regained its legs; up the whole line jumped with a yell, and the lion, which I had at first fancied was killed, continued his course the same as before, only, perhaps rather stupified by the shot, he abandoned the ford, and ran parallel to the stream, taking no notice of the people, many of whom shrunk back as they saw him nearing their part of the line. I began to cover him when he was still two hundred yards off, and I think I kept the gun up too long, for when I fired at half that distance I missed clean. I made a better shot with my next barrel, rather too far forward, but just catching the point of the fore-shoulder, and of course putting that useful limb *hors de combat.* The brute appeared to be as cowardly by daylight as he was daring in the dark, for instead of charging he bolted under a small tree and lay down growling, and in ten minutes every one who was coming—and three-fourths of the men did so—had made their appearance, and were formed in a compact body behind me. He had not waited all this time very patiently; but when I fancied I saw symptoms of his having a desire to slink away out of the reach of the fast-assembling relatives of his victims, I had all the dogs set at him, and though only a few would go, and they would not have even hampered his escape, yet they distracted his attention for the time.

Our plan was a very simple one. The five hunters and myself were to walk up as close as we dared, and fire in volleys of three, and if we did not kill, and he charged, we were to bolt behind the natives for shelter. We walked up within thirty yards, and I and two hunters stood up while three knelt in front of us and fired, the brute growling furiously the while, but not attempting to move. The moment, however, the balls struck him—and with a lion crouched flat as he was, it was not to be expected that they would kill him unless one hit the centre of the forehead—he came straight at us, roaring horribly.

My two companions, hardly going through the form of taking aim, pulled their triggers and joined those who had already fired. Fortunately he could not spring with a broken fore-leg, and though he looked most unutterably savage he did not get over the ground very fast, so I took a steady shot at the centre of his big chest, fully expecting to see him tumble over, but you could not even see that it had struck him; and as he was getting very near I didn't take a much better aim with my second barrel than the two last hunters had, and, like them, missed, turning as I did so, and running away for bare life. I was surprised to see how the men behind had diminished in numbers, but still there remained upwards of a hundred, who so far showed no signs of flinching, and I bolted in behind them and commenced to reload, altering my position when once the powder was down, so that I could see what was going on.

The lion had charged up to within ten yards of them, and then, no doubt awed by their steadiness, he had pulled up, and was now walking slowly up and down like an officer in command, growling and showing his teeth, and looking a very noble animal with his heavy yellow mane floating round him. Very likely he would have remained like this until we had reloaded had not a young fellow in the front rank flung his assagai, with an insulting expression, at him, and as the spear-head entered he made two bounds forward, singling out the unfortunate man, who, however, met him pluckily, presenting him with his great six-foot shield to tear at, while he stuck him in the chest with his long and keen double-edged stabbing spear; as he did so, there was a sudden jerk, as of a steel trap closing, along the line, through which I was in time to catch sight of two more assagais being simultaneously plunged into the beast. All those that had run away hurried up, and a dense mass was formed, pushing and struggling to get into the centre, making the scene somewhat resemble a native football match I had once seen in the colonies. Such a contest could not possibly be continued long. Dozens of spears had been buried in the brute's body the instant it had reached the man, while, although I could tell by the shouting that they were still stabbing it, it was probably only a dead body on which they were wreaking their vengeance. Be that as it might, it was nearly half an hour before I could find any opening which led to the lion's carcase, and I do not think there was one solitary individual among all who were out that day who had not gratified himself by plunging his spear into it; at any rate, its skin was a perfect sieve, and had at least five or six hundred holes in it. The price at which the victory was gained was comparatively small, only one man having received a fatal wound; while the one upon whom the brute had sprung escaped with some severe gashes and a broken arm. The lion itself, though apparently still retaining all his powers, was so old as hardly to have a tooth in his head, and was one of the largest and heaviest I ever saw.

It was wonderful that it should not have fallen to our bullets alone, the marks of six of which were quite plain. Two had struck it in the head, one partially shattering the jaw, the other entering above the eye; a great round hole in the very centre of the chest marked my second; and one had gone into the neck, and had driven through the whole length of the animal; while the shot that had rolled it over in the first instance had also struck in the neck, and had grazed the bone. The noise the men made in going home was deafening. They never ceased singing the hunting-song at the top of their voices the whole of the six or seven miles we had to go; while man after man, amid the shouts and acclamations of the others, sprang out of the ranks and performed the bravery-dance. Old Tekwane, whose stinginess to his own people, whatever it might be to Europeans, was a proverb, forgot himself in slaughtering two oxen, and a good deal more than half the night was spent between feasting, singing, and repeated bravery-dances.

The other instance to which I have referred occurred at the Nkwavuma. I had just arrived there from the Pongolo, and the men I had sent on a couple of days previously had formed a rough camp round a solitary clump of bush, which stood in an open surrounded on all sides but that which faced the river by dense ukaku thorns. I arrived at dusk, and while lying down resting an hour afterwards, I was disturbed by hearing a rustling sound, and once or twice by the breaking of a rotten stick, and turning to a boy by me, who was learning to be a hunter I asked him if he had heard it. He said yes, and, after listening for a minute or two more, we took up our guns and stole out, thinking that as the camp had so lately been formed the game might not have discovered it, and that some stray buffalo which had been lying in the reeds might be grazing near us. After going about twenty yards from camp we caught the sound again, seemingly proceeding from the shadow of some large trees under which the vegetation was particularly rank. I whispered to Usikoto that I thought the tread was too light for a buffalo; and on his asking leave to fire in the direction, I at once gave it, and stood clear of the flash, so as to see anything he might disturb, but, to our surprise, not even a rustle succeeded the report, and after waiting a few seconds to see whether the sound would be repeated, we returned to camp, where the impression was that it must have been a hyena, though I, though without any idea of what it really was, silently differed, on the ground that if so we should have heard it rush away when Usikoto fired.

In the middle of the night the camp was roused by two consecutive shots fired from the part exactly behind where I was, and as we were in a sort of half expectation of an attack from some outlawed Dutch boers with whom we had already had a conflict concerning our equal right with them to these hunting-grounds, the panic was tremendous, and one which it was fortunate the Dutchmen did not see. On going round to the other side I found a sharp contest going on among the hunters, those who had been wakened by the shots pitching into the men who had fired them for causing unnecessary alarm, when it was only a prowling hyena which they had heard, while they contended that it was a lion, and dared their reprovers to go out in the dark and look, and although three-fourths of the camp said "Bah, it was a hyena," no one stirred.

From what they told me I very much doubted it being a hyena. One man had wakened during the night and had heard the noise of crunching and tearing at some buffalo-meat hung up on a fallen tree, the trunk of which was in camp, while the big branches on which the meat was were some five yards beyond. Being still half asleep, the idea of our dogs being the culprits was uppermost in his mind, and he called out "Get away," and flung a small brand in the direction. This was answered by a low growl. Now it is a well-known fact that the hyena, whether with the intention of deceiving people or not, utters under circumstances like these a growl that may easily be mistaken for that of a lion, and the man was not sure what he had to deal with, but thought it wisest to awaken the next man, who was a half-caste Hottentot, and whispering to him what was going on, they silently took up their guns and listened. In about five minutes the crunching was recommenced, and as the loom of the meat could be seen they both fired under it, but dead silence was all that resulted. If any one had stirred out to look, as was suggested, they would certainly have found a lioness lying crouched flat beneath the meat, but, as no one did so, the camp, after a short discussion, was soon asleep again.

When morning dawned and I went round to that part of the camp, I found that who our midnight visitor had been was already settled beyond a doubt, for some of the men awaking while it was yet dim twilight had seen a large animal slink off in the direction of the reeds, and the footprints showed that it had been a full-grown lioness. The mark she had left on the ground proved that she must have spent much of the night under the meat, a large piece of which was missing, and my suspicions being raised that it must have been the identical animal Usikoto had fired at on the previous evening, I went to look, and found her spoor encircling the camp.

I was at home all the next day, my knee, which had been hurt by a buffalo some months previously, having been overworked in coming from the Pongolo, and I noticed a singular disinclination among the dogs to go far from camp, and an occasional anxious snufling of the wind as it came up from the reeds, which led me to imagine that the lioness had not gone far away, and just as I was about to turn in, most of the camp being already asleep and quiet, the dog that was lying outside by me got up, and looking in the direction of the nearest thicket, uttered a low whine, put its tail between its legs, and went inside among the sleeping Kaffirs, saying as plainly as possible that it smelt something uncanny and did not like its position away from the men. However, as I much doubted the animal returning, I heaped more wood on the guard-fire, and slept without interruption till daybreak. It was unfortunate that I had not kept watch, as I had half thought of doing, for the brute had paid us another visit during the night, and had this time carried away two large pieces of buffalo-meat, weighing at least eighty pounds.

Next night I watched the spot from the time the camp became quiet till daylight, but no doubt she had carried away enough for her wants for the time, and my watching was in vain. A feeling, however, had sprung up that the brute was always near us, and as the old hunters had unfortunately said in the hearing of the camp-boys that they had no doubt she would take a man if she got the chance, it became difficult to get firewood, and the following evening, after the arrival of some of the Bombo natives, who told us that it was certainly the lioness that attacked every camp in the district and had already carried off two men, on finding my water-calabash empty and ordering it to be filled, I was surprised at the dead silence, instead of the usual "Yebo, Nkosi" of ready obedience. Turning to my head servant I said, "What's the matter? have the boys struck work, or what?" "They're afraid of the lion," I was assured. So, taking up my gun, I told them to come with me, and was astonished to find over thirty boys from different parts of the camp turning out with their masters' calabashes to take advantage of my escort.

The path to the Nkwavuma, about a hundred and fifty yards distant, passes through two dense bushes just on the top of the reeds, and we had reached here in safety, when I suddenly heard a rustle a yard or two off. Stopping, with my gun at the charge, I could quite distinctly hear the heavy soft footfall, evidently approaching; and so could the boys, for one and all took to their heels and left me face to face, and divided only by the darkness, from the treacherous man-eating brute. It was by no means a nice predicament, and I stepped backwards foot by foot, momentarily expecting to be attacked. However, the cowardly brute, noticing no doubt with its cat-like power of seeing in the dark, that I was always facing it, feared to spring on me, and I reached camp in safety.

But it was not to be borne that we were to go to bed thirsty, so I turned out all the hunters, reassembled the boys with torches, and marched back again, firing a couple of volleys into the two bushes before we reached them, and however near the brute may have been crouching it was overawed, and did not betray itself by any movement. Nothing more was heard of it till next afternoon, when two of the hunters saw it rolling on its back in a thicket about two hundred yards off, but the ground being unfavourable they were afraid to fire at it.

The number of people in my camp was at this time so very large, there being about sixty hunters and upwards of a hundred carriers, besides my own servants, that for the sake of escaping from the continual din, I ordered a new one to be made on the edge of the very thicket in which the lioness had been last seen. A space of about twenty yards square was cleared, and the thorn branches thus obtained were formed into a strong and high fence. Two huts were next built, one for myself and my servants, the other for a dozen of the older and more steady hunters; and as the latter was completed that day I moved into it, my own not being yet sufficiently thatched. Each hut was a long low shed with two small entrances, before each of which a fire was built, and about five yards off a small tree had been left to hang our meat upon.

In the middle of the night the Kaffir next me awoke me by saying that the lion had come, and I jumped up just in time to see a shot fired from the lower entrance, opposite which my bed was. It met with no response, and must therefore have missed, and the hunter who fired said he only had a glimpse of the brute as it cleared the fence. Umdumela had happened to awake some few minutes before, and wanting to go outside, had just got his head out (the entrance was so low one had to crawl through on all-fours), when he saw the lioness standing under the tree. It at once perceived him and growled, and he turned back for his gun, awaking the next man as he did so, who, being ready quicker, got to the door and fired the shot I have mentioned.

We had all grown so accustomed to the brute's presence that, tired as every one was with their hard work on the previous day after buffalo, sleep overpowered them again in half an hour. I had, however, been out and seen that no meat had gone, and had put some wood on the fires, and coming back, I waited till the hut was quiet, and then taking my gun and blanket, I lay down in the entrance to watch for its return. Judging by the past it would certainly do so, probably as soon as the fires got dim, but the flickering flame had quite died away, and I caught myself dozing at intervals before anything happened. I suppose my eyes, tired with watching, must have wandered from the place, for the first thing I remember is seeing a dim outline standing where before all had been darkness. It was the lioness; and my heart thumped against my ribs like a steam-hammer as I saw her almost imperceptibly glide forward to the tree, and raising herself attempt to seize a piece of meat. This action enabled me to see a faint glimmer of white under her, and I put the sight as near on it as I could, and fired. I have often heard lions roar with rage or pain, but never anything like this one; the very ground seemed to shake while she flung herself against the roof of the hut, making the men inside tremble while she fairly bellowed forth her rage. She next sprang on to my unfinished hut, and then over the fence, where her furious roarings gradually toned down into low mutterings, and at last died away.

Before this I had gone outside, where I was joined by one or two of the more plucky hunters, and had piled

"IT WAS THE LIONESS"

wood on both the fires, so that in a few minutes the whole encampment was lighted up, and all the men came out. When the silence had continued several minutes, and while I was peering through the hedge with a torch to try and see something of the animal, which we fancied was dead, we heard a voice out of the darkness asking to be let in, and on removing the bushes that closed the entrance through the fence we found a hunter called Dick —who, having been forced to have a private camp of his own on account of an accusation of witchcraft from his brother hunters, had had the wonderful pluck to leave it when he heard the shot and the roaring of the animal and come to ours in the dark, running the risk of meeting the wounded lioness. It was a thing I certainly should not have dared to do, and one of the pluckiest I ever heard of.

Our people, now fancying that the animal must be dead, struck up a triumphant hunting-song, but it had hardly broken the stillness before it was silenced by a deep growl close at hand, several of which, though growing fainter and fainter, and mingled with a sort of choking cough, were uttered in the next half hour. Daylight soon after broke, and then we sallied out and found it not ten yards off, stone dead. The shot had been a most fortunate one, the ball having gone in between the shoulder and the chest, and come out on the other side of the same shoulder, merely inflicting what appeared at first sight to be a slight flesh wound, though some large artery must have been cut as she had bled to death. She was a large gaunt lioness, reduced by illness and starvation to a mere skeleton, and evidently unable to procure food in any way but by that she had taken to. I do not think that she was, properly speaking, a man-eater, for so long as she found meat handy she did not go further, but she certainly had the name, and had killed two men, and would, no doubt, if hard pressed by hunger, have killed more, so that she was as well dead.

A lion will seldom stand much bullying. He may, and often will, get out of your way, nay, even leave his prey if you approach it, and, should you follow him, will perhaps do so a second time, but that is about the extent of it. He seems to argue, "I've retired twice, and here you are at me again; well, if you must have it, come on nearer, if you dare;" and then, if a male, he growls deeply, and makes his mane bristle up round him; or, if a lioness, crouches down like a cat, lays her ears back, and shows her teeth, and in most such cases, when the brute is fairly roused, a charge is inevitable, whether you advance or retire.

On one occasion I disturbed a lion once too often, though he did not charge, but warned me back by a low threatening moan out of the reeds where he was concealed, a sound that I well knew meant that he was in a bad temper, and that I had better not come too close. I was out hunting, and was walking along the bank of the river, when suddenly the brute got up and roared a few yards off. I could not see him, but the sound made me jump, and, when I recovered myself I went round the thicket and saw a dead buffalo, from which I had disturbed him. As the skin was almost perfect, I told my boys to take it off, and meantime I went after some water-antelopes I could see about half a mile off. I could not get near them, and on my way back through some thickets near the river I stumbled on the lion again, and catching a glimpse of his body as he sprung away, I fired, missing, and went back to my men. Soon afterwards, hearing a shot or two across the river, I again took my gun and went down to the reeds, thinking that it might be buffalo, and that some of them might be driven in there for shelter. Just as I reached the top of the bank I saw the reeds shaking within a few yards of me, and my head being full of buffalo I at once descended, and was in the act of entering when I heard the low moan I have spoken of. For a second I thought it was uttered by some large animal in pain, but as it caught my ear a second time I recognised it, and knew what it meant. The brute might easily have sprung on me in our present relative positions without even giving me a chance to defend myself, and I was glad enough to regain the top of the bank.

I was an eye-witness to another instance, ending fatally, of the folly of pushing a lion to extremity. I was out with four hunters, and we were returning from following the spoor of a herd of elephants on which we had slept two nights, but without being able to catch up to the fast-travelling animals, and were all slightly scattered, looking for something to shoot for food, when up jumped four three-parts-grown lions in front of the man furthest to the left. He and I fired at them as they galloped away in different directions, both missing, and I thought nothing more of it until I saw one of the other hunters running across me, and on shouting to him heard that "April" had followed them as soon as he had loaded.

I was very lame at the time, but I set off running too, and on getting clear of a small thicket that obstructed my view, I saw him about a hundred yards behind one which had separated from its mates, stopping when it stopped, and sometimes covering it, but always keeping about the same distance between them. The other hunters had all passed me by this time, and I could hear them shouting to him to wait till they came up; but he was always an obstinate fellow, and I had not run many hundred yards more, when I saw that the lion had pulled up again, and that he was covering it, and this time he fired.

I saw him abandon his gun and make for a tree close by, but the lion caught him with two springs at the foot of it, and threw him down, seemingly not trying to injure him, and eyeing the other men, two of whom were well up, the other, Mahlatine by name, and far the fastest of the three, having climbed up a tree when he saw how things were going. The two men pulled up about thirty yards off, I now shouting to them to wait for me, and one levelled and fired, only striking up the dust, and then turning in disgust, rushed to the tree where Mahlatine was, and climbing up, wrenched his gun from him, giving him a nasty fall in the process, and at once returned to the scene of action.

The other man, Untabine, the best shot I ever saw at dangerous game, left to himself, walked a little nearer, and despite my cries of "Wait a second," as I panted up, knelt down, and taking a deliberate aim, dropped the lion dead over its victim, shot through the brain. It is possible the poor fellow might have lived had there been medical assistance on the spot, for the wound in his thigh, though deep, did not seem to me a mortal one, but he died the next day, probably as much from weakness and loss of blood as anything else. We carried him up on a rude litter to the village where we were staying, and hard tiring work it was for us four to carry the moaning man the twenty miles we had to go, but we thought we might save him, and he certainly would not have lived in the flats during the rainy season.

Although I do not think that the lion deserves the title of king of beasts, as the elephant is more sagacious, and the black rhinoceros (upetyane) is certainly more dangerous, and either of the two could kill him in a few moments, with but little danger to themselves, I consider him the most noble-looking of all.

Perhaps the most beautiful sight that I ever saw in connexion with them was on a morning when I had gone out to hunt with one bearer at dawn. I had not got far from camp, and, most carelessly, my gun was still unloaded while I was examining some buffalo spoor, when on looking up I saw my gun-bearer, who had my cartridges, running away at full speed. Knowing that he must have seen something to frighten him so, I did not shout, but went to where he had been standing a few yards ahead, and there, sure enough, not twenty yards off, were a pair of lions; they were both full grown, and the male had an immense mane, and formed altogether as handsome a pair as I ever saw; the lioness was rolling on her back, playfully striking out at her lord and master with her forepaws like a kitten, while he stood gravely and majestically looking on. I stopped a moment to watch them, though the ground was quite open, and they must have seen me if they had looked round, and then I rushed off after my Kaffir to load. The position they were in was good, and I might have killed one to a certainty, if not both, but when I had succeeded in getting him down from the top of a big tree and went back, they had gone. I suppose they must have got our wind. No doubt they had been hunting all night, and had been down to the river to drink preparatory to going to bed.

I once had the pleasure of, unobserved myself, watching a lion family feeding. I was encamped on the Black Umfolosi in Zululand, and towards evening, expecting a friend, I went out to meet him, and, instead of taking a gun, which I should have done ninety-nine times out of a hundred, I only took up one of the Kaffirs' spears, not intending to go beyond a couple of hundred yards. However, not meeting my friend, I went on, and at about half a mile from camp I saw a herd of zebra galloping across me, and when they were nearly two hundred yards off, I saw a yellow body flash towards the leader, and saw him fall beneath the lion's weight. There was a tall tree about sixty yards from the place, and anxious to see what went on, I stalked up to it, while the lion was still too much occupied to look about him, and climbed up. He had by this time quite killed the beautifully-striped animal, but instead of proceeding to eat it, he got up and roared vigorously, until there was an answer, and in a few minutes a lioness, accompanied by four whelps, came trotting up from the same direction as the zebra, which no doubt she had been to drive towards her husband. They formed a fine picture as they all stood round the carcase, the whelps tearing and biting at it, but unable to get through the tough skin. Then the lion lay down, and the lioness driving her offspring before her did the same four or five yards off, upon which he got up, and commencing to eat had soon finished a hind-leg, retiring a few yards on one side as soon as he had done so. The lioness came up next and tore the carcase to shreds, bolting huge mouthfuls, but not objecting to the whelps eating as much as they could find. There was a good deal of snarling and quarrelling among these young lions, and occasionally a stand-up fight for a minute, but their mother did not take any notice of them, except to give them a smart blow with her paw if they got in her way.

At last one of the whelps, having probably eaten as much as it could gorge, began to wander about, and in a few minutes came my way. Seeing it so near, the idea of catching it entered into my head, and descending to the lower branch, I waited till it came underneath and dropped down over it, seizing it with both hands; but I had counted without my host; the little beast snarled and bit and tore at my bare arms in such a fashion that I was glad to fling it away, and scuttle up the tree again as fast as I could out of the way of the enraged mother, who was coming down at full gallop, her tail carried out straight behind, and looking the very personification of fury. She rushed right against the tree in her blind hurry, and then rearing up, glared at me and roared terribly. I might easily enough have sent my spear into her; but as there was not the faintest chance of its killing her, and it would answer no useful purpose, I refrained, and watched her instead as she flew at her offspring, and drove it, yelling at her rough treatment, towards the others. There was now little left of the zebra but a few bones, which hundreds of vultures were circling round waiting to pick, while almost an equal number hopped awkwardly about on the ground within fifty or sixty yards of it; and the whole lion family walked quietly away, the lioness leading, and the lion, often turning his head to see that they were not followed, bringing up the rear.

In the valuable work on "The Lion and the Elephant," written by the late Charles Andersson, and edited by Mr. Lloyd, the following passage occurs, when speaking of the former of those two animals:—"Occasionally, moreover, he attacks and kills the buffalo," and this was commented on in a review of that work in *Land and Water* in the following words:—

"This is rather a mild way of putting it, when the lion is well known to almost live on buffalo in such districts as they are common, urged thereto by the fact that, keeping under cover, and sleeping, as they do, during nearly the whole day, they are more easily stalked by his majesty than the open flat-loving and wary antelopes."

It would not have been necessary to mention this here had not Mr. Lloyd, while writing to find fault with other criticisms in that review with which we have nothing now to do, written the following paragraphs, the perusal of which by one ignorant of the subject might lead him to believe that the statement of the reviewer in *Land and Water* was incorrect, and that the lion does not principally feed on buffalo under the conditions enumerated by him:—

"Other faults have been found by your critic with Andersson, especially as regards a statement of his respecting the animals on which the lion preys; but as another little work of his is likely shortly to appear, in which, since it not impossibly will be shown that your reviewer's assertions are as groundless as those he makes with regard to the Ama Zooloo lions, it is needless for me to enumerate them here."

From my experience, the reviewer was right and Mr. Lloyd wrong; indeed, I can hardly imagine the well-informed Andersson lending his name to any statement to the contrary. I have probably, at different times, found between one and two hundred animals killed by lions, and I have seen at least treble that quantity of game killed by hunters and broken into by lions. Among the first there may have been twenty zebra, and ten cases in which some of the other kinds of antelopes, gnu or water-antelope for instance, were the victims, the remainder being buffaloes, as in nine cases out of ten they were among those left dead by the hunters.

Among the numerous times on which I have seen lions hunting by daylight, I cannot call to mind a single instance when the game they were after was not buffalo, and times without number I have found a herd of buffaloes that I had been after all day scattered and dispersed by lions during the night.

On the other hand, I would not go so far as to say that buffalo-meat is their favourite food. Were a zebra, a fat rhinoceros, and a fat buffalo to be killed and left out, it is probable that they would be eaten in the order in which they are named. Soft succulent fat is what the lion probably considers most toothsome, and zebras supply this in a higher degree than any other animal save the rhinoceros and the hippopotamus, neither of which he is able to kill; but, on the other hand, the zebra, precisely in the way stated by the reviewer in *Land and Water*, confines himself to the open as far as possible, never approaches within springing distance of a thicket, and rarely, unless when going to water, gives the lion a chance. Buffalo, on the other hand, are nearly always in and close to cover, presenting continual opportunities for a successful stalk; and though the danger in attacking them is much greater, as is proved by the by no means rare instances of lions being maimed, and even killed, in such contests, yet for the above reason they form their chief food. It is said lions will go an immense distance to the carcase of a rhinoceros; and a half-mad hunter of mine, who also had a mania for its flesh, and used to go and camp alone by the dead body when one happened to be killed, and was indeed currently reported to get inside and sleep there, often told me that he had seen eight and ten tearing at it at one time.

They are by no means too proud, as I have said, to eat game killed by other people, particularly when killed so late in the day that it cannot be broken up; and even when the hunters are sleeping by it they will come almost within the glare of the fire, and tear and crunch away, taking no notice of shots or stones, but an occasional growl, unless hit, when they are pretty certain to make one spring into the centre of the camp and do all the mischief they can.

Apropos of this, I remember hearing of a very plucky thing done by a native hunter of a friend of mine. He had killed a buffalo and was sleeping out by it alone, and during the night he heard a crunching going on that only a lion's powerful jaw could produce. He got up, and by the dim light of a third-quarter moon could just make out the outlines of two lions, about twenty yards off, and, taking a steady aim—he only had a single barrel—he fired at the nearest, which made a bound upwards and fell dead. The other took no notice, and after a minute resumed its meal, upon which he quietly loaded and shot it dead upon the spot. It showed great pluck, for alone in the dark with two lions, and only one shot to trust to, is anything but a pleasant position. Sometimes I have heard the most extraordinary concerts going on round game the lions were feeding on, hyenas and jackals keeping up a continual round of howling, squealing, and laughing, which, being interpreted, meant, I suppose, that they were very hungry and wished the lions would clear out and let them begin. It is by no means unusual to find a hyena or jackal lying dead, punished on the spot for daring to approach too near the bigger robber's supper, and I have often seen the spoor of where a lion had chased hyenas several hundred yards away from his prey.

Sometimes, when attracted by meat, they will come and roar all night within a few yards of the camp, and I have often had sleepless nights from serenades of this description; cases have also occurred when the smell of the meat has been irresistible, and they have forced their way to it. I remember one man, a European, who had to spend the night in a tree watching a male who had sprung into the camp and seized a piece of meat, kindly taking no notice of the terrified scramble he caused, and who, after roaring a little, was joined by two lionesses, the three proceeding to eat all the buffalo-meat in stock, one always keeping guard while the other two went to water, roaring all the way there and all the way back. This habit of keeping guard over their food they have been forced to acquire from the depredations of vultures, hyenas, and jackals, which, if not prevented, would pick the bones clean in a few minutes.

Sometimes a lion when prowling about will come across a man, perhaps strayed, or watching a water-hole, and in such cases will very likely kill him and leave him where he found him, not eating the body. I know a Dutch hunter, a very powerful man, who was once sleeping out near the Nkwavuma. He had been unsuccessfully pursuing game all day, and had made no camp-fence, or other protection, as he had got no meat with him. During the night he was awoke by something catching hold of his arm, and thinking that it was a hyena, he made a tremendous effort to free himself, striking out at it with the disengaged arm. The blow was such that if it did not knock the animal down, it at any rate drove it back, and enabled him to snatch up his rifle and fire. The lion, as to his astonishment it turned out to be, jumped away roaring, and next morning was found dead a few yards off.

Much has been written about their roar, and I must confess to having been disappointed in it at first; but after a time I discovered that, though it had no resemblance to thunder or anything of that sort, it really was a very awe-inspiring sound. It commences by a low booming growl, repeated two or three times, and increasing in loudness until it becomes a roar that fills the air, and then dies away again in a low muttering. Lions coming from different directions will often keep it up for half an hour, answering each other; and it shows how the animal is dreaded, that the moment it is heard near camp there is a dead silence, more wood is hastily heaped on the fire, and all the natives uneasily shift their positions, and take up their guns and spears. It can be heard for an immense distance in the clear atmosphere of the tropics, and I have frequently heard it plainly when it could not have been less than two miles off.

The most likely places in the bush country in which to find lions, as far as my experience goes, are the ukaku thorns, the dense evergreens which line the rivers, and, during summer, the reeds on the margin of lagoons or streams, while in the open flats any patch of reeds or tall grass suffices to conceal them. The best chances for killing them are obtained in the first-mentioned spots, as you often come across them asleep when you are stealing about after game. It is better not to fire if the brute's head is towards you, as, even if you shoot it through the brain, its dying bound may land it on the top of you; but if you see one in that position, go round, and try and get a shot at its back—they always lie on their side—and then there is a good chance at the head or breast, with a possibility of breaking the backbone. Sometimes the bush is too thick for you to go round, in that case hide and break a twig, or give a low whistle, and it will get up uncertain what has disturbed it, and give every opportunity for a steady shot.

Sometimes one meets them in bad places, where it would be very dangerous to fire if alone, and when, if seen, it is best to stand one's ground, not attempting to make any offensive movement, and *not to kneel down*, as for some reason, probably because they themselves always crouch preparatory to making an attack, lions will rarely stand this if in anything of an ugly temper. When you do fire, try for the shoulder, or, if a very crack shot, and not at all nervous, the brain; in the latter case, do not aim too high, as the forehead is perfectly flat, and a ball is very apt to glance; in the former, in dealing with a male, take care that the floating mane which conceals the shoulder does not also cause you to aim too high, as when the brute is angry and bristles up, it makes it seem a far larger mark than it really is.

It should always be recollected, before meddling with lions, that if you do come to close quarters with them death is the probable result. There are cases within my own knowledge where, single-handed, and armed only with a spear, a native has succeeded in killing one that has sprung upon him, without receiving in return anything but trifling injuries; but these are only exceptions that prove the rule that where they strike they kill. Unlike other large game, they divide their attentions equally, springing from one to another, and fighting with tooth and claw in the most wonderful manner. It is a grand sight to see one charge a native regiment sent out after it, as they sometimes are, springing over the heads of the first line right into the centre, flying about, knocking men down with every blow, until, a complete sieve of assagai-wounds, it dies fighting.

Few hints can be given that can be of any service when the lion is once fairly charging and your gun is empty. When you have to take refuge in a tree, go up it as far as you can,—for if none of its bones are broken the lion will generally have a try at you, though if the branches are thick there is little danger, even within distance of its spring. In a case where a few seconds' delay may save your life, it is worth while to know that anything thrown down—a hat, coat, etc.—will first be torn up with a crunch of the teeth or a blow of the paw before your pursuer resumes the chase. It has, to my knowledge, saved more than one man at a pinch.

CHAPTER VI.

LEOPARDS.

As might have been expected from the immense herds of antelopes scattered all over Africa, the wild animals which prey upon them are very numerously represented. Lions, leopards, panthers, tiger-cats, hyenas, jackals, wild dogs, and the smaller varieties of the cat and weasel tribes are all common, and among them, passing over the lion, the first two mentioned are best worth the hunter's attention. There seems to be some little confusion among naturalists as to how many species of these exist in Africa, but in the south and eastern portions of the continent there are undoubtedly three, and in my experience no more. Which of these, correctly speaking, is the panther,

I am unable to say, as the African hunter learns to know animals chiefly by their native and local names, and the whole there are colonially spoken of as "tigers."

The "ingwe," the most common of them, is, I have no doubt, *Felis leopardus*, and inhabits almost every strip of jungle in South and Eastern Africa, and has been found wherever travellers have as yet penetrated. It is the second in size, and is distinguished by its peculiar markings, having little white spots in the centre of the black, but so unevenly inserted as to debar the black from being called a ring.

The "ngulule," or maned leopard, is very rare, I having only twice met with them. It is considerably larger than the ingwe, far more cowardly, and in many aspects resembles a young lioness or puma. My late friend Mr. Leslie, who had perhaps more acquaintance with this subject than any one else, wrote to me as follows about them:—

"I had three skins; a cub, a half-grown one, and a full-grown one. My Kaffirs did not know what the cub skin was. I got it first. The cub is grey, light, and furry, just like some kittens; the half-grown one, grey also, but the spots are rather faintly distinguishable. In the full-grown one they are perfectly so, but very dirty and undefined. There is also the peculiar grey hog mane. This is the ngulule."

The description of the latter skin, I may add, perfectly agrees with that of those which I have myself seen, and I have no doubt that it is the same animal which the late Mr. Andersson, the discoverer of the Okavango river —who, by the way, seems to use the terms leopard and panther as applied to the same animal[1]—saw in

[1] *Okavango River*, p. 204.

South-Western Africa, and speaks of in the following terms :[1]—

"Being in advance of the waggons, I suddenly came upon an animal, which, though considerably smaller, much resembled a lion in appearance. Under ordinary circumstances I should certainly have taken it for a young lion, but I had formerly been given to understand that in this part of Africa there exists a quadruped which, in regard to shape and colour, is like the lion, but, in most other respects, totally distinct from it. The beast in question may be said to be nocturnal in its habits, to be timid and harmless, and to prey for the most part on the small species of antelopes. In the native language it is called Onguirira, and would, so far as I could see, have answered the description of a puma."

Andersson here so exactly describes this animal—which, though its spotted skin on a closer view would have shown him to what species it belonged, at a little distance so strongly resembles a lion from its tawny yellowness and general shape, that I was once, as will afterwards be seen, myself deceived by it—that I have not the slightest doubt that it is identical with the ngulule of Eastern Africa, though, as far as I know, it does not exist in the South.

The third, which is the smallest, and in my opinion not a distinct species, but merely a variety of the first mentioned, like it goes under the generic name of "ingwe" among the natives, and "tiger" among the colonists, and is only distinguishable by the jet blackness of its spots, and the greater purity of the grounding, as well as by being the most fierce. It is also far less common, and its cubs, like those of the larger variety, have their markings complete at birth, though their coats are not so smooth nor the colour so clearly defined as in those of full growth.

[1] *Lake Ngami*, p. 149.

Common as the ingwe is, it is, owing to their nocturnal habits and the thickness of the jungles they lie in, seldom that one is seen, but any one who is continually hunting will occasionally come across them by accident, and on several occasions I have obtained shots at them in this way. Once, when hunting along the banks of the Pongolo, the dog that accompanied us suddenly wheeled to windward, and growling furiously, went slowly up in that direction. We at once guessed what it had scented, as no other animal would have made it show such anger, and at the same time so much caution, and it was not long before the fresh imprint of a leopard's foot in the soft sand by the river confirmed our suspicions. The brute had no doubt seen or heard us, and had made off in that stealthy manner they are accustomed to use when stealing away unobserved from some danger which their keen senses have pointed out to them, and it was not before we had gone nearly half a mile that we saw by the dog's bristling up, and its hesitation in advancing, that we were close to it. There was a small belt of thick bushes lining the river, into which the track now led, and I ran up to guard the one end of it, while the hunter who was with me stayed below. Hardly a second elapsed before the dog gave tongue, and soon afterwards we could tell that the leopard was at bay. I ran as fast as I could in the direction of the sound, but was only in time to see it, with its back arched and every hair on end, break away, and, without giving either of us a chance to fire, bound through the bushes, and passing through the waste high grass which concealed it beyond, head for another cover a little higher up. To this we at once followed it, still led by the dog, but found that it had passed on, and in a few minutes our guide rushed into a round patch of tambuti grass of about twenty yards in diameter, and began to bark furiously, while we placed ourselves on opposite sides, so as to command a shot if the brute again broke.

I had hardly taken up my position when there was a rustle and a rush, and its long spotted body was flying past me within a yard. It took me so much by surprise that it had almost reached the nearest bushes, some twenty yards off, before I could get my gun on it and fire, but the answering growl made me hope that I had hit it, and on crossing to the place we found blood dotting the leaves and running down the blades of grass. The smell of this so excited the dog that it went off in pursuit at full speed, whereas it had hitherto been almost too careful and slow, and in five or six minutes we heard it giving tongue again. As we neared the spot, which was in thick jungle, the angry cat-like spitting and snarling of the leopard was distinctly audible. But when I got close and could see the dog I could not place my eyes on the brute itself, until I heard a shot from the hunter on my left, and it suddenly fell struggling down from a branch of a tree above me and scarcely three yards off. The dog rushed instantly on it, but received such a blow as sent it back howling, thus enabling me to get a clear shot, and plant my two bullets in its chest. This nearly disabled it, and the dog was able to keep its attention engaged until I had reloaded, when another shot through the neck, breaking the spine, killed it on the spot, and we found that it was a large male, its size and the white spots in the centre of the black proclaiming it as belonging to the common variety.

On another occasion I came across two three-parts-grown cubs of the smaller variety. It was near sunset, but I was still following some buffalo which I had fired at through a patch of jungle, when my eye was attracted by something moving in front, and on standing still I soon made out that it was a leopard. It was quite near me, and as I could plainly see its spotted skin I might have fired at once, but noticing that its progress would necessarily bring it in a few moments into a small glade beyond, I refrained and waited. As it emerged from the bushes I saw that it was accompanied by another, and that neither of them were full-grown, but before I had time to raise my gun they began to roll and struggle together, playfully growling just as two kittens might, springing up into the air after their mock fight, and embracing the trunks of the trees with their claws, arching their backs and gambolling about in a way far too interesting for me to disturb them, until I had watched them. It was a very pretty scene, as this variety, whose regular black spots stand out in marked contrast to their almost white skins, are remarkably graceful in their movements. Sometimes they would lie down facing each other, their small heads laid flat between their fore-paws, and remain motionless for several seconds, their long bushy tails, alternately marked with white and black rings, alone betraying by their waving motion that they were not asleep; then they would jump up, springing round each other and striking out with their paws, one even performing the old kitten trick of trying to catch its own tail. At last one sprung into the jungle, and fearing lest the other should follow its example, and both disappear, I at once aimed at it as it stood broadside to me, and broke both its shoulders with the first shot, paralysing it. Its skin, which was made into a gun-cover, was, I think, the most perfect I ever saw, retaining all the softness and beauty of a cub's, combined with the well-defined markings of a full-grown one.

Perhaps the most common manner of finding leopards is either when they have killed a sheep, a goat, or an antelope, and the carcase is found and watched; and in this way I have killed several. The first one, which was also the first I had ever seen, had broken into a kraal of a farmer on the river Tugela, and had, without injuring the carcases, killed nine sheep. I was staying at the time at a farm-house on the opposite side of the river, and soon after daylight on Christmas morning a mounted messenger was sent across with the news, and to ask me if I would come over, as the brute was to be followed up at once. Of course, I delayed no longer than was necessary to get my gun and ammunition and to saddle my horse, and on arriving at the farm I found a strong body of natives headed by a Christian Kaflir with a gun, and two young Dutchmen from a neighbouring farm. The owner of the sheep was not himself going out, being in delicate health, but in his place he sent two noble Boer-hounds, great yellow animals as big as a young calf, besides which a whole pack of curs of every cross accompanied the natives, which, like their masters, disappeared as if by magic when we approached the leopard, and they discovered what they were after.

Our way lay up a broken kloof or glen, down which a small stream ran, and which was covered with dwarf thorns, aloes, and rank grass growing amongst great boulders and stones. It would have been all but impossible for us to have tracked the leopard here, but fortunately the keen and willing noses of the Boer-hounds enabled them to lead us over the more difficult ground, and when they were at fault on the various occasions when it had crossed water we always managed to assist them by finding the spoor on the soft ground on either side.

At last, on nearing a native village, a man came out and shouted to us that the animal which we were in search of had passed there at early dawn, and had, out of sheer mischief, for it could not possibly have been hungry, killed a goat, the carcase of which they had found a few hundred yards off. On hearing this the party was divided in opinion as to the best course to pursue; whether for one or two of our number to lie in wait by the dead goat, to which the leopard was nearly sure to return, or to follow it up at once. I was in favour of doing the latter, for the reason that as there was no moonlight it was quite possible it might approach unseen, even if it did not defer its visit to the following night, when the meat would be higher and therefore more in accordance with its tastes, and also because from the behaviour of the hounds I felt no doubt that we should be successful in our search, and after some little argument it was decided that it should be so. Striking the track again, therefore, at the spot to which the native had followed it, we proceeded without a check for some two hours, momentarily getting into steeper and more broken ground, until we reached a mass of great bare boulders and exposed rocks much resembling a Highland cairn.

Here the hounds began to give evident signs of being

near the animal, and the cowardly Kaffir curs slunk away with their tails between their legs, to be soon followed by their masters, who one by one dropped out of sight, till we who had guns were left with only the two men who were leading the hounds. It soon became extremely difficult for them to retain their footing among the rocks, and at the same time to restrain their charges, which, bristling up and growling deeply, tugged at their collars in such a way as showed the leopard could not be far off. On a sudden, and without giving us any warning, one of the Dutchmen fired, aiming at the rocks above us; and the leopard, which he had seen lying on a ledge, sprung down with a snarl, coming straight to us. We all immediately fired at it, but, I think, without hitting it, unless, indeed, with my second barrel loaded with slugs, and in another second it would have been among us, had not the hounds loosed by the terrified natives sprung forward towards it, and meeting it a few yards from us, occupied all its time in defending itself.

These hounds, if they had been accustomed to the work, ought each to have been more than a match for a leopard, but as this was probably the only one they had ever seen, they did not seize it at the right place—behind the head at the nape of the neck; and though evidently much torn it was soon able to escape from them, after inflicting several nasty gashes, and to take refuge under a large rock about fifty yards off. Here we followed it, and unavailingly fired several shots in the attempt to make it bolt, but as we failed and the hounds could not get in, we were at our wits' end to know how to get at it.

It was dangerous work coming up close, but we all

did so and examined the place. It was a fissure between two rocks of some eighteen inches high, and a couple of yards broad, and the animal was evidently pretty far back, as the hounds were lying scraping at the entrance, unable to reach it. At last one of the Dutchmen laid himself down flat, and in spite of our remonstrances when we saw his object, pulled the hounds away, and holding his gun at full-cock in front of him, dragged himself to the entrance, so that he could see in. When he did so I raised my gun, and cocking both barrels, now both loaded with slugs, held myself in instant readiness to fire if the brute attacked him. A second afterwards he had fired, having first warned us with an exclamation, and as I heard the growl and rush of the animal, for I could not see for the smoke, I also fired, rather at random, I am afraid, but fortunately with the result of just catching it as it came out, and killing it on the spot. The Dutchman's last bullet, aimed between the two eyes, which he had seen glaring upon him out of the darkness, had struck it too high in the head, and had glanced, while his first had entered in the chest, and passed through its whole length. The skin, which, though a handsome one, was much spoilt with my slugs, we gave to the farmer whose sheep had been taken, and six years after, when calling there, I saw it still in existence.

Lying in wait for them is, however, an easier mode of getting shots, though it may occasionally become rather an exciting one. On the two occasions on which, when by myself, I have killed leopards in this way, the whole affair has been more or less tame; but I have heard of cases where the wounded animal has discovered its opponents, and seriously injured several of them before dying. On the first I was staying in a village in Zululand, from which a goat had been taken the previous night, and as I happened to see its owner while on his way to search for the carcase, I told him that if he found it he was not to touch it but to bring me word, and accordingly he returned towards afternoon to take me to the spot. It was nearly a quarter of a mile off, and the carcase was lying in the open in the shade of a tree on the edge of a jungle, in which, no doubt, the leopard had made its lair. It was a difficult spot in which to conceal one's-self, and I found that if I remained I must do so by standing behind the trunk of a tree, and must necessarily be alone; but as it is so rare to get a shot at leopards, and the wind at least favoured me, I determined to wait for its coming, and sent the man home.

I was forced to stand straight upright and not to move for fear of exposing myself, the trunk of the tree being of no great size; and as the scorching afternoon sun was shining direct on the back of my head, my position was an exceedingly irksome and disagreeable one, and was not improved as the sun went down by the advent of clouds of mosquitoes. My patience was not, however, tried long. Just as it became dusk I heard a rustle in the grass, and on cautiously looking round I saw the leopard itself standing over the carcase. It had not seen me, but some faint sound must have caught its ears, for it was standing motionless, listening. It did not see me even when I raised my gun, and fell dead a second afterwards, shot through the brain.

The next time that I lay in wait for one was on the

top of the Bombo Mountains. Close by where it had left the goat, which, as on the former occasion, it had taken from the village where I was, was one of the little tiny watch-huts, just sufficiently large for a person to sit comfortably down in, and raised on stakes about four feet above the ground, in which the native girls sit when the crops are ripening, and drive off the baboons, monkeys, and birds, which would otherwise eat up the entire yield. It was late in the year at the time, and harvest was over, so that I was able to take undisturbed possession of the hut, which, however, acting upon the advice of a hunter who belonged to the village, I did not do till after dark. The moon was pouring down a flood of light as this hunter conducted me by intricate paths, sometimes through the forest, and at others through the maize-fields, to the hut, and left me there. The field on the edge of which I stood was merely a clearing in the forest on the side of a steep slope, over which great trunks of trees lay scattered, their charred outlines half concealed by creepers; while here and there some giant, which had resisted the imperfect tools of the natives, stood erect, but naked and bare, its base blackened with fire and its branches lopped off. The foreground showed white in the moonlight with the dry stalks and leaves of maize which covered it, causing the forest above to seem the more sombre and dark by contrast. Below only the spray of the trees could be seen, with a silvery gleam on them almost like hoar-frost, while thousands of feet lower down there was a dim greyness, without shape, which I knew to be the moon shining far down on the plains below, on the tops of innumerable acacias and other flat-topped thorns.

It was all so still and peaceful, that it required the cry of a leopard from among the great rocks and wooded precipices which surrounded me to recall my attention to my purpose in coming there; but it was not till near morning that the animal itself made its appearance.

The moon had become concealed by the forest above me, though it was still quite light, when my eye first caught a glimpse of something moving stealthily towards me. The gait of all beasts of prey changes according to their object, and when approaching anything that they have formerly killed they seem to take as much care as if it was still living, and required to be stalked. Obedient to this instinct, the leopard, after leaving the shade of the forest, stole from trunk to trunk, paused, and even crouched down once or twice, before it caught sight of the carcase, after which, apparently reassured, it came on more rapidly, and soon stood beside it. I had, on my first arrival, so placed my gun in one of the supporting posts of the hut that I could take aim without hardly moving, and as, from the position of the animal, I feared that my ball might glance if I aimed at the head, I took it between the shoulders, and pulled the trigger. With a muffled roar it sprung forward, its fore-paws catching on the frame-work on which the hut was placed, while its head was on a level with me, and not a yard off. The other barrel was loaded with slugs—a precautionary measure which I think should always be taken when after leopards,—and without a second's delay I fired them straight into its face, the charge taking effect like a ball, and blowing its skull to atoms, while the whole head was scorched and blackened with powder. Of course, it instantly relaxed its hold, and after a convulsive struggle or two, lay dead beneath me, where it was found next morning when the villagers came down, with me sound asleep above it, curled up in the hut. It turned out to be one of the smaller variety; but for some reason or other its skin was rough, and not in good order.

As I have before mentioned, I have only seen the ngulule, or maned leopard, twice. One afternoon as I was nearing camp, drenched through and through by a violent thunderstorm, I saw two animals sitting on their hind-quarters watching us about half a mile off, and turning to my gun-bearer I asked him what they were. "Lionesses" was the answer, and as I was not then acquainted with any animal so much resembling them, or which sat in that peculiar position, I had no doubt but that he was right, and at once passed on to camp, which was close by, to get a fresh gun instead of the one I had, which was wet and would not go off.

On returning a few minutes after with two hunters whom I happened to find in, we soon saw the animals walking away nearly a mile off, and made towards them as fast as we could, still under the belief that they were two lionesses, and it was not until we crossed their spoor that we saw that it differed in formation from that of those animals, as well as being smaller and lighter, and one of the men who had before seen it at once declared what they really were. They had in the meanwhile disappeared in a patch of jungle, but keeping up our pace, we sighted them again as they emerged from it and, still walking, crossed the open towards another cover; before, however, they could reach it, we were within a hundred yards of, and were noticed by them, upon which they both crouched down and faced us.

I was in front, and shouted out to the nearest hunter, "Will they charge?" but at the sound of my voice they both sprang up and made off, and I fired right and left at the largest, striking it with the first shot, and bringing it to a standstill just outside the cover into which its companion had disappeared. The two hunters instantly ran, one on each side, to try and cut the latter off, while my plucky gun-bearer wavered, turned back, and then, in spite of my shouting, ran frantically after, but a long way behind, one of the hunters, leaving me alone to finish off the wounded brute. Had I then known as much as I do now about them I should have walked straight up and shot it, but accounting it a leopard (ingwe), and knowing well how dangerous they are, I did not care to do so in such an open spot, where, if it charged, my life would depend upon my two shots; so, keeping my eye on it, I started across for the cover near which it was, and there disappearing, I stalked up to the part nearest to it, and fired when about fifteen yards off. My bullet brought it on to its legs again, and it blundered forward at right angles to me, so that I could place another behind the shoulder, this time inflicting a mortal wound, though as it still breathed I walked up close and finished it off. It was a male; its tawny, dirty, skin with its faint irregular spots and the peculiar mane have been already described; otherwise, its limbs were large, and showed more power than activity, and in size, as well as somewhat in general appearance, it resembled a three-parts-grown lioness. The other one escaped.

While returning, I naturally asked many questions of the natives about this animal, which I had sometimes heard of, but had never before seen or formed any particular idea of. They told me that it was very rare; that in this part of the country it was principally found in the rocky gorges in the Bombo Mountains, among the dense jungle of which it lay concealed, though it was occasionally, as in the present instance, seen hunting in pairs through the plains; that it lived chiefly on the smaller antelopes, and was harmless and cowardly to a degree. As an instance of its great resemblance to a lioness, one of them related a story of a hunter who met his death by chasing one of the latter animals, under the impression that it was an ngulule.

On the other occasion on which I came across them I found the fresh spoor of a pair soon after starting out hunting early one morning, and, as the rain had been heavy on the previous night, and the tracks would therefore be distinct, I determined to follow them, despite the entreaties of my gun-bearer, the same man who had been with me on the former occasion, and who stoutly maintained, though of course he knew better, that it was the spoor of two young lions.

I tracked them for some hours without intermission, and had an interesting study of their mode of stalking and their movements while hunting before I reached the greater part of the carcase of an impalla which they had killed, upon seeing which I hesitated as to whether I should go on, or wait by it for their return; but as I hoped to find them fast asleep in some thicket close by, gorged with meat, and overcome with the heat of an unusually hot day, I decided to do the former. It was lucky that I did so, for their spoor almost immediately entered some bushes which lined an old dry water-course, the thickness of which I knew by experience, and into which I did not think it advisable to take the native, who was evidently afraid, and might by some involuntary start rouse the animals.

After going about two hundred yards I distinguished something tawny through the darkness of the jungle, and on placing my foot on the lower branch of a tree which stood convenient, I saw the two lying within a few feet of each other, one of them, laid flat on its side with outstretched limbs, being in full view. It was a most tempting shot, and I only wished they had been a pair of lions, so taking a steady aim at the exposed one, I pulled the trigger, and the instant after I did so, the one at which I had not fired bounded under the tree and stood listening, evidently not knowing where the sound that had disturbed it came from. A second afterwards it was staggering away, shot through the lungs and with a broken shoulder, while I, getting down, went to look after the first. I found that it had hardly moved, and was lying quite dead in almost the same spot in which it had been asleep, my ball having fortunately—for such a shot can never be anything more than a "fluke,"—smashed its spine, and caused all but instant death; and when, after loading, I followed the wounded one, I found it in scarcely a better plight, lying beneath a bush unable to rise, but as it still breathed I had to shoot it again.

The common leopards, *i.e.* the two locally known under the name of ingwe, are much to be dreaded when brought to bay, and anecdotes innumerable might be related of instances when they have killed or seriously injured both white and black hunters. The virus of their bite is very great. I remember once seeing seven men belonging to a Zulu village awfully torn and mangled by a single animal, and the wounds remained open for a long time, and ultimately left great scars. On the other hand, I know of several who have died where the injuries received were not such as to have been generally fatal, though I am ignorant of the precise details in each particular case. It has been asserted by Mr. Layard,[1] on the authority of Messrs. Chapman, Andersson, and Holding, all names of great weight, that leopards even attack human beings without provocation; this, however, is so contrary to their general disposition and habits, for they are the most retiring and secretive of carnivora,— I should almost have said timid, were it not for their extreme ferocity and pluck when wounded,—that no one well acquainted with the African species would consent to believe it without positive proof, and I incline to the belief that the well-known travellers whose names have been quoted must have been deceived, unintentionally, no doubt, by their servants.

Travellers passing rapidly through a country, more particularly if they do not thoroughly understand the language, are very much guided by what their native attendants tell them, and this will be admitted by all who have been much in Africa to be a very misleading method of gaining information. In many cases the servants belong to other tribes, and have heard reports which they

[1] Letter to the *Field*.

believe to be true, and consequently pass on to their masters. These are very often erroneous. Natives of the country are not much to be trusted unless they imagine you know too much to be easily led astray; besides which, they are naturally so polite that if you ask them about any custom or fact it is by no means unusual for them to say they know all about it, rather than disagree with you. Taking this into consideration, and as it does not clearly appear whether these travellers spoke from hearsay or not, I am inclined to believe the former, and that they were misled by their informants, though, at the same time, it is possible that some exceptional case may have occurred in their own experience of a man-eating leopard, strange and unlikely as it may appear to me.

Another statement made by Mr. Layard deserves notice, as being at variance with my own experience. He says,[1] "The leopard will gorge himself on any carrion." Personally, I have always found the exact contrary to be the case, for I have never once heard of or seen a leopard going near dead game, unless killed by itself, or even condescending to look at other than a live bait. Cases may, and no doubt do, occur, when the animal, pressed by hunger, will do so, but, as far as my experience goes, it is quite the exception, though it is but fair to add that Mr. Layard supports his assertion with well-authenticated instances of the use of a dead bait being successful, and it is only another instance of how different people in the same country, and under apparently the same conditions, may arrive at widely different results.

The hyena, colonially known as the wolf, is exceed-

[1] Letter to the *Field*.

"TREACHEROUS, COWARDLY & SAVAGE"

ingly common all over the country outside the colonies, and its mournful howl is to be heard every night as one reaches the more thinly populated districts. Three species have been observed by different travellers in Africa, with only one of which—*H. crocuta*, or the spotted hyena—I am personally acquainted, though both the other two occur in the districts of the east coast through which I have travelled. The former, which is the largest, most powerful, and most savage of the three, is distributed over the whole of Africa below the latitude of 17° N.[1] They exhibit a great variety of markings, and differ considerably in colour, the spots being sometimes light and indistinct, at others, on the contrary, dark and well defined. It has been suggested that the variegated species found on the east coast, and mentioned by Speke, is a cross between *H. crocuta* and the striped hyena of the northern deserts, but, though its size, markings, and colour give a shadow of probability to the idea, it is extremely doubtful whether such is the case.

Treacherous, cowardly, and savage in their habits, as all the species are, they are invariably killed whenever opportunity offers. I have at different times shot specimens of the common spotted kind; sometimes at night, when they have come prowling round our camp in search of anything they could find—despising nothing edible between a sleeping child and a leathern strap; sometimes as they lumbered homewards at their ungainly gallop when daylight has overtaken them while still at some distance from their holes; and, more rarely, after having put them out of some dense thicket, in which they had made a tem-

[1] *Heart of Africa*—Schweinfurth.

porary lair. Cowardly, when there is the faintest suspicion of danger, daring when there is none, stealthy and cunning to the last degree, and provided with great powers of scent and hearing, added to immense strength, there is no animal so universally hated, or that causes more trouble and annoyance to both hunters and the peaceful natives.

The amount of damage they do in a season to the former by breaking into their game and destroying the hide when time has failed to skin it, can hardly be calculated; not to mention such trifles as shoes, straps, and in fact anything and everything left outside the camp during the night. To the villagers the number of cattle they annually kill is a most serious loss. They choose the darkest nights, generally when it is raining, and going to windward of a village allow the cattle to smell them, when, if the kraal-fence is not strong, the terrified animals break out, and at once become an easy prey to their cunning foe, who, selecting a young beast, will soon run it down and kill it, two or three sometimes assisting each other in doing so; or, worse still, it will attack a number of cows in succession, seizing them all at one spot, namely, the udder, which, with their powerful jaws and great strength, they soon tear off, and go on to the next. I have known no less than seven cows mortally injured in this way in a night, and the natives said there were only two hyenas concerned in doing it. This is not all: the cowardly brutes will even attack a human being when asleep, though, as I will afterwards show, they dare not touch a harmless antelope, scarcely living, but aware of their presence. I have seen many men who had been mutilated, while they slept, in the most horrible way; their noses wanting, the whole mouth and lips torn away, or half a cheek gone,—for it is curious that it is the face which always suffers, possibly because the rest of the body is rolled up in the blanket natives invariably wear, and is not exposed. It is commonly said that a man who snores runs more danger than one who does not, as the brute selects him, feeling sure that he is asleep. I have never had a case in my own camp, nor has one ever occurred when I have been present, but I have seen a boy who had been dreadfully bitten in the face only a few days previously. Shaw[1] mentions no less than forty instances in a few months, and within his own knowledge, of wolves, as hyenas are locally called, taking youths and young children, and even adds that they prefer human food, passing by calves to take children. He gives two examples, one of which may be interesting:—

"The first I shall mention is that of Dapa's great-grandson, about ten years of age. The wolf had previously seized a younger brother and torn away a part of his face. Another night he came into the house and took a second, and carried him completely off, of whom nothing more than a fragment was found. On his third visit he seized the lad just mentioned by the left shoulder. The little fellow, awakened by the grasp, struck him with his hand; the wolf left his hold, and, grasping him on the opposite side, broke his collar-bone. The poor boy still fought with his left hand, and his antagonist, letting go his hold a second time, seized him by the fleshy part of his thigh, and ran off with his prey; nor was it till he had carried him a quarter of a mile that he could be made to drop him, when, biting away the precious mouthful, he left the little sufferer with his thigh half-severed, but fortunately the bone was not broken. In this state he was brought to us for help, and by daily attention he is perfectly restored."

[1] Shaw's *Memorials of South Africa*, 353.

In this case it is probable that the animal had become a confirmed man-eater, and had to some extent overcome its natural cowardliness, otherwise I should have been surprised at the perseverance it displayed. Another instance of the same kind is mentioned by Mr. Skertchly[1] as occurring on the West Coast. He says,—

"At three in the morning I heard a great outcry. On inquiring the cause, I found that a hyena had entered a hut and seized an infant sleeping in its mother's arms by the head, but being frightened by the screams of the inmates, had dropped its prey and decamped. The poor little fellow was quite dead, its skull being crushed in by the teeth of the monster."

I remember one evening severely wounding a doe impalla, one of the most timid of antelopes, which, however, I was unable to get from want of light, but as there was no meat in camp, I followed it up the first thing next morning, and before we had gone far on the track, which was literally drenched in blood, we noticed the marks of a hyena, and I gave up all hope of finding anything except the bones, but ultimately we came to it, still alive though unable to stand, and untouched, though the hyena had absolutely gone within a yard of it, had, indeed, walked round it, and then, seeing that it was living, had slunk away, afraid to touch a harmless doe antelope so wounded that it could not stir, so long as breath remained in its body.

Common as these hyenas are, it is very unusual to see one, they being, like most animals of prey, night-prowlers, and retiring to their holes at the earliest dawn. Regular beaten paths lead to these burrows, along which they invariably go, both when coming out and returning; indeed,

---

[1] *Dahomey as it is*, by J. A. Skertchly, 331.

unless they scent food, they always make use of paths in their nocturnal rambles, whether made by themselves or by men or game.

In a primitive state there is no doubt that they are chiefly dependent upon the lion for their daily food, and it is equally certain that they must be able to go without eating for immense periods. The old hunters declare that their numbers have much increased within their memory in the districts in which there is most hunting, and as so much game goes away and dies unseen of its wounds, which the hyenas are easily able to find by the blood-track which they leave, to say nothing of the amount of meat that is purposely left for want of a use for it, there is every reason to think that they must find man a better purveyor than the lion, and increase accordingly.

Among the flocks and herds there is no animal whose ravages are more dreaded than those of the wild dog (*Canis pictus*). Fortunately their visits are rare, for I have known as many as fifty or sixty sheep missing after one, though of course not a third of that number had been killed by them; and so daring are they that I have seen them dash into a herd of cattle feeding not a hundred yards from the house, and drive out a beast, disappear over a rise in the ground with it, and kill it and pick its bones before we could get the saddles on our horses and follow them. It is a marvellous sight to see a pack of them hunting, drawing cover after cover, their sharp bell-like note ringing through the air, while a few of the fastest of their number take up their stations along the expected line of the run—the wind, the nature of the ground, and the habits of the game all taken into consideration with the most wonderful skill; and then to see them after they have found, going at their long unswerving gallop, so close together that a sheet might cover them, while those which had been stationed, or had stationed themselves, it is hard to say which, drop in one by one as they find themselves unable to make the running any longer; and the chase, generally a gnu or a water-antelope, pressed first by one and then another, though it may distance the pack for a while, soon comes back to it, and is in the end almost invariably run into. The only thing to which I can compare these animals, and their instinct, as people call it, is a pack of hounds hunted and whipped in to by members of their own body, and combining in one human reason and brute cunning and power.

I have personally met with them on several occasions, and have shot three or four at different times, though with some compunction, for the sake of their skins, which make beautiful gun-covers. At other times I have not dared to meddle with them. Once, when shooting in the Free State, I was out stalking gnu on the immense plains of which the country is formed, and was lying behind an ant-heap watching a herd, when I saw them suddenly whisk their tails up and rush away, evidently alarmed at something, and in a few seconds more an old bull of the same species came into sight, crossing me at right angles about two hundred yards off, and from his manner of running seeming to have come a long distance. Keeping on, he soon disappeared over one of the long wave-like undulations which form an African plain, and in a few minutes a pack of about ten couple of wild dogs showed themselves on his track, running mute, with sterns down and heads up, an occasional whimper of impatience from some of the younger of them alone showing their appreciation of the hot scent. As they reached the top of the rise two of those which were leading singled themselves out, and, as far as I could see, went off at a long slanting angle to their former course, and in a few minutes a burst of music announced that the pack, which had kept straight on, had run from scent to view.

In the meantime, my stalk being spoilt, I had got up, and was looking in their direction hoping to see something of the run, when I noticed the old bull, having made a long circuit and probably turned by the couple that had taken a line of their own, reappearing over a distant rise, and heading directly towards me. There was an unusually large ant-heap close by, and I went and stood on the top of it, and could then see the pack running in full view of their quarry, sweeping along in a compact body, well together, and, having given vent to their feelings on coming into view, now mute again. They seemed to be gaining but slowly, and I thought the run likely to be a long one, till I heard one or two of them speak, and then saw one race forward, at a pace which showed how much they were going within themselves, and push the antelope for several hundred yards, finally dropping back to its companions.

They were now getting so near that I feared lest I should be seen, and got down and concealed myself behind the ant-heap, and in a few minutes the bull came up, now only leading by a bare twenty yards, and showing by his open and foam-covered mouth and heaving flanks that his race was nearly run. As he passed by me I had a magnificent view of the pack, now gaining at every stride, but still maintaining their order and monotonous pace.

It was evident, from their superior size and well-developed frames, that the leading hounds (it is difficult to speak of them as "dogs") were the pick of the pack, the next being small and lighter, and probably ladies, while those behind were undoubtedly young hounds and three-parts-grown puppies—all but one, which seemed to act as whipper-in, and rivalled the best of them in its proportions. There was not even a whimper now; not a sound but the dull patter of many feet as they swept along; but they had scarcely passed the spot where I was concealed before they ran into the antelope, which, good use as it can generally make of its horns against dogs, had now no opportunity to do mischief, being pulled down in a few seconds.

Those accustomed to see hounds break up their fox can form some idea of the scene which now ensued: of famished hunger satisfying itself before life had left the animal's body; of quarrelling and of fighting. It is sufficient to say that I was glad to crawl round to the other side of the ant-heap, and to remain quiet while it was taking place, and that I was not sorry to see the pack, having in ten minutes reduced their prey to a skeleton, take itself off in a contrary direction.

Two species of wild-dog are mentioned by some authors, but I have only met with one, of which Burton[1] gives the following account:—

"The Waraba or Durwa is, according to Mr. Blyth, the distinguished naturalist, now curator of the Asiatic Society's Museum at Calcutta, the Canis pictus seu venaticus (Lycaon pictus, or Wilde Honde of the Cape Boers). It seems to be the Chien sauvage or Cynhyène (Cynhyæna venatica) of the French tra-

[1] *First Footsteps in East Africa*, Burton, p. 83.

veller Delagorgue, who in his *Voyage dans l'Afrique australe* minutely and diffusely describes it.

"Gordon Cumming supposes it to form the connecting link between the wolf and hyena. This animal swarms throughout the Somali country, prowls about the camps all night, dogs travellers, and devours everything he can find; at times pulling down children and camels, and, when violently pressed by hunger, men. The Somal declare the Waraba to be a hermaphrodite; so the ancients supposed the hyena to be of both sexes."

That they do not show the slightest fear of man I have repeatedly proved. I remember once coming upon a pack scattered asleep in the long grass on the side of a hill, and walking right into the middle of it before I knew they were there. One jumped up at my feet, and running a few yards, faced round and began to give tongue, upon which the grass seemed to become alive with them, more jumping up all round me and joining in the chorus, but not one attempting to run away. I was rather alarmed, as I was alone, and picking out the two most clamorous, I shot first one and then the other, after which the others slowly retired, giving vent to their anger in their sharp metallic bark as they did so. They are curious-looking animals with their erect ears and variegated skins, but would, no doubt, become invaluable to the hunter if they were broken and trained. That they can be trained is proved by Schweinfurth,[1] who saw one in captivity; and Livingstone mentions that the natives of the Kalihari desert break and train them for the chase.

Perhaps the only animal of this genus that causes no annoyance to the inhabitants of the country is the jackal. Of these I am acquainted with two, the silver and the grey. They are pretty little creatures, whose

[1] *Heart of Africa*, Schweinfurth, vol. ii. p. 274.

only use to the hunter is to indicate the proximity of lions; for when seen prowling about in the day-time, particularly if vultures are also wheeling round the spot, or sitting in the neighbouring trees, it is almost certain that a lion has killed and is feasting upon some animal close by. Neither they nor the hyena always escape scot-free in their attendance upon his majesty, for I have at different times found three of the former and one of the latter lying dead near some bones which they had approached too closely. I much doubt the common opinion that they accompany the lion's footsteps, even at a respectful distance; for they possess such wonderful powers of scent that they can easily discover anything that has been killed for several miles round.

CHAPTER VII.

HUNTING WITH DOGS.

ONE year during my sojourn in South-Eastern Africa having severely hurt my right arm I was unable to shoot, and after in vain trying the consolations of the country fishing—which, at its best, is about equal to punt-fishing on the Thames—it struck me that something might be done in the way of coursing the antelopes, with which both the jungles and opens were well stocked.

The idea had been first suggested by my having met a deformed native (rather a rarity, by the way, in Africa), who I knew could not hurl a spear from the malformation of his arms, on his way to join a hunting party; and on my asking him the use of his going, he pointed to a great black hound which a boy was leading behind him, and said that it would kill more antelopes than all the spears put together. This had been in the morning, when going to the river to fish; and as I was coming back later in the day, the boy who accompanied me exclaimed, "Look, there's a reed-buck being chased. Yes! there are the dogs; that's Makambi's black one leading." On looking in the direction pointed out, I saw a doe bounding with great springs down a slight rise, while almost at her heels, with its long body laid flat upon the ground, ran the black hound I had seen in the morning, followed at a considerable distance by half a dozen more. We were in a first-rate position to see the chase, the ground slanting down towards the depression in which we were, and then gradually rising towards a ridge of small hills about a mile off. The doe was heading directly towards us, and in five or six minutes more she crossed within twenty yards of us, now going somewhat heavily, the black dog still retaining its relative position, while the rest were nowhere. It was all I could do to restrain the excited boy from hurling his spear as they passed. He would very probably have succeeded in his aim, and so, by drawing first blood, become part owner in the antelope with the master of the hound, and his consequent grumbling was loud and long. In the meantime the hound, gradually gaining, forced the exhausted animal to slightly alter its course to one nearly parallel to us, and in a few minutes more, running clean past her, he seized her by the throat, contrary to the custom of most native dogs which generally commence at the other end, and after being dragged a few yards and a short struggle, he brought her to the ground. We then went up to the place, no one appearing in sight, and the boy satisfied his longing for action by plunging his spear through her vitals, the hound still holding her by the throat, and giving us some difficulty in inducing him to leave go.

Knowing that a reed-buck doe is by no means easy to run down, especially on ground such as this, I examined her captor with much interest and with the intention of, if possible, making him my own—particularly as my boy told me that he was well known as the fastest and most plucky dog in the neighbourhood. He was a fine-looking animal, approaching a staghound in height, but longer and more powerful both in the chest and hind-quarters, though in other points resembling a greyhound, all except his long ears, which, standing erect like those of the wild dog (*Canis pictus seu venaticus*), gave him a most curious and wild-beast appearance. I describe him thus particularly, as he was a good representative of the only pure breed of native dogs that I have ever seen in Africa, the Amaponda greyhound. They differ in colour—black, tawny, and white being the most common, and the latter being the most prized by the Kaffirs—and they differ in some having more of a deerhound and others more of a greyhound form; but all are distinguished by the same erect ears and smooth short coat, as well as by possessing great speed and but little power of scent. The best dog for antelopes that I ever owned was the second cross of one of these with an English foxhound. It was undistinguishable from the Amaponda breed in form and speed, and gained from its other ancestor an undeniable nose and great pluck.

Acting upon the advice of my boy, I said nothing

about buying the dog when its triumphant owner came up, but next day I sent a native to act for me, thus escaping with the payment of a milk-cow, instead of the two I should certainly have been asked for if I had gone myself. As I already had a young English greyhound, I at once commenced coursing on the arrival of the other; and in about six weeks ran into and killed no less than thirty-seven antelopes of various kinds. Usipingo, as my new purchase was called, killed almost all of them, and I am afraid a few more that no one knew about, for he often used to break away and not return till nightfall, being so powerful that it was all a man could do to hold him when he saw game, and I have seen dog and man both sprawling on the ground when a sudden unexpected bound had upset the equilibrium of the latter. Ultimately this trait caused his death.

Many of the number of antelopes I have mentioned could hardly be said to have had fair play, as I sometimes used to attend the great native hunting parties, when upwards of five hundred men would form a circle driving the game inwards, while those who depended on the speed of their dogs would stand outside at such spots as their experience suggested would be chosen by the antelopes to break out at. The poor brutes had thus to undergo the chasing of scores of curs, and then to run the gauntlet of dozens of spears before they reached the place where the fast hounds were stationed, so that it was no wonder that many were caught; indeed, it was extraordinary how many escaped under all these disadvantages.

A description of one day may serve for all. The meet was about ten miles from the native village where I was, and a message had come to say that, as it was getting so hot, the earlier we could manage to start the better. I therefore sent the hounds on at daylight, and after breakfast followed them on horseback. The formation of each native tribe being very similar to that of each nation, *i.e.* a lot of small clans incorporated together, each division forms a separate band at hunting parties, marriages, and dances; though at tribal assemblages they drop these distinctions, in the same way that in national gatherings all tribal distinctions are lost. On my arrival there, I found only one such clan on the ground, squatted on a ridge like a row of baboons, waiting for the rest. Soon, however, band after band came up singing their hunting-songs, and before taking their places with the rest, forming a semicircle and dancing before them; and when at last all had come I estimated them at about eight hundred men.

The country about to be beaten was a nearly level one —slight depressions marking the "vlies," or damper parts, where tangles of water-loving bushes grew, overshadowed by the great water-boems; and in places where the dampness had resolved itself into a stream small patches of jungle lined the banks. Large quantities of the rank grass had been burned off, leaving their sharp stems protruding—a fruitful source of lameness both to the dogs and unshod natives.

After a short performance by the head of the hunting party (the man who had called it out)—which chiefly consisted in asking the "amadhlozi," or shades of their ancestors, to give them luck—the two wings were sent round to form a circle, while the centre, in which the older and less active men remained, proceeded more leisurely, after having waited long enough to hear that the two sides had met and that the circle was complete.

It was the latter portion of the party that I joined, partly to escape the extra work that I should have with the others, partly because the game, which would mostly be put up by them as our side would advance very slowly, would consequently chiefly come our way. In a few minutes the hunt began; antelopes of various kinds, but principally duiker and reed-buck, could be seen on foot, each attended by its pack of curs, while the black forms of the natives gleamed in the sunshine as they flitted to and fro, guarding what small gaps occurred between man and man. Now and then, as an antelope broke through them, the tribal hunting-cry of the men could be heard as they flung their assagais at it. At last an unfortunate duiker, having so far escaped the many dangers from men and dogs with which it was threatened, ran within a few yards of my next neighbour, who having, like myself, a fast hound, had remained outside the now rapidly converging circle; this he slipped at it, and a few seconds more decided its fate. Hardly had my ear caught the bleat that told of its capture, before a loud shout warned me something was coming my way, and almost instantly three reed-buck broke covert below me, and came straight up the rise. I crouched in the long grass until the foremost, a doe and a yearling, had passed within a few feet of me, and then, springing up, slipped my black hound, whose head I had hitherto firmly held between my knees, and cheered him on to the buck that followed them; and at the same moment my boy slipped the other hound. Away they went like lightning, the reed-buck taking great bounds over the long grass which so much impeded his pursuers. I made for a cabbage-tree close by, and climbing up as far as I could, watched the chase, while my boy ran in the direction which he thought they would take. The hounds made nothing of it at first from the length of the grass. Indeed, as the buck fairly got the steam up they rather lost, until they reached a level mile of the burnt ground, over which they really seemed to fly, the black one drawing in closer and closer, and the greyhound losing nothing; so that the chase was fain to wheel sharp to the right, and make for a wet bottom not far off, where, not many minutes after, I heard the hounds baying. I then got down and went towards the sound, finding on my arrival that my boy had come up and killed it —the united efforts of both hounds only bringing the animal to its knees, while in the scuffle the greyhound had got a deepish scratch on her haunch.

After getting men to carry it home, I returned to the hunting party, where in an hour or two Usipingo caught a couple of duikers. One rather curious incident happened. The men were just finishing a beat, and were consequently almost touching one another all round the circle, when a large reed-buck doe rose from some rushes, and probably not seeing, although she had heard the people, cantered quietly off until she came to those opposite. Here she was received with a storm of spears, some of which no doubt struck, if they did not hurt her, while all the curs came yelping up. Bolting round, she made off at full speed in the opposite direction until she reached our side of the circle, when, noticing the men, she pulled up for a second; but having seemingly made up her mind, she came on again at full swing. Luck befriended her, and the score of assagais that came hurtling through the air all fell wide, and she kept on until not a yard from one of the men; just as I expected to see her fall to his poised spear she made a tremendous bound over him, and in a second more was galloping away in safety, leaving him stretched on the ground, with some nasty cuts about the head and chest from her hoofs. It was the only time I ever saw such a thing done, though I not unfrequently heard of it, and once or twice saw men scarred in a similar manner.

I remember once, at such a hunting party, seeing a free fight among the natives. They had quarrelled about the possession of an antelope, and in two minutes after the first blow was struck upwards of four hundred men were engaged in a series of single combats with their sticks and knobkerries, and, no doubt, when much pushed, making use of their spears. The whole side of a hill was covered with them, and I remember being much struck by their mode of treating the conquered. One man had knocked another down, and by one or two well-aimed blows on the head kept him there. He then proceeded to turn him on his side, and lifting his arm out of the way, to beat him for several minutes with a stick, much as one would thrash out corn or beat a carpet, on the ribs on that side, and then, turning him over, repeat the operation on the other. Ultimately one party ran away, and the other ran after it, and I saw nothing more of any of them that day.

Soon after my return to the colony, after one of my trips into the interior, I went with some friends to shoot a jungle in Victoria county, attended as usual by Usipingo, and while going along the outside scrub a male bush-buck got up, and was missed by the nearest gun. The hound, noticing that the boy who led him was not attending, made a sudden spring and got clear off, and in ten minutes had run the antelope, one of a very slow species, to bay in an open near the stream; and when I at last got down there through the thick and precipitous jungle I found an assemblage of natives standing at a safe distance, with one great tall fellow, who, fearing to go in front, had just managed to put a charge of buckshot into the beast's hind-quarters, occupied in loading his gun, while a cur lay yelping on the ground more frightened than hurt, and another snarled at the buck's heels, distracting his attention from Usipingo, who, all covered with blood, stood just out of reach of his lowered horns. Just as I arrived the furious animal wheeled round, and catching the unfortunate cur that was yelping behind him on his sharp horns, tossed it howling into the air, while with a jerk of its head it again marked Usipingo, who had taken the opportunity of springing at its throat. Unfortunately the moment my dog saw me he redoubled his efforts, and rendered it difficult for me to get a certain shot; but at last I did so, and the noble brute—for the male bush-buck is the finest in appearance, as well as the most plucky, of all the smaller antelopes—dropped dead. My dog had in all seven cuts, two of which were nasty ones; but he recovered with a week or two's care, and seven of these fine bush-buck were ultimately killed by him without any help. That same day he caught two red buck (*Cephalopus Natalensis*), which rush so violently through the jungle that they are anything but easy to catch in it, and often give the stationed gun an impression that something larger is coming. The small blue-buck, however, was quite beyond him, and unless he nailed it at the first spring, he used to stand and watch it dodging through the under-brush with a comical air of disgust, but latterly he would never attempt to run one.

Some time after this, long after Usipingo's death, and when I had succeeded in getting a very fast lot of hounds together, I was asked to pay a visit to a friend of mine on the Noodsberg, and went up, taking two of the fastest with me. The very afternoon I arrived I met an old fellow—the head man of a neighbouring village, he told me—carrying an oribi, and followed by six or eight half-starved crosses of the Amaponda breed.

"Where did you get that from?" I asked.

"The dogs caught it."

"Nonsense! An oribi is faster than a reed-buck, and would give one of these," pointing to my hounds, "all its work to do. You must have stuck it."

No, he hadn't, he persisted; and as I could find no mark on it I went on, satisfied that the oribi was not as fast as people said it was. I had shot them often enough, but had never coursed them. So that evening I said to my friend that I should like to take one of the hounds out next day and pull an oribi down. The other was a little lame, and I didn't care about working her.

"Is your dog very fast?" he asked.

"Fastest I've got," was the answer.

"Did he ever run into an oribi before?"

"No."

"Well, I think I'll come with you to-morrow and see the fun;" and with this understanding we went to bed.

Next morning three of us started, well mounted, and with my boy leading Babey. The Noodsberg is a great flat table-land, broken by a few streams, and covered with short grass, and we had not far to go to find an oribi; but as they rose rather wild I did not at first give the signal to slip. My friend at last spotted one lying flat on the bare ground, and, edging round so as to form a half-circle, we got within twenty yards, when she rose in front of the hound, and the two got away on fair terms, and we, as soon as they were fairly off, raced after them. In the first two minutes Babey lessened the distance between them by one-half, and I thought the affair was settled, when I suddenly saw the antelope, seemingly having just become aware of its danger, shoot away in such extraordinary bounds as left the hound as though it were standing still.

I had often seen Babey go, but I never saw him go better than he did that day, though quite unavailingly, for the antelope, keeping a bee-line, gradually increased his distance, and sinking a small rise disappeared from view; and the hound after half an hour's absence returned quite done up and with a clean mouth.

"I thought your dog would be a good one if he caught an oribi by himself," was my friend's remark, "though he certainly runs well."

"Why, I met a nigger yesterday who pretended they had caught one," I said, much disgusted, for I had thought Babey could run into anything with four legs.

"Oh, that would be the old induna! I tell you what:

Come along and you shall see him catch one. He'll go out for me; and if he does, he is nearly sure to kill."

"You don't mean to tell me that those half-starved brutes can run alongside of Babey?" I asked contemptuously.

"Come along and see for yourself," was the answer; and putting our horses into a canter we soon reached the village, upon which my friend began, to my great discomfiture, to relate to the grinning heathen how Babey had been beaten off; and the man, nothing loath to show off before a stranger, at once consented to come and show me how his dogs did it, and off we went. They were not led; and as soon as we got to the ground and he sent them away, they formed an irregular line of sixty or seventy yards broad, and beat the rise some way in front of us. Up got an oribi to the extreme left, and away went the nearest dog in pursuit; but an ear-piercing whistle brought it back at once, and prevented the others from following it. At last an old buck, that had lain quietly until we were close to him, got up in their middle. "Nansia 'nyamazane," shouted the old fellow, and away went his curs. For the first twenty yards the buck ran straight, and then I could see him throwing his head round to watch his pursuers, and at once catching sight of the one furthest to the left he bent his course the other way; but he had not run long in this direction before a yelp, yelp, almost alongside, met his ears, and he found that he had avoided the frying-pan only to tumble into the fire. Wheeling slightly, he tried to run straight away, but the dogs on the left—which, instead of following him in his former digression, had kept straight on—

headed him at once. He now got stupid, ran first one way and then another, and after a run of nine minutes allowed the dogs to pull him down, making scarcely any effort to escape.

The moral that I gained from this day's experience, and which I afterwards repeatedly proved true, was that a single hound will rarely run into an oribi, but that two or three, even though not very fast, will do so with comparative ease, if they run cleverly.

I have already alluded to the death of my first dog, Usipingo. It occurred in a very sad way, viz. by my own hand. It happened while we were shooting a jungle on the Natal coast. I was stationed so as to command a narrow footpath, and my boy was standing with the dog a few paces further back. He had been told not to slip it without my telling him to do so, principally in order that it might be at hand if wanted for a wounded antelope, and should not unnecessarily damage itself with the great thorns. However, a female bush-buck rushing past within a yard was too great a temptation, and the dog was either allowed to go, or, as the boy said, broke away; she passed through a patch of jungle, and then, turning, crossed the path I was watching. I knew nothing about Usipingo's being after her, and fired, breaking the antelope's back, and it was not till half-an-hour afterwards that on going to the place I found the dog on one side and the antelope on the other, both dead. I had fired with large shot, which had scattered a great deal, and a single pellet had struck him on the head. I afterwards had faster dogs, and some with better noses, but I never had his equal in common sense. When he got accustomed to the gun he showed no anxiety to get away, as he used to before, unless the game was very near, and no persuasion would induce him to follow any antelope that I had fired at and missed for more than two or three hundred yards; while on the other hand he would follow any that were wounded, however slightly, until he killed them.

In the interior there is only one species of small antelope, if we except the springbuck and blesbuck found on the great treeless plains to the north, that does not occur in the colonies—the roibok, or impalla. It is about the size of a small reed-buck doe, though more slenderly made, and the districts inhabited by it are most fatal to dogs. I shall afterwards have occasion to mention a scratch pack that I got up for the purpose of hunting pig, and on one occasion I had great sport with it and a herd of these impalla, which singly or in the open could easily distance any dog I possessed. The whole pack were following at my heels, and I was on a small promontory, bounded on three sides by the perpendicular bank of the river, when a herd of impalla numbering upwards of a hundred, starting from where they had been feeding beyond, attempted to rush past, and on two or three succeeding, the main body, always ready to follow where one has already gone, came on running in single file. In an instant the dogs were amongst them; and as, when taken by surprise and much pressed, they, in common with most antelopes, entirely lose their presence of mind and run in any direction, five were at once caught, three jumping over the bank into the river, and two being stabbed by the two boys who accompanied me; while the remainder passed me, many of them within reach of my hand, and although I held a spear in it, I was too much occupied in watching the unusual scene to remember it until too late. However, in less time than it takes to write it we killed seven of these handsome antelopes, besides getting two out of the three that had jumped into the river; the crocodiles probably accounting for the third.

Among the other small antelopes which I have coursed, I may mention the Vaal and roi raebok; the former, from the roughness of the ground on which they are generally found, it is next to impossible to hunt with dogs, but they are sometimes, though rarely, ridden into on horseback. The latter is slower than the reed-buck, but inhabiting a more hilly country does not afford so much sport. The steinbuck is, like the duiker, too easily caught; so that for the purposes of coursing the palm must, in my opinion, be given to the oribi and reed-buck.

Wild pigs were very common in Tongaland and on the Bombo flats where I hunted a great deal, and it often struck me that pig-sticking as performed in India would be some little change from the continual pursuit of buffalo and other large game, which, strange as it may appear, one does in time tire of. I do not mean that one ever really tires of the half-hour's fight with the wounded brute, when every nerve is on the alert to protect one's own life, and the excitement, so long as it lasts, takes away all remembrance of the previous hard work; but after months and months of it, one begins to feel that the necessary exertion is too great for the reward, and that no amount of danger or success can atone for hours and hours of walking and running under the glare of a tropical sun, without water, and often, after twelve or fourteen hours so spent without any intermission, having to sleep on the ground under a tree, taking your chance of rain, and without food or any hope of obtaining it, save by the repetition of another such day's work. Tired of it one certainly does get, though a week or two's rest is generally sufficient to make one as keen as ever, and it was during such an interval that I thought of pig-sticking. The idea was suggested to me in the following way: I had gone out shooting early one morning, and one of my dogs had followed me unperceived. It knew well enough that it would be sent back if I caught sight of it (for I do not, as some do, consider dogs necessary, or even, except under peculiar circumstances, desirable additions for large game hunting), and so kept itself well in the background, until I fired at, and as I supposed missed, a great boar which was rooting about in one of the glades of the jungle. It then made a rush past in pursuit, and some ten minutes afterwards I heard it giving tongue; and as the sound was steady in one place, it was clear that the boar must be at bay. Knowing from many a camp-fire story that a dog was nearly certain to lose its life in such an encounter, and this one being an especial favourite of mine from its skill and pluck in tackling wounded buffalo, I made an attempt to force my way through the jungle, here so thick as to be all but impassable; and while doing so I came on the spoor, not ten minutes old, of a troop of buffalo, which the noise made by the dog had disturbed, and which were making to-

"THE BOAR WAS STANDING FACING THE DOG"

wards an evergreen thicket, where they would be sure to stand. The first thing was to get the dog quieted, and so I went on until I reached it. The boar, an immense brute with tusks eight or nine inches long, was standing with his hind-quarters protected by a bush facing the dog, which I was sorry to perceive all covered with blood from the severe gashes it had already received. I would not fire for fear of driving the buffalo out of the covert, but took a couple of spears from my gun-bearer, and going up to within five yards of the grunting brute, hurled one into its ribs behind the shoulder. On receiving the wound—a deadly one, as these spears can be thrown with great force as well as precision,—it wheeled round, ploughing up a furrow with its curved tusk, and came straight at me. It was utterly impossible for me to have got out of its way; so, using the remaining spear as a leaping-pole, I planted it straight in between its shoulders, and leaning all my weight on it, sprang on one side just in time to escape his tusks. I lost my grasp of the spear, which was driven right down through him; but my Kaffir ran up and stabbed it as it struggled to rise, and the dog seeing its enemy on the ground pinned it by the ear, and in a few seconds it was dead.

After this I determined to send for all my dogs, some of which were absent with my native hunters, and buying as many more as I could, to increase their numbers by borrowing all those belonging to the natives, and then to try how pig-sticking on foot would succeed. Horses would not have lived where I was, on account of the tsetse. The one I had already killed was no criterion, as he, I afterwards found, had had his hind-leg broken by the bullet; he would otherwise hardly have come to bay with a single dog, or, if he had, would probably have very soon killed it. I have seen an old boar on more than one occasion deliberately go away, taking no notice whatever of half a dozen great Boer-hounds, none of them much smaller than himself—so long, at least, as they confined themselves to baying and did not attempt to bite. If one, bolder than the rest, did dare to come to close quarters, he would turn round with a sudden effective jerk, which either sent the dog away howling, or left it crippled on the ground. The tusks, forming a large section of a circle and of wonderful length, are, especially the lower one, as sharp as a razor and would break even a man's leg if they came fairly in contact with it.

There are two kinds of pig in South-Eastern Africa—one inhabiting the plains and the light thorn jungles; and the other frequenting heavy timber jungles, though also found, but more rarely, in the thickets in the thorns, and the dense reeds which line the rivers. The former, the "indhlovudawane," is not to be met with south of the twenty-ninth degree of south latitude, and is not plentiful before the twenty-eighth degree, while the latter is common in the colony of Natal, and far below it. The "ingulubi," as it is called by the natives, does an immense amount of damage to their sweet potatoes and fields, and has in consequence been exterminated in many districts. In no way is it the equal of the larger species, carrying tusks little longer than those of a domesticated boar, and affording comparatively little sport to either gun or dogs.

As soon as I got my small pack together, I commenced

work. The "indhlovudawane" feeds in small family herds of from two to eight or ten, and comes out to root in the glades and opens for two or three hours every morning and evening; so I knew both when and where to find them, and I had such good sport, after one or two comparative failures, that I kept on, and at the end of two months had killed a large number of pig at the expense of losing several of my dogs. My failures were at first caused by the dogs generally all tailing on to one unfortunate porker, rarely to a full-grown boar or sow, and allowing all the remainder to escape; but after tasting blood several times they warmed to their work, and it was nothing unusual for three or four (and I have seen six) pigs to be all held at bay simultaneously within a mile of each other. Two dogs would combine, and keeping themselves as clear as possible from the tusks, would ultimately seize the animal behind until it got furious and began to charge, coming to bay for a few minutes, and then breaking, only to be again brought to a standstill by the same manœuvres. They nearly always broke bay when I got up to the place, but the hounds, encouraged by seeing me, would rush in one on each side and lay hold behind, and allow themselves to hang there until the pig, tired of dragging them and mad with pain, would face round, and often, seeing me, would come straight on without any further notice; indeed, two out of every three were killed charging. A fair proportion used to escape into the innumerable hyena, ant-eater, and porcupine holes, and though I sent for a couple of spades from the waggon, I seldom succeeded in getting them out. They have a most curious mode of exit when they do bolt—a dangerous one if you are not up to it. As they emerge from the hole they turn a somersault on to the back of it, instead of coming straight out like an ordinary animal, and as that is just the spot where one would naturally stand, more than one man has had his legs ripped open before he learned wisdom of experience.

On only one occasion did I receive any damage, and it was from the largest boar, though not the best tusker, that I ever saw. I had only a couple of dogs with me—indeed, I was not out hunting, but was merely going down to bathe in the river, and in lieu of a gun, the usual walking-stick of wild life, I had taken a spear as being lighter, and the dogs had come of their own accord. Just as I reached the top of the steep bank which overhung the alluvial flat through which the river ran, I heard the rhinoceros-birds chirping below me, and catching my dogs, I peered through the evergreens to see what particular species of game they were relieving from the ticks that infest them all. It was an immense boar of such unusual size that for the first second I mistook it for a rhinoceros-calf, and was looking about for the mother; but my dogs knew better as the breeze brought up the rich scent, and escaping from me they rushed down full tilt at him. Anything more cool than his behaviour could hardly be imagined. He threw his head up with a grunt, and looked at the advancing dogs, then, curling his tail into a corkscrew above his stern, trotted off for a few yards, and as they overtook him, turned round, and faced them. "Leauw," a great yellow dog, so called from his size and resemblance to a lion, but too rash for pig, went straight at his head; the boar gave himself what seemed to be a slight shake, and down went the dog, *hors de combat*. The other, a wise animal, confined himself to the flanks and rear, and though its antagonist made some very nasty-looking twists round it never caught him with its tusks. I was very savage at seeing poor Leauw so treated (though I did not then know that the wound was mortal), as he was one of my best dogs, and ran down as fast as I could to the assistance of his comrade. When the boar saw me, he as usual trotted off grunting, but so slowly that in five minutes I was alongside, the dog holding on to his stern; and then, carefully picking out the exact place behind the shoulder which practice had taught me led to the heart, and using both hands, I rammed the spear home with my full strength. As I made the thrust he wheeled, and with a rapid movement stretched me at full length on the ground, while a sudden pain in the calf of my leg followed by the warm rush of blood proved that he also had not missed his aim. I lay still for a moment, half expecting another attack; but on raising my head and not seeing the animal, I got up, and could then just make it out disappearing in the edge of the reeds, the spear still sticking up and the dog in attendance. On examining my cut, I found that it was a nasty gash, though cleanly done as if by a knife, and the blood flowed so freely as to give colour to a suspicion that some important artery was severed—a most unpleasant one when the means of stopping hemorrhage are totally wanting; and as my spear had been carried off, there was nothing for it but to get back to camp. Finding on my arrival there that the bleeding still continued, though to a less degree, I remained at home, but sent half a dozen men and all the dogs with orders not to come back without the boar, which they were not long in doing (though it was all they could do to carry it), as they found it lying perfectly dead three or four hundred yards from where I had stabbed it, and my other dog, also dead, a few yards off. In this case the pig certainly had the best of it, though he had only two stumps of tusks worn away to almost nothing; but on other days I have killed, morning and evening, a considerable number with hardly a scratch among the whole pack.

Of course it was to be expected that we should occasionally fall in with other animals, and I have already referred to the impallas, and in another place to a buffalo. Sometimes we came across troops of monkeys, when the dogs would tree them, and we would spend an hour or two throwing spears and stones at them for the sake of their skins, which are prized by the natives as an article of dress. We also killed a baboon. The latter happened in this wise :—I had not got far from home on a pig-hunting expedition, and the dogs were still in leash, when I heard the booming call of a male baboon, and on looking about I saw him—a very large old fellow—sitting on the top of a great ant-heap, resting from his labour of grubbing up roots. The ground was open with here and there a tree, and as it is rare to find a solitary baboon, I determined to try and stalk as close as I could, and then run him down with the whole pack, and get up and kill him before he could do much damage; for they will decimate a pack in ten minutes. He was sitting with his back towards us, and we got within a hundred yards unperceived, and then as he made off I had the dogs slipped, and they had him at bay in a quarter of a mile. He got hold of one that ventured too near and simply tore it to pieces with his great claws, upon which the others formed a circle through which he could not break, but they would not go within his reach after the previous example. I was the first to reach the scene of action, and running in hurled a spear at him; it missed its mark, but stuck quivering in the tree against which he was, and he instantly drew it out and shied it back at me, though it came crossways, and not point first as a spear ought to. In hurriedly trying to throw a second time I slipped and fell; but my aim was more true, and it struck him under the forearm, and as the natives declared—I could not see—the brute snatched the weapon from its body and would have stabbed me, had not three or four spears been simultaneously thrown by the Kaffirs, one of which entering above the eye penetrated to the brain, and killed him on the spot. He turned out to be a regular old patriarch, with only one solitary tooth in its head, and quite grey with age,—a great big ugly brute, with a most disagreeable resemblance to human beings.

I have never had an opportunity of really coursing the larger species of antelopes, though, from being on most occasions accompanied by dogs, I have several times seen them run into. My experience is that very few of them, if any, could escape from a well-bred greyhound, as far as mere speed is concerned, but that, from their size and strength, it would generally be impossible for it to bring them to bay.

The blue gnu (*Catoblepas taurina*), which I had previously always held in contempt as utterly harmless, once gave me a lesson as to what it could do when baited by dogs. Solitary males of this, as of other species, are often seen wandering about, and one day an old fellow allowed me, partially concealed by a clump of bush, to get within eighty yards of him. As he whisked up his tail and wheeled round preparatory to taking to flight, I fired at him, and the two dogs that accompanied me immediately rushed off in pursuit, while I ran along a ridge parallel to their course, in full view of the whole chase. The bullet did not seem to have made the slightest difference to the antelope—if such, indeed, a gnu can be called,—and the dogs had to run hard and strong, although they were by no means slow, before they reached him. Each then tackled him after its own fashion, the older and more wary biting his heels, which, to judge by its usual effects, is about the most irritating thing that a dog can do; while its younger and less experienced companion ran on and sprang at his throat. The horns of a gnu are bovine, and, on a miniature scale, much resemble those of a cow buffalo, though the curve does not take them so far back; and I was now to learn for the first time what deadly use he can make of them when roused. With a wheel that, active as all these animals' movements are, seemed like a flash of lightning, he caught the younger dog on his horns, and sent it spinning and howling a dozen yards away, at the same time making a vicious rush at the other.

Old Shot was, however, far too clever an animal to be caught in this way—it was nothing unusual for him to be chased about by a wounded buffalo for half an hour, and he evidently did not mind it in the least,—so he now took to his heels, with his tail well tucked in between his legs, until the gnu, finding itself unable to catch him, gave up the chase, and turning made off in the opposite direction. Upon this Shot returned to his former position, and kept the enraged old bull so well occupied in making continual rushes at him, that I was enabled to overtake them. The idea of there being any danger to myself to be anticipated from the animal never for an instant crossed my mind, and I advanced to shoot it as I would have done an impalla, or any other harmless antelope; and even when, after an unsuccessful raid upon the dog, it came straight on towards me, it never struck me that it could be charging. However, by the time that it was ten yards off I saw what it meant, and as I couldn't run away, I did my best to shoot it in the middle of the forehead, and luckily succeeded. It was the only time that I ever saw a gnu fall lifeless, as they are without exception the toughest of all the wild game that I have met with; and it was also the only time that I was ever charged by one, though, when I told about it at the camp-fire that night, almost every old hunter had a similar experience to relate.

Neither the koodoo (*Antilope strepsiceros*) nor the water-antelope (*Kobus ellipsiprymnus*) are remarkable for their speed, and in one of the most beautiful scenes I ever saw in Africa, these two antelopes, brought to bay by a lot of Kaffir dogs, played a prominent part. I was at the time encamped about two miles above where the river Pongolo, forming a deep gorge through the Bombo mountains, escapes into the Amatonga flats beyond, on its way to join the Sutu. The natives who live on that range had sent down a message to us that a strong body of them was to come down on the morrow for the purpose of hunting as trip of country some three miles long by two broad which lay between the river and the mountain, and to request that I would send my hunters to guard the fords across the river, as well as a narrow pass in the gorge, on the condition that they should give us all the hides of the large game killed, while they could take all the meat away. Of course, I had no objection to this arrangement, which suited both parties, especially as I knew that the ground to be beaten generally contained a few buffalo, and always a large number of koodoo and water-antelopes; and so next morning, after watching the long line of natives wind down the almost perpendicular hill, on which they looked no bigger than a file of ants, we all started to take up our positions—some (for we were many, and the fords few) crossing over and joining the natives, while each of the remainder chose a station along the river banks, and I wandered from one to another as the game got driven further and further down. I was, however, unlucky in getting shots, though the frequent firing, both after I had passed and in front of me, and occasionally a glimpse of game rushing along the opposite bank in search of a ford, proved that my men were getting their share; while the continual hunting cries raised by the natives concealed in the jungle told that they were not allowing all the game to pass unscathed. At last I determined to go down to the pass in the gorge through which I was sure that at least some of the water-antelopes would pass, and while on my way there I saw two koodoo bulls break out of the bush, with an old water-buck close behind them, and followed by a small pack of Kaffir dogs.

There was a ford some little distance beyond, where I thought it probable that they would attempt to cross, and I started for it, running at full speed in the hope of cutting them off. Before, however, I could reach it, I heard the dogs yelping below me, and as from the sound they seemed to be stationary, I turned off to see.

I soon found myself on the top of a precipitous bank, clothed with evergreens, and overhanging the river, which here formed a vast horse-shoe of calm, still water, in which several small sand-banks showed themselves above the surface. Widening circles marked where the disturbed crocodiles had plunged in, while a keen eye could distinguish a few of their log-like forms still resting on the more distant shoals. Opposite lay a peninsula formed by the river, the monotonous hue of the long waving grass relieved by the flat-crowned mimosas, and here and there by the more striking shape of the green cactus-like euphorbia; while nearer in, and bordering the river, were a number of immense white-stemmed wild fig-trees, crowded with paroquets and turtle-doves feeding on the half-ripe fruit. Half a mile off was the narrow, rock-guarded defile which the river, by the unceasing toil of centuries, had worn through these mountains, which, otherwise without a break, raised themselves wall-like and impenetrable from the level plain, and stretched away on either side into the dim distance; and now and then the booming call of the baboons, which inhabit the masses of dense bush that clothes every hollow and fissure in them, could be heard answering to the shouts below, while over all and above all was shed the glorious sunlight of the tropics.

My eyes were, however, fixed upon the river, for there, on a small sand-bank, stood the two noble koodoo bulls at bay. Two or three dogs had also gained a footing, and made the air ring with their sharp barking, re-echoed back again and again by the precipice on which I stood; while several more swam about trying to stem the current and regain the ground which they had lost. One of the antelopes stood with lowered head, and his long circling horns pointing towards the dogs—a picture worthy of a Landseer,—and in his side I now saw that a spear was half-buried; the other, evidently unwounded, but unwilling to leave its companion, remained motionless, his nostrils thrown forward, as if to catch the first taint of the human pursuers sure to follow in their dogs' wake, and his equally magnificent horns resting almost on his haunches. Twenty yards above them was the water-antelope, which had probably followed the others under the impression that it was a ford, and was now unavailingly trying to scramble up the perpendicular bank.

I enjoyed the scene without moving for several minutes, but as from my elevated position I could see down on to the peninsula, I soon noticed several natives running to the spot, guided by the yelping of their dogs, especially of those that, not daring to enter the water, had remained on the other side, and as I by no means relished the idea of all these glorious horns falling into their hands (one pair belonged to them already by the hunters' law of first wound), and although I would willingly have let the antelopes alone if no one else had been there, I at once made the best of my way to the spot where they were at bay. Just as the natives emerged from the bush I aimed at

"ON A SMALL SAND BANK STOOD THE TWO NOBLE KOODOO BULLS AT BAY"

the still motionless koodoo, and fired, the precipice rolling back the sound in repeated echoes for a couple of minutes after. My bullet, after passing through the antelope, which with a bound fell back dead, struck the water, and then I saw it throw up the sand not a hundred yards in front of the advancing natives. I had not taken into consideration the chance of its passing through the koodoo's body, and was considerably alarmed at seeing it do so; however, no one was hurt, though the natives, thinking that it was one of my hunters who had fired, began to swear at me, until they got such an answer back as they knew no black man durst give them, and immediately shut up. The water-antelope, which had succeeded in gaining a footing on the bank, was so astonished by the report of the gun right above it that it jumped back into the river and swam down, and after three shots at its head I succeeded with the last in killing it. The natives then shouted to me to shoot the remaining koodoo for them, and that some of their number would then come round by the ford, and entering the water from my side, would fetch out all three. This I did, and a dozen men soon made their appearance, and dashing in with a great deal of noise and splashing to frighten the crocodiles, they dragged the two koodoos ashore. The water-antelope was floating in deep water, and it was anything but a pleasant task to swim out to it, but a couple of men consented to do so on condition that I should fire an occasional shot to keep off the crocodiles, and though the river was swarming with them, it was performed in safety. It was even more remarkable that none of the dogs had been taken, especially before I began to fire; but these reptiles are miserable cowards, and must have been alarmed at so great a disturbance, and feared to seize their favourite morsel. I ultimately bought the other pair of koodoo horns from the man who had wounded it with his spear, and taken as a whole, the three pair, which I kept in remembrance of one of the most beautiful and thoroughly characteristic African scenes that I ever saw, were the finest specimens which I had in my collection.

Owing to the koodoo when disturbed invariably making for the roughest and most stony ground which it knows of, added to the fact that in the districts where it is found horses cannot live on account of the tsetse, it is very seldom that an opportunity occurs of chasing them on horseback, and only once have I seen one ridden into.

I had been at a hunting party given by Prince Usibepe, a cousin of the Zulu king, with whom I was at the time staying. I had not, however, killed anything during it, as owing to the immense number of men, at least five thousand of whom were out, I considered it unsafe to follow the example of either my host or of one of the king's sons, who was also there, who both banged away whenever they saw hair, regardless of their people's lives. Nobody was hurt, as it so turned out on this particular occasion, though it is exceedingly rare for a great hunting party to pass off without a few casualties from stray bullets.

Usibepe and I had both ridden down from one of his kraals, a distance of ten or twelve miles, for being, like all those of the blood-royal, a big, heavy man, he found it a more easy mode of progression than marching at the head of the men after the usual Zulu fashion, and when the hunt was over we remounted and started back. The ground at first was so densely wooded that we were forced to walk our horses, but the moment it became more open we rode as hard as we could, as there was a heavy thunderstorm gathering, and we feared lest it should break before we could reach our destination. As we topped the second rise we suddenly came upon a koodoo bull looking up in surprise at the sound of our horses' hoofs, which he had no doubt mistaken for those of a herd of zebra. Usibepe instantly tore after it at a mad gallop, firing as he went, while I, restraining my horse, who wanted to race, lay back out of reach of the flying pebbles. The koodoo headed direct for the kraal which we were going to, and did not gain very much, but the Prince's weight soon began to tell, and he had to drop his gun and use the little rhinoceros-hide whip which hung from his wrist to enable him to keep in front of me. Even this did not avail for long, and I passed him without in any way increasing my pace, which, as the ground was much broken, I did not yet attempt to do. The Prince, who, like all the great chiefs, possessed a capital breech-loader, resumed its use as soon as he saw that he could not catch the antelope by sheer speed, and his bullets came whistling past my ears in very unpleasant proximity, until, as we dropped down on to a level bottom and increased our pace, he fell too far behind and gave it up. When we got on to the level I was about ninety yards behind, and feeling that now was the time to make a push, I urged my horse to its utmost, and soon found that I was gaining rapidly; indeed, within ten minutes I had so far lessened the distance that I might have made pretty sure work with my gun, but finding that my horse showed no signs of distress, and seeing that the koodoo was already flagging, I thought I would keep on and try to ride it to a standstill. Maintaining, therefore, the same pace, I gradually crept up until we reached more stony ground, when I urged my horse a little more so as to get him alongside, and just as his head was level with the koodoo's haunches the latter made a stumble, and in trying to recover itself lurched forward and fell on its knees, and from this position it did not stir even when, after pulling up and getting my horse turned, I rode up to it and dismounted, when, pitying the pain its laborious breathing showed the poor brute must be in, I at once put an end to its sufferings by shooting it.

The dog which I have already mentioned as having been gored by the gnu recovered from the wound, and was afterwards instrumental in saving my life from a lion. Native huts are, as everybody who has opened a book about Africa knows, magnified bee-hives, and if the reader can imagine what sleeping in such an erection during the suffocating heat of a tropical night in summer must be, he will not wonder much at my turning out, after an hour or two's restless tossing, to lie on the ground outside, particularly if it be remembered that for nine months previously I had never slept with anything, unless a tree, between myself and the sky.

Once in the open air again I soon slept, but was awoke in the middle of the night by this dog, the only one I had with me, growling savagely, upon which, placing my hand on my gun never far off in these wild countries, I tried to discover what was disturbing him. In Africa everything goes by extremes; on a clear moonlight night it is so bright that you can see to read, and it only differs from the day in that the light is softer, more subdued, and more beautiful; but when it is dark it is a darkness that can be felt. On one occasion Andersson, speaking of his experience of night-shooting says, "So black was the night that I could not discern even the muzzle of my gun;" and in another place, "though the impenetrable darkness prevented me from seeing anything, I could no longer doubt that I was in the immediate vicinity of a lion," and on this night my position was, as regards a total want of light, much the same.

The dog, which had been lying close to me but on the side opposite the fence which protected the village, now rose, and standing over me, growled louder and more fiercely than ever, while I fancied I could distinguish some faint sound in the direction in which his head was turned. On passing my hand up on to his neck and mane I found his hair all bristling up, and for several reasons the idea of its being a lion at once took possession of me. I argued that if it had been a hyena the dog would long ago have rushed out after it, and that even if it had been a leopard he would have warned me by barking, while I remembered that on the occasions, neither few nor far between in that country, on which he had seen lions or got their wind when with me, he had growled in a similar manner. It was not an altogether pleasant idea that close by, perhaps within a few yards which it could clear at a single spring, a lion was prowling about on the search for food, for with no other purpose could it have come here. However, I could not help myself, except by sitting up and noiselessly cocking my gun, and in that position I remained for I should think half-an-hour, listening intently, but unable to distinguish anything; the growling of the dog, after becoming so furious that I every instant expected him to fly out upon the midnight prowler, gradually becoming fainter and fainter, until, after momentarily disappearing in the darkness, he again lay down by my side; and nothing more happened to disturb us that night. When morning dawned the first thing I did was to go and look for spoor, and there, sure enough, were the animal's great footprints. He must have been a cowardly brute, for he had jumped the fence, walked round the hut where the goats were tethered, which must have been too terrified to even bleat, and then after coming in my direction had turned sharp off and jumped out again, but if the dog had not been there it is more than probable that he would not have despised the human morsel lying so temptingly in his path.

Three days after this, with the usual bad luck with dogs that has always attended me, I accidentally killed this one. I had been stalking a mixed herd of gnu and zebra, which in all might number a couple of hundred, but they had taken to flight before I was ready to fire, and in doing so had raised such a dust in the dry red soil that they were perfectly concealed by it; as also were my dogs, both of which had bolted after them. Of course, I could take no particular aim, and so fired both barrels into the thickest of the cloud, thinking that among so many my bullets could hardly fail to prove effective. I could not have given them both the same elevation however, for when the dust settled there was a zebra trying to hobble away, and ten yards on this side of where the herd had passed, as we could see by the spoor, lay my poor dog shot through both shoulders and quite dead. I was never more sorry for the death of any animal.

The hartebeest is one of the fastest antelopes in Africa, and possesses such strength as well as to render it almost impossible for anything under a whole pack of strong and swift hounds to bring it to bay. It is common in the great level grass plains to the north-west of Zululand, and on several occasions I tried coursing them there with two very fast crossed Amaponda greyhounds, but although they could run up to them when they had a fair start, they never once succeeded in bringing one to bay, or even in causing one to separate from the herd. The natives of the districts having often seen me unsuccessfully stalking them, or trying to ride them down, and being much interested in a supply of meat being obtained of which they would get a share, came to me and said that they would show me how I might easily get a shot at close quarters. Breaking the regular surface of these plains are deep indentations formed by the water during the heavy thunderstorms of summer; they are often from ten to twenty feet deep, with such perpendicular sides that not only is it impossible to see them at a hundred yards' distance, but they are often uncrossable for upwards of a mile. The subsoil being principally formed of a strong red clay, the shapes the rain and the wash of the torrents cause it to assume are as peculiar as they are curious; piles of bright red columns, which bear a singular resemblance to those to be seen in the sea-washed caves of Staffa, sometimes standing in rows of several hundred yards, while all the various forms to be found amid icicles and stalactites are here reproduced. This curious freak of nature is by no means peculiar to this part of Africa, but is found everywhere where the country presents the same features; and I have always been surprised that travellers have never thought it worthy of mention among the numerous lesser details which are generally to be found in their works.

It was by taking advantage of the crossing-places in these gullies that the natives proposed to enable me to get within shot of the hartebeest. They said that some of the herds when driven from a certain direction and pressed invariably crossed at the same spots, and wished me to conceal myself in them while they drove the game to me. It was in the afternoon when they made this proposal, and I asked if the hiding-place was far off; and on receiving an answer in the negative, I went at once with them to examine it. It turned out to be similar to any one of the hundreds which I had before seen—half a dozen paths leading in and out, while the inequalities of the centre were worn smooth by the continuous trampling of many feet. But I found out all that I wanted to know, namely, whether I could conceal my horse as well as myself, and finding that it would be perfectly easy to do so, I told the men that I would be ready for them on the morrow.

By ten o'clock some ten men had come, who, on being joined by all I could spare from the waggon, went off to do their part of the work, taking all my dogs with them, and I, mounting my horse, trotted down to my hiding-place. I could see three or four herds feeding in different parts of the plain, and as until they came near there was no danger of frightening them by the exposure of my head, I sat and watched them. The men did their best, and the dogs did theirs; but herd after herd utterly refused to go in the required direction, one of them making back right in their faces, and perversely offering splendid shots to those who had no guns. The last herd seemed at first to be going right, but at the last minute they also turned off and made for a crossing-place about a mile above me; so that after wasting some eight hours I went home without a hartebeest having come within half a mile of me. The natives, however, when they came in, said that I was not to be discouraged, and that I would certainly be more successful next day, and as I really wanted meat to sun-dry for provisions, and had so far only managed by firing at long distances to kill two of these antelopes, I consented to sit for one day more in the scorching sun, which glared on the white and red clay of the gully, whose perpendicular banks prevented a breath of wind from entering, and made the atmosphere all but unbearable, so that, indeed, I had to spread a handkerchief over my guns where they lay, partly to prevent the barrels burning my hands, and partly with a half-defined idea that they might go off of themselves if they got too hot.

Next day four of the men appeared on horseback, riding clean-limbed active-looking little mares, with a sack for a saddle, and a grass rope for a bridle. They suggested that as there were four crossings which the hartebeest were likely to make for, and only myself to guard them all, stops should be placed at the other three, who need not unnecessarily show themselves (and so give the game an idea that it was surrounded), unless a herd tried to pass their way. In other respects the arrangements were the same as on the day previous, and we could see more game even from the waggon than there had then been.

I had not long to wait to-day. The first herd when disturbed made off up to a spot which I knew was tenanted by a stop; the second, however, came direct towards me, the native horsemen following in their wake with naked arms and legs flying like moving windmills, and yelling and shouting at the top of their voices. I watched them until the herd was within three hundred yards, and then ducking down I ran to my battery, and cocked in succession all the six barrels of which it consisted. As the foremost of them reached the descent they exchanged their lumbering but swift gallop for a trot, and in a few seconds the whole space in front of me was filled with dark-red bodies, jostling and pushing in their hurry to get across. As soon as I thought that there was no possibility of their breaking back, I covered a shoulder and pulled the trigger. The struggling mass got wild with fear and plunged forward, and again and again, almost as excited as the beasts themselves, I fired at successive shoulders, and as the last of them disappeared over the further bank I stood with empty guns and an aching arm, while four, out of upwards of forty, hartebeest lay either dead or dying in front of me.

I had hardly loaded one out of the three muzzle-loaders, when the shouting above made me run to the top of the bank and look over, and there I saw another herd, the same one that had been first started, and which had been turned by the stop, galloping down the side of the gully. I had only time to ram cartridges into my breech-loader when they reached the crossing; but whether they smelt the powder, or whether they saw the dead bodies of their comrades, they swerved at it and continued their former course. This the heavy rush of their hoofs told me, and again running to the bank with my guns, I fired all four barrels at them from between sixty and a hundred yards. One fell, and I heard the bullet tell on another, but the other two must have been clean misses. In the excitement of the moment I had not gone after the first troop on horseback, as I had at first intended, but now I rushed to my horse, jumped on to its back, and extricating it as rapidly as possible from the gully, galloped off in pursuit of this one. They were then leading by about four hundred yards with one of my dogs not far behind, while its companions, having followed them since they were started, were lagging some just before and some just behind me, the Kaffir dogs having turned off to the one that had dropped in its tracks, mortally wounded.

My horse, stiff from standing, and impatient from having had nothing to do for so long, was only too glad to be allowed to go; but after the first quarter of an hour of hard galloping, during which I had rather improved my position, I had to check him, as it was impossible that he could keep that pace up for long, and I had been too often beaten off not to know the staying powers of a hartebeest, even when, as was the case with one of these, it had a bullet somewhere in its body. No ground could possibly have been more favourable for a trial of speed, it being as level and clean as a race-course, and the shortness of the grass preventing any mistakes in the hyena or ant-eater holes. Before long, too, my horse, which had had plenty of similar experiences, and knew the value of saving himself as well as I did, settled into a steady gallop, so that I could drop the reins on his neck, and if necessary guide him by the pressure of my knees alone. A horse thoroughly well trained to this kind of work should require no guidance whatever from the reins; should, indeed, put its rider alongside of the game of its own accord, while it should render implicit obedience to the slightest pressure of the knee, wheeling round so long as it can feel it, and should also be taught to stop dead on the spot when informed by a pinch on the withers that its rider wishes it to do so. A good horse will not only do all this, but will carry you alongside of elephants and other dangerous game, and will sheer off of itself in the nick of time the instant a charge is made. Much of the pleasure of this kind of sport, which can, however, bear no comparison with shooting on foot, lies in watching the instinct with which your horse will work, it asking no more than that you should retain your seat—not always an easy matter during the sudden swerves it makes to escape danger,—and that you should fire at the proper time, in order that it may enable you to overcome any game that you may show it, and which it possesses speed enough to overtake.

I had noticed one of the mounted Kaffirs galloping across the line of the hartebeest when we first started, but he had shortly afterwards disappeared, and in the excitement of the moment he had passed from my mind; but now, on seeing the herd suddenly swerve, and make a rush, at the same time altering their course, I was surprised to see that he was the cause. The gully by the side of which we had been going had taken a long bend, and the native, aware of the fact, had taken advantage of it to ride straight and conceal himself in it; and as the herd reached him he sprang up and raced them at full speed for nearly half a mile, by which time his little mare was blown. But it had been of immense service to me, pushing and tiring the hartebeest, and causing them to alter their course so much, that, without increasing my pace, the distance between us was lessened by one-half. Thinking that it would be a good thing if I could press and tire them now before they had time to breathe again, I spoke to my horse, and in a few moments we were flying across the flat at the top of his speed. The antelopes were settling back into their regular stride as I did this, and I had gained another fifty yards before they saw me, when they jumped away as fast as ever. For upwards of a mile we maintained the same pace, when my horse showing symptoms of becoming distressed, I steadied him, and the hartebeest then soon resumed the pace that they had been going at before.

For the next two miles there was no change, and we had been going so fast and so long that I began to think that the chase would end as all the others had, when I noticed that one seemed to be lagging a yard or two behind its comrades. My fastest greyhound was the only dog now with me, and it had settled down into galloping alongside of my horse; but, although distressed, it was not dead beat, and answered at once when I spoke to it and urged it forward, and in a few minutes it ran up to within twenty yards of them and gave tongue. This had the effect of causing them to make a spurt, and to my great delight, I saw that the gap between them and the hindmost one increased every second. My dog saw it too, and immediately ran up to it and tried to seize its throat, but was instantly shaken off, and beyond possibly delaying the animal a few seconds, did no good. My horse was considerably distressed, but I roused him up again, and when he caught sight of the now almost solitary hartebeest he did his best to run up to it. However, all we could do was to force it to leave the rest, and to take up its own line, and I was obliged to save my horse, now getting very weak under me, as much as possible. My dog also would not answer my voice any further than to look round at me, while the hartebeest kept on its steady gallop, its skin, dark red at all times, now seeming almost black as it steamed and shone with perspiration. I felt dizzy myself from the great heat, and for choice the antelope seemed the most likely of us to win the day. I was gaining, however; yard by yard the brute came nearer to me, till I could count the rings on its crooked horns, and it seemed to be failing more at every stride, but so was my horse. The latter sobbed under me as I lifted him on, and I knew that he would drop soon; yet I had not the heart to pull him up, with the chase so near, and in a condition of such evident exhaustion. At last I thought I would try the gun, but the lumbering way in which my horse was galloping made me miss, and I had scarcely reslung it, when with a long quiver as if he were breaking his heart, he fell beneath me, though, as I felt him going, I did not get a fall. There was still one chance left—a chance that was but a slight one, with my arms aching, and my whole body exhausted with the hard riding; but I knelt down, took a long breath, and was just going to pull the trigger when the hartebeest stopped of itself. The dog had kept on, and it now ran up to it, tried to fly at it, and then lay down by its side, and I knew that horse, antelope, and dog were all three dead beat.

The first thing was to attend to my horse. I loosened the girths, took the bit out of his mouth, and moistening my handkerchief with a little water which I had in a flask, I put it over his nostrils. This was sufficient, and in a few minutes he stood up, and replacing the bit, I led him forward towards the antelope, which, having seemingly run until it could run no more, paid no attention whatever to our approach. Hartebeest do charge sometimes, but this one, though a bull, did not even seem to look at us, and fell to my first shot. On going up to it I was surprised to see the dog dragging itself to me instead of rising; and fancying that it must be exhausted from the great heat and from want of water during its long run, I opened the hartebeest, and taking out the stomach, squeezed the grass I found there until my hands were full of water, which the dog eagerly lapped up, and I repeated the operation until there was none left. After examining my prize, and finding to my surprise that it was not the one which I had wounded, I turned to go, but finding that the dog would not get up and follow me, I left him there, intending him to rest and return with the men whom I should send for the meat; but he was dead before they got there. My horse, too, was long before it fully recovered from the effects of that ride, and I never after attempted, even under favourable circumstances, to ride a hartebeest down, unless he was hard hit.

CHAPTER VIII.

ANECDOTES OF ANTELOPES.

I HAVE already in another part of this book referred to the skill displayed by the gnu in the use of its horns. This antelope perhaps occurs more frequently than any other, but is so extremely wary that fewer are killed by the native hunters than of any other species. Europeans, however, find them good practice in rifle-shooting, as they will stand in herds at a distance which they think secure, say three hundred or four hundred yards, and watch the passer-by. Only twice have I succeeded by fair stalking in getting quite close. In the first instance a native hunter and I were returning from breaking up a buffalo which I had shot the previous day, and on our way home we came across the fresh track of a white rhinoceros. This we followed; and while we were engaged in doing so, my companion suddenly said, "Look, are those not buffalo?" and on the opposite ridge, about half a mile off, I saw a black mass coming slowly down. Of course we at once left the rhinoceros, and set off towards them, though I noticed on the way that the hunter kept looking very earnestly. At last he sat down, laughed, and taking his snuff-box out of the slit in his ear, prepared to indulge in that luxury. "What's the matter?" I wonderingly asked. "They're not buffalo, they're gnu," was the answer. I had not killed much game in those days, and thought a gnu very nearly as good as a buffalo, at any rate sufficiently so to make me say, "Well, I'll go and stalk them while you are taking snuff."

The old hunter looked amused, but nodded assent, and off I started. There were a number of small thorn bushes between me and the spot where they were feeding, and running stooping forward, though not taking any particular pains to conceal myself, I always managed to keep one of them between us. It was twilight, and the herd was feeding, or I should most certainly have been noticed, but as it was I reached a little bush, not two feet high, some two hundred yards from them, and as they were grazing in my direction, in a few minutes the whole herd was within fifty yards of me, many of them within ten. It was a long time before I fired. Even a very young and keen sportsman cannot fail to be interested in watching a large herd of wild game peacefully feeding, unsuspicious of danger, within a few yards of him,—so interested sometimes as to forget that he has a gun.

However, I did not do so that evening, for I did not care to go back empty-handed. The only difficulty was which to choose among so many, but chance solved that for me, for a cow, walking up to within five yards of the bush, would in another second have discovered me had I not shot her.

The other time was after what I believe was the most creditable stalk I ever made. A large herd was scattered over a couple of acres, some feeding and others lying down, and a few standing motionless in the shade of the thorn-trees. They were at the bottom of a gentle slope, on the top of which I was, in a perfectly open place, without a tree between us, and the grass being burnt clean off except where they were actually feeding, the ground was quite bare. I wriggled, serpentine, for fully half a mile, taking advantage of every stone and little ant-heap, watching intently every fresh movement, more especially of those whose heads were towards me, until at last, with my hands and wrists all bleeding from the sharp stumps of the burnt grass, and my knees and elbows completely skinned, I found myself close to this great herd of upwards of a hundred gnu, the nearest of which was barely twenty yards distant. Much surprised at my success, and having only once before, and that many years previously, been so close to them, I lay for upwards of an hour watching their movements. A cow and a yearling calf particularly attracted my notice. The old lady was lying down, peacefully chewing the cud, but the young one wanted her to get up, and kept butting at her, until, wearied by its failure, it would walk away, though on looking round and seeing that its mother was not following it, it would return and repeat its unavailing attempts. Presently a patriarchal old bull came up from where he had been feeding some hundred yards away, and roused in succession every one that was lying down. Something about the place did not please him, and he was going to drive them all from it. Could it have been that instinctive knowledge of something wrong which we call presentiment, and which the natives often affirm that this animal shows, even going to the length of calling it the "Umgoma," or wizard; or was he merely thirsty, and wanting to take the herd to water? He was very peremptory about it anyhow, and if any of them did not go in the right direction, did not hesitate to use his horns, which seemed so large that I coveted them for a friend who had asked me to get him a pair. The herd was already up, and those which had been lying down were stretching themselves preparatory to moving, so that I had to make up my mind whether to fire at him, or at a cow for the sake of her meat; but as they are not very good eating, the fat being hard and nasty, and the flesh dry, I chose the former, and put a bullet through his shoulders. He managed to keep with the herd for a little while, but ultimately left it, and after a good deal more stalking, and three more shots, I finished him.

I think I said that it was the only time when I had been so near them. I was mistaken. I was once, though accidentally, nearer. It was during the most terrific thunderstorm that I ever witnessed, and I have seen a good many. Although it was mid-day it had grown so dark that I could not see ten yards in front of me, and I was walking through a sea of water, with trees for islands, which not an hour previously had been dry land, parched and cracked with the great heat. The thunder was crashing continuously, and with such violence that I staggered under each successive peal, while the lightning either blinded me as it struck within a few yards, or shimmered in broad dazzling sheets of light through the watery air, and one loud, continued roar went up from earth and sky, mingling with the distant rumble of the thunder as it died away. While this was going on, I walked, hardly knowing where I was going, right into a herd of gnu. I did not see them until I was almost among them; but even had my gun not been hopelessly soaked, the fearful storm made self-preservation and not destruction one's chief thought. They were standing huddled in a mass, their heads together, and their sterns outwards, and they positively only just moved out of my way, much the same as a herd of cattle might have done.

I have already spoken of the wonderful tenacity of life displayed by these antelopes, and I think that the most extraordinary case in illustration of it that I ever witnessed came under my notice in 1869. While out hunting I saw a gnu running some two hundred yards off, seemingly edging my way, and as it came nearer I could not but observe its peculiar action. It was inclining over at such an angle that it seemed as if it must momentarily lose its balance, and was running, so to speak, on one side of its body only. It did not seem able to guide itself, and kept coming nearer, until, at about fifty yards distance, I shot it in the shoulder, when, after spinning forward a few yards—I know of no other word that would describe its mode of progression—it fell. On going up to it I found a bullet-mark in its chest, and that the other shoulder was broken, and when half an hour afterwards a hunter came up on the spoor and claimed it, he told me that he had fired at it standing not more than twenty yards off, that it fell on the spot as if dead, but that, instantly jumping up, it had since run six miles in this circular lopsided fashion. On cutting it up we found that his ball had passed through the chest, had broken the shoulder-blade, and running down outside the ribs had splintered the upper bone of the hind-leg. So difficult is it to kill them, that I have shot, and seen shot, as many as a dozen in a single day, not one of which was got, and for all that we rarely, if ever, found one dead of its wounds, while on the other hand, there was an old bull that we knew had three bullets in him, one of which had broken his shoulder, which I used to see every day for nearly two months, and which had then almost completely recovered.

It is unnecessary to describe at length the marks by which the four different species of zebra are distinguished, and it will be sufficient to say that there are only two which can be known apart at a glance, viz., the true zebra and the quagga. The former well-known animal is, as a rule, only to be found in the thorn districts, while the latter, which is larger and very differently striped, inhabits the immense treeless plains of the Free State and Trans-Vaal Republic. Both can be ridden into without much difficulty, though there can be but little pleasure in killing them in comparison with other animals more truly game, and, except by the natives who are passionately fond of their flesh and even prefer it to all other kinds, they would probably go unharmed by man were their skins not an article of commerce. One trait common to the whole genus is a curious one. When any of them are killed, the remainder, as soon as they become aware of the fact, utter a very peculiar and melancholy wail, and will wander about near the place plaintively lamenting their loss. There can be no doubt that it is a sort of dirge or wailing, as though I have often listened to it for hours during the stillness of the night, yet it was only uttered by the herd that had lost one of its number; the other herds, of which there were plenty, remaining quiet. Many a lion has lost his supper through it, for the natives, guided by the cry, will make search in the direction indicated, and should they find the carcase will scream and shout to scare the lion, and if successful will hardly leave it a bone.

The water-antelope (*Kobus ellipsiprymnus*) is an extremely fine animal, and so plentiful that there are, perhaps, more of them shot than of any of the other large antelopes. It may be classed with the reed-buck, in the same manner that the Nyala, hereafter to be mentioned, may be classed with the larger bush-buck. The large ringed horns, which in males crown its brow, bear a strong resemblance to those of the reed-buck, while the habits and general appearance of both species are almost identical. Both frequent thickets and reedy places near water, and are principally found in pairs or in small groups. They differ, however, in colour, which in the water-antelope is of a dark iron grey, with a remarkable white line passing down each haunch. The hair of the species inhabiting Eastern Africa is very long and coarse, though that of the one found in Central Africa (*A. difassa*) is remarkably soft, and is highly prized by the natives as being so.[1]

---

[1] Dr. Schweinfurth's *Heart of Africa*, p. 338.

The most curious shot that I ever made was in connection with one of these animals. I was walking along outside the reeds of the Nkwavuma with my gun-bearer, and had seen nothing for several miles. At last, the day being extremely hot, we sat down to rest on a large rock which overhung them, and a minute or two afterwards the native, after looking earnestly at one spot, directed my attention to it, and as the breeze bent the reeds forward I caught a glimpse of part of the head of some animal. After watching it for some time, we decided, from what seemed to be its long ears, that it must be a doe water-antelope, and when the wind next enabled me to see it, I fired, aiming at where I judged the shoulder would be. Utter silence followed the shot, but on descending into the reeds we found the animal, which was of the species which we had thought it was, lying dead. On proceeding to see where I had hit it, I was much puzzled by the number of bullet-marks, there being no less than three, all of necessity made by the same ball; and, after taking into consideration the way in which it had been standing, *i.e.* broadside to us, and the size of the holes —that of entry being always smaller, from the difference of velocity of the missile, than that of exit,—and after breaking it up and tracing, as well as we could, the course of the ball, we made out that it had gone first into the neck close behind the ear on the right side and had come out below the ear on the opposite side; had gone in again on the left side about eighteen inches behind the shoulder, and passing through the body had stopped in the skin where the shoulder and neck join, where we found it, not more than twelve inches from where it went in. It is very difficult to account for this, unless, indeed, it was licking its side when I fired, which, at the time, I certainly did not think it was, or unless it might have been caused, as the natives thought, by some sudden start it had given when first struck.

I also remember once seeing one of these antelopes browsing on some leaves above it in a curious manner. I was going through a line of jungle which edges the river Pongolo, when I noticed the branches in front violently agitated, and at first thought it was caused by monkeys. However, on stealing forward a few yards, I was much surprised to see the head of a doe water-antelope; for, in the first place, I had always thought that they confined themselves to grass, and in the second, I could not conceive how she could get so high up, unless, indeed, she was standing on an ant-heap, and that did not seem to be the case, as her head kept bobbing up and down as if the support could scarcely bear her weight. On moving a little on one side to where my view was not obstructed by the bushes, I saw that she was raising herself after the manner of a goat on her hind-legs, and after grasping a branch of leaves descending again. This she did several times in succession while I was watching her—until, in fact, I shot her. On relating the incident to the hunters in camp, I found them as sceptical as they dared to be with me, and though conviction was forced upon them by the contents of the animal's stomach, one and all declared that they had never either heard of or seen a water-antelope browsing on leaves, or raising itself on its hind-legs in such a fashion.

We all know how the first of anything lives in one's recollection, and there assumes an importance utterly incommensurate with its real worth; how the boy's first day with hounds, his first grouse or partridge, or his first salmon, remain, even in old age, distinct and vivid pictures. In the same manner the killing of my first antelope, and all the details connected with it, are far more clearly impressed on my memory than the death of many a rhinoceros, buffalo, or lion that I have since witnessed or taken part in effecting. It occurred during my first journey, in 1862, over the Drachensberg Mountains and through the Dutch States into the northern interior, but we had not as yet reached the confines of the colony of Natal, and had outspanned the oxen for the night on the hills above Bushman's River. Next morning, hearing that there were plenty of antelopes of the Vaal raebuck species to be found close by, I started early with a Hottentot named Klaas to try and get one, the Dutch owner of most of the waggon-train with which I was travelling agreeing to my request that they should only go on a few miles and then wait for me.

The ground over which we were to shoot was very broken, consisting of bare stony hills without a vestige of cover, and very rough to walk over, and a great part of it had lately had all the grass burned off by one of those fires which are so common in autumn, when the country gets so dry that a chance spark may often burn an enormous tract. I have since more than once travelled two or three days at a time (a hundred miles or more) without seeing any green thing; the ground—except a few dark-coloured ashes—being as bare as a floor, and not a sign of life to be seen anywhere, save, perhaps, a few locusts that had escaped the fire, or a solitary hawk sitting motionless on the top of an ant-heap. The immense flats of the Free State, or Trans Vaal, after a great fire has recently passed over them, present, perhaps, as perfect an idea of utter desolation as could well be conceived,—the whole country seeming almost literally to be in sackcloth and ashes, while the air, charged with gas such as may sometimes be observed in the glare of an intensely hot sun, is filled for days afterwards with minute blacks.

These fires are sometimes very picturesque, and one which I saw a short time previously to this was so much so as to merit description. The spot on which it took place was a flat of some three miles broad and two long, bounded by two streams, which, at the further end, converged until they formed a narrow path of not more than a hundred yards broad, the tall tambuti grass, some six or eight feet long, then giving place to equally dry reeds of double the height. The streams then made an outward curve, though the reeds continued up to the foot of a low range of hills a few hundred yards beyond. It was autumn, the season during which the annual grass-burnings for the sake of insuring young grass during the winter take place, and the fire having been lit on each side of the broader end of the flat in fifty or sixty places, presented soon after dark a most peculiar appearance. The wind was light and variable, and the numerous lines of fire retreated and advanced, or joined together, and after a bright flare for a few seconds, died out, and in general moved about in a curious and irregular manner as they were influenced by it. But little imagination was required to see in the smoke-obscured lines of fire a resemblance to an engagement; the rapid advance of one side as the wind favoured it causing for the same reason the apparent wavering and hesitation of the opposing lines, while, when they did meet, the blaze of flame that then took place might not inaptly have been taken to represent a hand-to-hand conflict.

Later in the evening the wind changed, and increasing, blew down the plain, and the various lines soon merged into one which rapidly neared the narrow pass between the streams, leaving behind them hundreds of minute fires, the smouldering of which enveloped the ground with smoke. The grass got longer and longer, till at last the reeds were reached, and then for several minutes the spectacle was magnificent. Nothing could be seen but immense tongues of lurid flame shooting out of a molten sea, and carried forward by the wind, licking the tops of the reeds twenty yards in front. The sound, even at the distance at which we were, resembled the low rumble of thunder, and the whole country and sky were lit up as if it were day. Half an hour sufficed to take the fire to the foot of the hills, up which it climbed in as good a line as the inequalities of the surface would permit, but before it had reached half-way it was much broken up and detached, and as the distance now gave each fire the appearance of being stationary, the whole hill looked as if covered with an innumerable number of watch-fires. But perhaps the most curious spectacle was yet to come. When the fire reached the top it was still more broken up into single detachments, apparently a yard or so apart (though really much more), which at that distance appeared to be stationary, and burning quite quietly and steadily, so that the hill seemed crowned for more than a mile with a row of lamps.

But to return to the antelopes. I had not very long to wait before I made their acquaintance. Before we had scarcely gone a mile, I was startled by a sharp, prolonged sneeze, apparently close by, and at the same time Klaas clutched me by the arm, and pointed to three grey objects that looked remarkably like the stones among which they were, but which on the strength of my companion's word I believed were antelopes. They gave no sign of life however, but stood there on the next hill, facing us and motionless; and though the eye could just distinguish them from the surrounding stones, yet if you looked away it was very difficult to find them again; every now and then they uttered their cry, which has the peculiarity, whether exercised at will or not I do not know, of seeming close at hand when really distant, and not being any louder however near they are. Of course, having been seen first rendered it useless to attempt to stalk them, and unfortunately it was but an earnest of our day's work. We saw great numbers, but in no case were we unnoticed by them, and from daylight till four o'clock I toiled up and down these hills, sustained by hope alone. At last, however, my patience was rewarded. I got to the top of a ridge, and on peering over the side of a big rock saw three unsuspiciously feeding about a quarter of a mile off; and after watching them for some minutes, and seeing that they were gradually coming nearer, I determined, as the wind suited, to remain where I was. In three-quarters of an hour they were about two hundred yards off, still feeding in the same direction, and quite unsuspicious;

but just when I was noting a big stone in their path as the spot which I would allow them to reach before I fired, and was calculating the exact distance, Klaas choked, and after a vain struggle to suppress it, began to cough violently. They instantly stopped feeding and looked up, and just as the leader, a male, began to turn away, I pulled the trigger. He made a magnificent bound into the air and fell dead, rolling twenty or thirty yards down the incline. My second bullet made the chips fly from a stone between a smaller male's feet as the pair rapidly disappeared round the face of the hill, and then I lost no time in going down to examine my first antelope. He was an old male, and a fine specimen. The species to which he belonged, though almost approaching a fallow-deer in size, more nearly resembles a chamois in other particulars; indeed, it has been called the African chamois, and so far deserves the title, that it certainly possesses many of the characteristics and habits of the European species—decidedly more so than any other of the antelope genus found in South Africa, with the exception of the klipspringer. Their colour is light grey, the hair being somewhat long and coarse, and the horns are straight, and by no means unusually large for the animal's size. They are never found but on the bare hills, among rocks and stones, and their powers of springing are wonderful. It seems extraordinary how their delicate limbs escape injury, when they take bound after bound, like an indiarubber ball, in places that a cat would shudder at. I do not suppose that they are really more shy than some of the more wary antelopes, but the nature of the ground which they inhabit makes it appear so. That it is hard to get near them no one will deny, and it is equally difficult to drive them, unless, indeed, you happen to know the particular troop, have often seen it, and been accustomed to notice the direction they usually took when disturbed. In such a case, you may have a shot at them within ten yards, for they always follow their leader, and he having once determined to go through some special pass or hollow, will do so whatever may happen—would, there is little doubt, go over you rather than turn back; and that this is a common characteristic of several of the shyest of African antelopes has already been mentioned in this book, and is one that I have many times had experience of.

That night Klaas told me over the fire, among a lot of other hunting stories, how a Dutch Boer in whose service he had lately been had exterminated all the raebuck in his district by galloping them down on horseback, and cutting them off by taking advantage of the above-mentioned peculiarity of never swerving from the direction first chosen. Klaas, to his other accomplishments, added that of first-class liar; so, though my curiosity was roused by his story, I waited until I saw the Dutchman with whom I was travelling in the morning, and on finding that he knew that such a thing had been done, I determined to try myself, and had the horses got ready at once. I rode Monarch, a great sixteen-hand brute with a ewe neck and a mouth of iron, but which, despite its ugliness, was remarkably fast, a good stayer, and very game; and I mounted Klaas on Pig, my own shooting pony, with orders to try and keep me in sight if he could. I carried a short breech-loading Terry, very light, and handy for horseback.

As on the day before, we soon found the game. It was a troop of five, and they were feeding on the face of a not very steep hill, crowned with a flat top, for which they made on discovering us. I allowed them to disappear over the rise, and then followed, scrambling up as best I could, and rather repenting of my rashness in thinking of galloping over such horrible ground. Just before I reached the table-land I gave my horse's bridle to Klaas, and went forward on foot to see if they were still in sight. It was lucky that I did so, for they were standing some two hundred yards beyond looking back. Resting the rifle on a rock, I fired, and one fell on the spot, the rest making off at full speed, and as soon as I could get my horse I followed as hard as I could. They were heading for the further end of the table-land, about a mile off, nearly a quarter of which distance they had of start; but Monarch's long stride soon came into play, and at the end of the first four hundred and fifty yards I found that I was gaining rapidly, particularly on one that was lagging and was already some way behind the rest. What exciting work hard galloping is, both to horse and rider! Monarch fully entered into the spirit of it, and required no urging, while the antelopes did not seem to be pushing themselves; at any rate, they were going no faster than at first, and as we neared the descent I was not twenty yards from the hindmost one. For the first time using my spurs, I simultaneously cocked my rifle, and just as the antelope disappeared over the rise, not five yards from me, I pulled the trigger; a sudden swerve, a feeling like descending out of a blanket after being tossed too high and hitting the ceiling, and I remember nothing more till I woke up to find myself jammed between two big rocks, with an uncomfortable feeling in my left arm. With some difficulty I got into a sitting posture, and found that if I had not broken, I had at least considerably hurt it. Monarch was standing, looking very much ashamed of himself, a few yards above, and close by I could hear the antelope bleating, though it was concealed by the rocks. Just then Klaas arrived, and dismounting helped me up. On examination I thought that I had no bones broken, though I was severely bruised about the side and my arm was very painful. The horse, which unfortunately was not mine, was slightly cut on one leg, but otherwise uninjured. Of course, I had no inclination to resume the chase, and we went down to where the antelope was lying. It was by no means dead, and scrambled up on seeing us, and, though it could not get away, gave Klaas some trouble among the boulders before he caught and killed it. We found that it had been struck by the former bullet—the one that had killed its companion—while the last shot had missed it clean. I was never quite clearly able to make out how I had so completely come to grief; but I suppose my firing just as we were on the verge of the descent, combined with the extreme badness of the ground, had put Monarch, usually the most sure-footed of horses, out of his stride, and it had ended in his coming down. However, I had killed two, an old and a young male; and though it turned out afterwards that I had damaged a rib and severely strained my arm, I did not at the time think much of my hurt, and returned to the waggons rather elated at my success than otherwise. On the whole, however, I do not think I should recommend galloping antelopes on the hills to any one who had much regard for the safety of his neck; though, what between the ant-eater, hyena, and porcupine holes on the flats, and the branches of trees and thorns in the thorn covers, it is rather hard to say which is the more free from danger.

Perhaps the most beautiful of all the antelopes that I have seen is the Nyala; the white lines with which it is striped being more numerous, more regular, and much better defined than those of either the koodoo or the striped eland, which, as far as I know, are the only two animals which possess them at all. Unfortunately it does not exist except in the low, fever-stricken districts, and I have never seen it south of the Bombo range, about the twenty-eighth degree of south latitude. It frequents the densest thickets it can find, and is wary and difficult to stalk; indeed, I should fancy that more people have caught fever by hunting this antelope than by the pursuit of any other animal in Africa, except, perhaps, the elephant. Of course, as with most game, early morning and evening are the best times during which to look for it, and early dawn implies being wet through above the waist by the heavy dew, and the subsequent drying of one's things by the heat of the sun, a pretty certain method of getting fever; evening, on the other hand, means not getting home till hours after dark, and breathing during that period the fatal miasma which as soon as the sun sets begins to rise from all over the great lagoon-dotted plains where this antelope is chiefly found.

Nyala-shooting and fever are all but synonymous, but to those who have already had the latter, and with whom the mischief, as regards injury to the constitution, is

PERHAPS THE MOST BEAUTIFUL OF ALL THE ANTELOPES IS THE NYALA

already done, ample amends are made by the graceful beauty of the antelope and the magnificence of its skin. Its horns almost exactly resemble those of a koodoo of eighteen months or two years old, though if anything, they have rather a broader spread.

Only one of the antelopes already mentioned are to be found in the colonies at the present day, and some of them, it is probable, never existed there. There are, however, at least ten distinct species, which, though inhabiting other parts, are nowhere found in greater perfection, both as regards numbers or single specimens, than in the colony of Natal. These ten may be said to naturally divide themselves under three headings, viz., those existing only in the forests, those which live entirely in the open, and those which, although not found in the forests, will occasionally take refuge in them, and are fond of lying in small patches of thicket, and in the thorn scrub, as well as in the open.

The first-mentioned consists of three species, which never leave the shelter of the forests, unless occasionally to feed on their edges at early dawn, or to cross from one to another, viz., the great bush buck, the red buck, and the tiny blue buck. The former of those, the male of whom is known as the "nkonka," and the female as the "imbabala," and which differ so greatly that experience is necessary to teach one that they are of the same species, is undoubtedly the finest in every way of all the antelopes, whether found in the colonies or interior, that are known to the hunter as "small game." In size it resembles a full-grown fallow buck, weighing, according to age and condition, from nine to thirteen stone; its colour is a dark reddish brown, often verging into black, and with indistinct markings on the sides, haunches, and legs; it has a great deal of hair, and a considerable mane, while the neck, which is thick out of all proportion, is nearly bare. The last-mentioned peculiarity detracts from the otherwise graceful outlines of its body, the more so perhaps from its head being so finely shaped and small. The horns are nearly straight, rough and ringed for about three inches from their base, and then taper away, smooth and polished, to an almost invisible point; they vary from nine inches to a foot long, and from the way in which they are set on the skull, the immense strength in the neck and shoulders of the animal, and their extreme sharpness, form about as formidable weapons as could well be imagined, especially as their owner is the most plucky antelope, without exception or consideration of size, with which I have become acquainted in Africa. I do not think that in all my experience, and I dare say that I have killed not far short of a hundred of them, I remember a single instance in which an nkonka has not tried to charge when wounded and brought to bay, and no one, even after a very moderate experience, would ever allow any dog on which he placed any value to attack them.

On one occasion I had a narrow escape from one at which I had fired. I was out buck-shooting, having with me about a dozen natives to act as beaters and one hunter, and after unsuccessfully trying several places we came to a large jungle known to contain all the different species of bush buck, as well as an immense number of baboons and monkeys, and, report said, probably truly, one or two leopards. It was, however, far too extensive for us to attempt to beat it all out, and we selected a long, but narrow strip which ran out from the main jungle as more suited to our numbers. The spot chosen by me as a station was a clearing in the bush about half a mile from where the beaters went in, and which divided the jungle into two parts. It had originally been the same as the rest, but had been cleared some few years back by the natives as a maize garden, who had now, after exhausting the soil, permitted the scrub which covered it to the height of some three feet to grow up. It was on the slope of a very steep hill, and as the best pass, being near the bottom, did not command the upper portion, I sent the hunter above me. For some time after our arrival everything remained quiet, the silence only broken by an occasional shout from the beaters; but at last the dogs that accompanied them began to give tongue, and it was evident from their notes that several head of game must be on foot. The antelopes seemed to be circling about, doubling on their pursuers, and unwilling to break cover, but after some minutes I heard a slight rustle in front, and a second afterwards a little blue buck, having succeeded in throwing the dogs out, stole along the path which I was watching. From the height of the underbrush it was necessarily very near before I saw it, or could fire, so that when I did so it dropped lifeless on the spot, and before reloading I removed its body from the path for fear that its presence there might turn anything else that came that way. Suddenly, while loading, I heard a great uproar in the jungle below, and was warned by shouts of "nkonka enhla" that one of the great bush bucks was coming our way.

I could hear the dogs in full cry after it, and hurried on my loading to the uttermost, and just as I placed the cap on, a red buck, breaking out with one of those tremendous rushes for which these antelopes are famous, and which so often makes the hunter think that he has something larger to deal with, almost brushed past me, so taking me by surprise, for I had thought that it was the nkonka, that I missed it clean. Half a second afterwards my hunter fired a shot from the top of the bank, and as he did so I saw the head and horns of the nkonka appear over the brushwood, about thirty yards above me, making at full speed for the jungle beyond. Wheeling round I got the gun up and covered it, aiming through the low scrub for where I considered that his shoulder ought to be, and when the smoke cleared the animal had disappeared. At that instant two of the dogs came up to me, attracted by the shot, and as I thought that I might have wounded it, I climbed up the bank with them without delaying to load, in order to put them on the scent while it was still quite fresh. The ascent was nearly perpendicular, and I had some difficulty in reaching the spot. Just as I did so the two dogs ran forward, and instantly I saw the head of the nkonka rise out of the underbrush, and springing to its legs, the brute charged straight at me. I was certainly not three yards off, and my gun was empty. Dodging was impossible, and I had only time to club my otherwise useless weapon, and, bringing it round with a swing, to strike the antelope on the side of its head, the force of the blow unfortunately breaking the stock of the gun, which, as it happened, did not belong to me. As I did this I half lost my balance and fell forward

ANECDOTES OF ANTELOPES.

across the animal, but luckily the blow had made it swerve, and one of its horns, instead of coming in contact with my body, merely made a long scratch on my leg. At this second the hunter above me fired, placing me in greater danger from his bullet than I was already in. Fortunately the man was a first-rate shot, and it struck the antelope in the haunch, and drove lengthways right through the body, causing the blood to spurt out all over me as the beast sprang down, and after an unavailing effort to keep its legs, fell lifeless just below me. The natives, who had come up by this time, were much frightened when they saw me all smeared with blood, and the long tear in my clothes where the horn had entered, and would not at first believe that I had escaped with a mere scratch. On examining the dead nkonka we found that my first bullet had passed clean through the neck above the withers, and had temporarily stunned it, the teeth of the dogs, no doubt, first restoring it to consciousness.

I do not think that fatal accidents, except to dogs, often happen in the pursuit of this antelope, formidable as it undoubtedly is. Only one has ever occurred within my personal knowledge, though another of a somewhat similar nature, but of which, however, I do not know the exact details, happened during a hunt on a sugar plantation on the coast of Natal, the victim in that case being a Kaffir. I was an eye-witness of the one to which I have referred, though the distance at which I was rendered me unable to afford any assistance to the unfortunate man. I was staying at the time with a planter, who, though he had been but a short time in Africa, was a keen sportsman, as well as a capital shot. His bungalow was nearly surrounded with dense jungle, except on one side, where a large clearing had recently been made for the purpose of planting coffee, and which was as yet a mass of fallen trees and branches awaiting the time when it should be sufficiently dry to be burnt and give place to the coffee-plants. This jungle was swarming with leopards, which were so bold that they used to come almost every night and prowl round the bungalow, carrying off any dog that might be sleeping in the verandah, as well as every fowl that was allowed to remain out. My friend A. had already fired at two from the windows, one of which was killed, and the other, as could be seen from his blood-marked trail, severely wounded; but the brutes were such a nuisance that at last he got some large double-springed steel traps, with which on my arrival he had succeeded in catching two more of them. One morning, shortly afterwards, he asked me to go round the traps with him, saying that, besides the chance of finding a leopard or an antelope in them, we were pretty certain to get a shot at some of the latter on the way, and I, of course, at once consented. The first three traps were, I found, set round the carcase of a goat, and had been undisturbed, though the bait had been there so long that no leopard within a reasonable distance could have failed to become aware of its presence. A. told me that he had resorted to a dead bait, which had however been, so far, unsuccessful, on account of the leopards succeeding on several occasions in killing and carrying off the live ones, without springing the traps, but that he thought that merely setting the traps in the paths they frequent without any bait was a better plan, as all that he had killed had been caught in that way. We then set off to examine the other trap, but on getting to the place we found it gone. His short experience had already sufficed to teach my companion that if a trap was attached to an immoveable weight, the leopard or antelope, as the case might be, generally succeeded in drawing out its foot; sometimes even leaving it in, and escaping with its loss; he therefore had wisely adopted the plan of securing it to an oval piece of iron-wood, the great weight of which rendered it impossible for the animal caught to go far, while its shape secured that it should always so far yield to its efforts to free itself that there was no fear of the limb giving way.

A few moments' inspection of the ground served to inform us that it was an nkonka with which we had to deal, and the way in which the ground was torn up, and the marks upon the trees, showed how furious his struggles had been. The trail left by the weight he dragged behind him was easily followed, though we did so quietly and cautiously, hoping to see him first and to wound him mortally before his struggles should render the task more difficult. A. was leading, and after going fifty or sixty yards down a slight incline, he suddenly pulled up and exclaimed "By Jove! what a sell!" "Why, what's the matter?" I asked, and on peering over his shoulder I saw the empty trap lying a few yards in front, with the wooden weight closely jammed between the projecting roots of a tree. Our first impulse was merely to reset the trap and then turn homewards, but curiosity having tempted me to examine the antelope track, I at once noticed that it was dead lame, and even if its fore-leg was not broken it was at least evidently unable to put it to the ground. On communicating the fact to A., who was still employed in loosing the trap, we decided to follow it up, and the task of tracking it having fallen to me, as the more experienced, we at once proceeded. It had gone steadily forward for nearly half a mile, until, on reaching a detached piece of jungle, overlooking and partially surrounded by the clearing, it had turned off at an angle and entered it. It being almost certain that when disturbed it would retrace its steps and make for the main jungle, we decided that A. should remain here, while I followed it in, and in a few minutes, despite all my precaution in advancing quietly, I heard it breaking to my left, and a second afterwards a shot from A., and then his voice shouting, "Look out, it's coming back to you." I, in consequence, kept myself quiet, and before long heard it crashing through the bushes in my direction, but owing to the thickness of the cover, I could only get a snap shot at it as it passed. Judging from the sound, I thought it would probably break cover below me, and crossing part of the clearing enter one of the jungles beyond, so I hurried out, and arrived in time to see it some distance below me, striking across as I had expected. Some of A.'s men were employed here in cutting up and heaping the felled forest for burning, and their attention having been attracted by the shots, they saw the antelope, and several of them rushed forward to turn it. One man, a coolie, was conspicuous; he was considerably ahead of the others, and was waving his turban and shouting, and by dint of hard running he managed to head the brute, which, however, instead of swerving, kept straight on, and almost instantly a wild shriek, and his falling to the ground, announced that it had charged and gored him. A., from his prominent position, had, as well as myself, been able to see everything that happened, and I had hardly pushed my way through the group of coolies and Kaffirs who surrounded the unfortunate man, before he joined us. The brute had gored him right through the abdomen, and his bowels were protruding in such a fashion as to tell us that there could be but little hope of his recovery. A. however at once sent off a man with orders to despatch the horse-keeper for the nearest doctor, and a litter having been extemporized from the branches which strewed the ground, the man was carried to the lines. After this had taken place, A. said that he hardly liked to go after the antelope again while his man's life hung in the balance, but that there was no reason why I should not; indeed, that he thought that the men would take it ill if no attempt was made to avenge their companion, and that I might take as many of them with me as chose to go. One or two of the coolies, of whom, however, there were not more than a dozen altogether, offered to accompany me, but as they are, unless trained Shikaris, utterly useless for such work as we had before us, I preferred taking three or four of the Kaffirs.

In my hurry to reach the wounded man I had only preserved an indistinct idea of the direction taken by the nkonka, and it was no easy task, although I was ably assisted by the natives, to track him among the fallen trees and branches, and it took us some hours before we finally traced him into the jungle in which he had taken refuge. It was but a narrow strip, not thirty yards wide, and not more than a hundred yards long, lining a steep bank overhanging a stream, on the other side of which the ground was open. I then asked the Kaffirs whether they had any objection to go in and drive the brute out, pointing out to them that, although both in front and across the brook there were jungles sufficiently large for him to make for, yet it was all open in the direction from which he had come, and that therefore there could be but little fear of his attempting to break back in spite of them, and as they at once consented to try, I went forward and took up such a position that I could command a shot whether the animal crossed the brook or came straight on. But a few seconds elapsed after the men had entered before I heard the bushes breaking, although the animal was evidently not going fast, and then the sound ceased, apparently but a few yards from where I stood concealed. I instantly guessed the real truth: he was standing, as they often do, on the very verge of the thicket, uncertain whether it would be necessary for him to break, but the shouts of the men getting louder and nearer, it at last sprang out at the slow gallop which constitutes their ordinary pace, and passed me within fifteen yards; upon which I fired right and left with s.s.g., and dropped him on the spot. He turned out to be an old animal, with horns worn almost to a needle point, and his great neck scarred with innumerable marks of conflicts with others of his species. The man whom he had so seriously injured lingered for a couple of days, though from the moment the doctor saw him no hopes were entertained of his recovery.

Of all the antelopes preyed upon by the leopard there is none from which it meets with such determined resistance as this. Two sights which it has never fallen to my lot to witness have been described to me, by those who have been more fortunate, as being very grand,—a fight between two old nkonkas in the breeding season, and between an nkonka and a leopard. A hunter of mine shot two of the former while actually fighting, they having, in their preoccupation, allowed him to get within a few yards, and when the first dropped the other continued to charge the body, and ultimately fell within a yard of its adversary. I saw them half an hour afterwards, and both were horribly cut and scarred all over the fore part of the body.

One day, while engaged in improving a track across a stream so that our waggon might get over, I had occasion to send one of the natives who were working with me into the adjoining bush to cut a stout pole to aid us in removing an obstructing stone. A minute or two afterwards I heard him shout, and being only able to catch the word "nkonka," I took my gun and went in to see what was the matter. Within a few yards of the water was a precipice of some height, under which there was a considerable space of bare ground; here the native was kneeling down, examining something. As I got nearer I saw that the ground was deeply indented with hoof-marks, and in some places torn up, while fragments of hair and spots moistened with blood bore witness to some terrible struggle; this was continued for several yards, and I noticed that the trunks of the trees about were much scratched, and also marked with blood. The mute evidences of what had taken place there early that morning, while the baboons peered down upon the conflict from the precipice above, and shrieked and yelled out their hatred of the leopard, were plain enough without the body of the nkonka, as I now perceived it to be, over which the native was bending. The struggle must have been terrific; no doubt the great cat had sprung on its victim unawares, but it must have been thrown off almost immediately afterwards, and repulsed again and again by the antelope before it succeeded in killing it. The marks on the latter told their own tale: there was a line on the haunches where it had probably been first seized, and the whole of its shoulders and the lower part of its neck were simply torn to pieces, while four deep marks in the latter part showed how the death-wound had been administered. I wondered how that leopard felt as he stood there victorious in the cool grey of early morning, and was in the act of turning away rather disgusted with the sight, when the native called me, and showed me that one of the horns was dyed with blood up to the very forehead, and on examining it I found several of the leopard's hairs which had adhered to it, leaving no doubt whatever but that it also was severely wounded.

Having heard and seen too much of these carnivora to care to follow a wounded one up in jungle without the assistance of a dog, I sent the Kaffir back to the waggon to fetch two that were there, and to call some of the hunters who were with it, in the meanwhile drawing the bullets with which my gun was loaded, and replacing them with slugs. However, all my precautions were useless, as the dogs bayed a flat-topped rock above them, not fifty yards from where the nkonka lay dead, and there we found the still warm body of its adversary, stretched out in a position so exactly resembling sleep,

ANECDOTES OF ANTELOPES.

that, in spite of its taking no notice of our shouts, it was not until three or four stones had struck it that we believed that it was really dead. The antelope's horn had entered under the point of the shoulder, and penetrated directly into the vitals.

The nkonka is one of the few of the small antelopes which I have never killed right and left. I once, however, shot one with its consort in that way. I and my Kaffir attendant were returning home after being at a native hunting party, and while going along a ridge I suddenly saw an nkonka walk out of a large strip of jungle below us, and, after standing about for a few minutes, go into a clump of bushes about a hundred yards from it. Feeling sure that the instant it was disturbed it would return the way it came, I at once sent the native round to come above it, and then going through the jungle, I passed out into the open and concealed myself behind a cabbage-tree. In a few minutes the advancing Kaffir roused the buck, which cantered leisurely down, and passed under the shade of the very tree under which I was standing, falling dead just beyond, shot through the shoulder. As I fired, an imbabala jumped up out of the grass, where it had been lying, about thirty yards off, and instantly wheeling, I fired a snap-shot at it with my second barrel, and on going up to the place we found her also dead.

Of the other two species inhabiting the jungles, the red buck (*Cephalopus Natalensis*) is the larger, and also the least common. It is, as its name denotes, of a light yellowish red colour, mingled with grey on the lower parts, and its chief peculiarity is a tuft of hair growing out of the forehead, which gives a curious appearance to the hornless does, while it partially conceals the small horns of the bucks. Its flesh is anything but good, and it is difficult to shoot from the tremendous rushes it makes when disturbed. So fast and heedlessly does it run, that I once saw a buck that had passed me while I was loading entangle itself in a mass of creepers, from which, despite its struggles, it was unable to escape until I released it with the help of my knife. It was quite uninjured, and I kept it in confinement for some weeks, but, like most antelopes when caught full-grown, it ultimately pined away and died.

Of all game found in Africa, the little blue buck, or Pete (*Perpusilla*), is the most common; and it is very doubtful whether they have even decreased in numbers, as most of the jungles on the coast of Natal are perfectly alive with them, despite the way in which they have been shot down by the whites and extirpated by the immense native hunting parties.

It is, I suppose, the smallest antelope in the world, being considerably less as well as much lighter than a hare, and it is a beautiful little animal, its colour being a bluish mouse, and having tiny straight horns scarcely peeping over the little tuft of hair on its forehead, while it has the most graceful and delicate limbs imaginable. It feeds principally on certain berries and shrubs found growing in the jungles, and seems to be on the move, more or less, the whole day, though, in common with the rest of the animal creation, it is most often to be seen at early morning and evening.

Perhaps the most enjoyable method of hunting them is to steal about in the dense jungle—noiselessly, of course, or you will not see a single one—and shoot them as they patter about among the dead leaves which strew the game-paths, or catch them while feeding on some favourite bush. In this way you may not only kill several, but you will see the recesses of an African forest when the varieties of its shade and shadow are especially beautiful, and you are continually passing through the most lovely spots, which would never otherwise be seen. Nothing can be more pleasant than so stealing along in the cool of early dawn among the enormous trunks of the yellow-wood trees, from whose far-off tops monkeys silently peer down to watch you, having first so concealed themselves among the dense foliage, that you can scarcely distinguish them—they have a most wonderful power of hiding, even in trees comparatively open,—and where great baboons almost deafen you with their hoarse bark of alarm, mingled with defiance; but though a very delightful way, it is also an extremely difficult one to succeed in, especially to shoe-wearing Europeans.

Natives can, and do, attain to absolute noiselessness, so to speak, as do also a few whites who have learned young, and have been apt pupils; but very generally people come back after an hour or two, and declare that jungles well known to be teeming with game do not contain a single antelope. Of course, if you are heard, even by the birds, the alarm will spread, and you will see nothing, and in jungles so dense that for twenty yards at a time you are forced to crawl on your hands and knees it really is difficult never to rustle a leaf or break a dry twig. For this reason it is a very common plan to start an hour or two before the usual time, and after finding a well-trodden path, or a shrub bearing their favourite berries, to sit and watch for them a few yards off. You need not even be concealed if you remain perfectly still, as all bush antelopes seem to possess curiosity to such a degree that even after noticing you and making their shrill whistle of questioning fear, they will come nearer and nearer if you do not move, until you could almost touch them with your gun. This is more remarkably noticeable with the red buck already mentioned, which has actually walked up to within a yard of me, and stood staring and stamping its foot, seemingly unable to make out whether I was a stump or what. Of course, the wind has much to do with it, and the eddies caused by the trees, especially if there be but a slight breeze, render it exceedingly difficult to choose the best position to lie in wait in.

It has often struck me what capital sport might be had among these tiny antelopes with a few couple of beagles, and what a pretty sight it would be to watch them hunting their quarry round and round in the circle it would be sure to take. I have many times seen them hunted with packs of Kaffir dogs, but on no occasion did they break cover, unless for a few yards on their way into another jungle, their small size enabling them with ease to twist and double in and out of what to their pursuers are almost impenetrable thickets, thus rendering it their principal object to retain the shelter of the jungle. Many of these, in which pete abound, are not more than six or eight acres in extent, and therefore two or three people stationed inside would see the greater part of the run, even if, as in many places would be possible, they could not follow the hounds sufficiently fast to keep them in view. It would be well worth the while of any one going to South Africa, whether for shooting alone, or as a settler, to take two or three couple of these miniature hounds with them, if only for the sport they might have in pete-hunting.

Five distinct species of antelopes inhabit the open country, though, perhaps, it might be more correct to say that they are not found in the forests; namely, the oribi and steinbuck, the Vaal raebuck and klipspringer, and the reed buck. The two first of these exist on the treeless plains, the former preferring the flatter and more unbroken parts where the grass is short, the latter lying in the broken water-courses, on the ridges where the vegetation is luxuriant, and generally in such positions as it finds most sheltered and concealed. The oribi, which I have already spoken of as possessing a wonderful turn of speed, and being one of the swiftest antelopes in Africa, affords very fair shooting. Its peculiar colour so much resembles the soil on which it lies that, trusting to remain unobserved, it often allows you to get within fifteen or twenty yards of where it is squatting. It is a handsome and peculiarly graceful antelope, extremely good eating, and well worth the hunter's attention. One thing he should bear in mind is, that however slightly they may be wounded they will go and lie down within a few hundred yards if not chased by a dog, and will in such cases very generally allow him to get within shot again.

The steinbuck is a far smaller antelope, resembling the red buck in point of size, and though in some places fair bags may be made of them, they hide themselves so very carefully that they are hardly worth the labour of looking for. The late Mr. Leslie and I killed nine one afternoon in Zululand, besides several "knorhaan," but the spot had probably never been shot before, and we had both beaters and dogs, and on the very same ground not nine months afterwards I only saw one. They are very easily run down by moderately fast dogs, and on the whole I think that they may be classed with the red buck, as affording least sport among all the smaller antelopes.

The Vaal raebuck and the klipspringer (literally, the "rock-jumper") both inhabit mountainous, broken districts; the former being found on all the stony bare hills of the uplands, while the latter is confined to the most precipitous spots on the mountain ranges. The first has already been described, and it will be sufficient to say here that if a hunter desires to perfect himself in the art of stalking on bare hilly ground, these antelopes will afford him the very best practice. The klipspringer is a small grey antelope, its skin being of a remarkable and very beautiful grey, and in all points, except that of personal appearance, it is a miniature chamois. It lives in places all but inaccessible to the most daring hunter, and possesses power of springing among rocks and precipitous ledges only surpassed by the Alpine antelope. It is far from common, and unless especially sought for may remain unseen during a long sojourn in the country. The only part of Natal in which I have personally found it is the Quathlamba or Drachensberg range, and, beyond the limits of the colony, in the precipitous faces of the Bombo mountains.

"THE LARGEST AND FINEST OF THEM IS THE REED-BUCK".

ANECDOTES OF ANTELOPES.

Last, and perhaps most common of all, as well as without doubt the largest and finest of them, is the reed-buck (*Eleotragus arundinaceus*), males of which not unfrequently weigh thirteen or fourteen stone. Their colour also is grey, though of a lighter tinge than that of the last mentioned, very old cows appearing to be almost white; the horns, only carried by the males, being slightly curved and placed well back upon the head, and their general appearance being graceful in the extreme, though slightly detracted from in the case of does by the length of their ears, one of the weakest points of the antelope genus. They frequent reedy, damp bottoms, where the vegetation is rank, and in summer-time such spots on the hill-sides as afford good shelter and are at the same time dry and cool. Reed-buck shooting is, I consider, the most pleasant of any, without considering the fact that a fat doe of that species is probably the best eating of all the smaller antelopes. The winter season is the best, as the grass being then much burnt off, they principally lie in the bottoms which from their dampness and consequent greenness have been able to resist the action of the fire. These bottoms exist in parallel lines between the long undulating ridges which form much of the coast-land of Natal, and average from ten to sixty yards broad. Three men are all that are necessary to beat the ground for two guns, as when the reeds are broad and thick the antelopes lie on the edges on either side, rarely going inside, and with that number I used to go out accompanied by a friend on almost every day for about six weeks, rarely coming home without one or two head at the least. Our best bag on a single day was five reed-buck, one duiker, and a monkey, the latter of which I tasted out of curiosity, and found it not unlike chicken.

The two antelopes that principally inhabit thickets and thorn scrub are the duiker and the roi raebuck. The former, a small grey animal, may be found concealed in almost every clump of bush or patch of long grass on the coast, and in the upland thorn districts. It lies very close, and is often difficult to see as it rushes away through the long grass, though fortunately it cannot go far without springing into the air and affording a shot. It is perhaps more usually met with than any other antelope, and in my own game-book its name appears in the ratio of about three to one of any other species. They have straight sharp horns, resembling those of an oribi though not so long; and when wounded and brought to bay will sometimes make the most determined rushes at their pursuer, and inflict severe wounds with them. Of course, this does not occur often, and only on one occasion has one of these little animals dared to turn upon me. It had been put out of a bush about forty yards off, and I fired right and left at it as it ran across me, missing with the first barrel, loaded with shot, and breaking both its fore-legs just below the knee with the bullet I had in my second. On seeing from its peculiar running that I had wounded it, and having no dog, I gave chase as fast as I could, and after two or three hundred yards, overtook it; the instant it saw that it could not escape it wheeled round and came straight at me, to my no small astonishment at such a little animal daring to charge, but as it came right on, and my gun was empty, and as for the life of me I could not make up my mind to run away from such an insignificant antagonist, I had no choice but to club the gun and deal it a blow on the head, which stunned it, but at the same time broke the stock, an accident of no small importance in a country where the nearest gun-maker is very possibly five hundred miles off, and will probably charge you as much as would suffice in these days of cheap muzzle-loaders to buy the gun outright.

The duiker is also, among the small antelopes, by far the most tenacious of life, and I remember one that displayed that quality in a remarkable degree. Accompanied by two or three Kaffirs, I was driving a small piece of jungle, which was so thick that, except in the very spot where I was standing, I could not see a yard any way, and while waiting here a duiker came out and rushed past me within five yards; I had a heavy charge of s.s.g. in and five drachms of powder behind it, and without putting the gun to my shoulder—for there was no time to do so—I merely held it out at arm's length, so that the muzzle could not have been many feet from the animal's body, and fired. It did not, however, fall to the shot, but ran down the hill some seventy or eighty yards, where one of the Kaffirs caught and killed it. On following its track down I was never more astonished in my life, as the shot had made an enormous hole six or eight inches in diameter, and the vitality that could run seventy yards afterwards, and then had to be killed, must be accounted as something wonderful.

The roi raebuck, though inhabiting thorn districts, prefers such as are on stony and broken ground. It is a fine large antelope, but little smaller than the reed-buck, to which it bears a marked resemblance, though its colour is, as its name implies, of a redder tinge. It is far from common, even in those spots it most frequents, and though well worth shooting is too rare to afford much sport.

Among the smaller animals there are one or two that deserve a passing notice, although not belonging to the antelope genus. Ant-eaters, porcupines, rock-rabbits, and cane-rats are all common in different localities. The ant-eater, like the white ant on which it lives, is found everywhere, but being a nocturnal prowler is very rarely seen, although evidences of its presence occur every few yards in the shape of half-formed holes in the ground, seemingly made for no purpose whatever, and holes in the sides of the ant-hills. I once saw one while shooting on an open flat in Swaziland; the half-bred pointer that was with me was ranging rather widely when it suddenly came to a dead point, but almost immediately afterwards began to draw in. I shouted to it, and ran towards it as fast as I could, but it paid no attention to me, and in another second an animal which I did not recognise, but which from its rounded back and general appearance looked like some kind of pig, jumped up out of the grass before it, and after being smartly chased for a couple of hundred yards took refuge in one of the numerous holes which covered the plain. On my reaching the spot I at once saw by the marks of its five-toed foot that it was an ant-eater, and as I had never seen one before I determined to get this one out. I first tried smoking it out, getting great bundles of grass and shoving them down the mouth of the hole, and after setting fire to them, placing my coat over the outside to prevent the smoke escaping.

It was no good, however, though, as the hole was shallow, the atmosphere inside must have been something awful, and I distinctly heard the beast choking once or twice. On seeing that it would not bolt I sent off the Kaffir who was with me to the waggon for another man and two spades, and after clearing the entrance to the hole, I sat down out of sight myself, hoping that it might bolt when everything was quiet; but before the Kaffir had been long gone I heard it commence scraping instead, evidently preferring to go further in than to risk coming out, and for the two hours during which I had to wait the sound never ceased. As soon as the men came with spades I started them to work, but after half an hour we saw that unless we hit upon some better plan than digging behind it it would be dark before we overtook it, if, indeed, we did so at all; so, after listening carefully to hear where it was at work, I made the men sink a perpendicular shaft about a yard in front, and after an hour's work the animal, hearing the spades within a few inches of its nose, turned round and at last came out, when I shot it. A most curious animal it looked as it lay dead, with its long thin tongue protruding from the toothless jaws, its bat-like ears, and its pig-like skin, which is so thick that shot will hardly penetrate it, covered with a few bristles. Its tail was a short flat hairless stump, and its tremendous claws set on limbs which were a mass of muscle, seemed as if they would be, as report stated they were, dangerous weapons to encounter at close quarters. I tasted its flesh, but it was strong-smelling and as tough as leather, and it is only its skin that is of any value, being, when properly dressed, superior to the best pig-skin.

Porcupines also are common enough in many places, and going out at night after them with dogs, spears, and torches is a favourite amusement of the colonists; but personally I do not think it can be compared to cane-rat hunting. This animal, one of the greatest pests of the African sugar-planter, takes its name from its strong resemblance to a huge rat. It is, however, a rodent, subsisting entirely on reeds and jungle-grass, and where there is cultivation making great havoc among the canes and maize-gardens. In shape it resembles the animal after which it is called, though its head is rounder, and its tail looks as if it had been docked, and a male will often weigh nine or ten lbs. Its body is covered over with coarse bristles, which in colour and appearance are not unlike those of the porcupine, though not more than an inch long. Several varieties, if not distinct species, exist in different parts of the continent, and have been noticed by various travellers, that mentioned by Schweinfurth[1] as existing in Central Africa appearing, from the web on its hind-feet and the rat-like length of its tail, to deserve the latter name. As food, he says, it "is excellent when roasted; it is rich, and without being sweet and insipid like that of the rock-rabbit, it is free from any unpleasant flavour; in quality it is about equal to poultry, whilst in taste it may be described as being intermediate between pork and veal." Skertchly[2] also speaks of the variety found on the west coast as being a "dainty addition to an African bill of fare;" but the animal inhabiting South Africa is by no means so much appreciated, few Europeans eating it, and the natives, though they do not waste it, caring but little for it. The truth is, that the old ones,

---

[1] *Heart of Africa*, vol. ii. p. 448.   [2] *Dahomey as it is*, p. 124.

especially of the male sex, are somewhat rank, though I have frequently eaten and enjoyed young does. They should be roasted like a sucking-pig, the bristles scalded off, and the skin, which is the best part, allowed to remain. They do not form burrows of their own; but when forced out of the thick tangle of overgrown grass or reeds in which they lie—a task by no means easy of accomplishment,—they take refuge in any hole or crevice among rocks or stones, or in the deserted burrows of the ant-eater or porcupine. They are, as I have said, not only destructive to a degree among sugar-cane, gnawing down stem after stem, but most difficult to extirpate, so much so that on many plantations 6d. or even 1s. per head is offered for every one killed. In spots such as these they live in what fields happen to be lying fallow, and which, being covered with an impenetrable thicket of grass and weeds, offer them a secure retreat from which they can nightly issue forth into the canes. It so happened that I had a tiny little smooth terrier, whose great delight was hunting these brutes; and as from his size he was able to follow them through the runs they made under the grass, he was most effective in forcing them out, sometimes succeeding in a few minutes after half-a-dozen larger dogs and a lot of men had tried for hours in vain. The consequence was that wherever cane-rats were doing mischief in my neighbourhood, whether in a native maize-garden or in a sugar-plantation, a petition came for the loan of my dog, and when I had nothing better to do I often accompanied it.

When it was to a plantation that I went where the damage done had become serious, and the planter had in consequence vowed destruction to the whole race, I generally found that their strongholds, the fallow fields, had been divided into small squares round which narrow paths had been chopped, and that all hands had for that day been taken away from their other employments, while there was generally a contingent of Kaffirs from the nearest kraals on the look-out for the bounty offered.

Everybody, European or native, would be armed with spears, for besides the little chance there was of getting a shot, and the danger of shooting a man or a dog, the risk of firing the cane, especially as people generally used paper instead of wads, was sufficient to prevent guns being used. The plot would then be surrounded, a line of men with poised spears standing in each of the cut pathways, and the dogs would be turned in. My little terrier used to immediately disappear under the grass, from which he would not again emerge until wearied out, though his shrill yelp could continually be heard, and before long he would force the cane-rat out, while the big dogs would dart about making pounces at places where the scent was strong, though, except by the noise and confusion they caused, they in no way aided in making the unwilling animal break cover. When at last it did so, it was as often as not only to be missed by the nearest spearman, and to take refuge in the next patch, where the operation had to be repeated. In this way a dozen or more were often killed, but they were never more than thinned, and a fallow cane-field was at all times a certain find.

Better fun was to be had in the autumn after the first grass-fires had taken place, and large patches were still left unconsumed near the native maize-gardens. The tangle was less thick, and the numerous open spaces gave a better chance of taking aim, besides sometimes enabling the larger dogs to catch the animal, which would often scuttle from patch to patch, escaping our spears, and ultimately take refuge in some fastness under a rock or big stone, from whence if possible it was dug out. It was generally advisable, too, to have a boy close behind you with a gun, as we often put up duiker, and sometimes a reed-buck, while it was seldom that I came home without a brace or two of partridges.

GROUP OF OSTRICHES.

CHAPTER IX.

GAME BIRDS.

PERHAPS one of the greatest charms of African shooting is the immense variety it offers, and though in the large-game districts bird-shooting is not of much consequence, yet, as it is one of the chief resources while the long journey to and from them is being made, it well deserves some notice.

The ostrich among birds holds the same position that the elephant does among quadrupeds, and like it, is being rapidly exterminated. This, however, is not of so much consequence in its case; for, besides only being valuable for its feathers, it has already been domesticated, and ostrich-farming has become a recognised industry in the eastern province of the Cape Colony. Shy and wary in the extreme, and principally frequenting the great treeless plains and deserts in the north, it is a bird that affords but little sport to the hunter, seldom offering him a shot, and requiring an unusually fast horse to ride it down, and having mentioned its name, I will at once pass on to those more likely to be met with, and therefore more deserving of notice.

Next in size to these giants comes the pauw, a species of bustard. Under this name, which was given by the Dutch colonists, and means peacock—to which bird, however, it does not bear the faintest resemblance—are included three well-defined species, viz., *Eupodis cristata*, *E. caffra*, and *E. Ludwigii*. The former, commonly called the crested pauw, from the immense top-knot it carries, is of great size, some specimens even weighing as much as fifty pounds, and measuring from fifty-six to sixty inches. They are not common, being seldom, if ever, seen in the more populous districts, and only found in sparse numbers in the spots they most frequent, which are generally districts dotted over with thin and scattered thorn-trees. The most that I have ever killed in a day is five, and four out of that number were scarcely full-grown birds. Shot I found of little use; but as they will often allow one to get within fifty yards, their great size renders them easy marks, even when a bullet is used. Mr. Layard, indeed, when speaking of the common pauw (*E. caffra*), mentions having killed them with No. 7 shot, but the following extract from my journal will show that my experience has been very different, as regards the larger species at least :—" I got a shot at a crested pauw to-day, a cock bird. He would not rise at first, but kept running before me about twenty-five yards off, till by quickening my pace I forced him to use his wings, and as he cleared the ground I gave him the whole charge in the back at certainly not more than twenty yards. The effect was merely to stagger him a little, and to knock out a cloud of feathers, and to my astonishment he flew away quite strongly." The charge used was buckshot (S.S.G.), with four drachms of powder, fired out of a close-shooting gun of 10-bore. The only way in which I have succeeded in killing these birds with shot has been by getting very close, and then aiming at their heads, and under those circumstances only can I understand No. 7 shot proving fatal.

E. caffra, the common upland pauw, is much smaller, rarely reaching to twenty-five pounds, and averaging eighteen to twenty-three pounds. It is found all over the larger table-lands in small flocks of from three to six, though more generally seen in pairs, and is considerably shyer than the former, seldom allowing you to walk within a hundred yards of it, and when much shot at not within three times that distance, though, being more common, it affords the most sport of any of the three kinds. Frequenting the opens, and from its height and length of neck being able to see over the grass, it is difficult to stalk on foot, and the most usual method is to shoot it from horseback. Like others of the bustard tribe, it often resorts to squatting, under the impression that it has not been noticed, especially when resort is had to the artifice of riding one's horse round it in a convergent circle, and in this way shots are often obtained within thirty or forty yards. It is often able, however, to carry off the charge, but as it is a heavy and slow flyer, it is generally possible by hard riding to keep it in sight and to mark it down, when the same operation is repeated, though it often takes four or five shots before falling. Shooting them on foot with the rifle is, I think, prettier work, as shots can usually be obtained within a hundred yards, and the bird cannot go far with a bullet through it. In either way though three or four are often killed in the day, particularly on the upland flats, where they are most numerous.

E. Ludwigii is hardly to be distinguished from the last mentioned, except in size, measuring some six inches more, or about forty-four inches, or forty-six inches, and by its only frequenting the coast. All these species possess the same habits and mode of living: stalking over the flats in search of locusts and small snakes; forming a very rude nest on the ground, often nothing more than is caused by their sitting in the long grass; laying two eggs of considerable size, and leading their young about as soon as hatched.

Besides the three above mentioned there are several different kinds of bustard to be found—as many as eight having been mentioned by some naturalists,—but they all so strongly resemble each other in their general appearance and habits, that to describe one is to describe all. They are colonially known as "knorhaan," literally, scolding cock, and are scattered all over Eastern and Central Africa, different species existing on the uplands and open plains, and in the thorn-jungle, though they are not, as far as I know, found in any of the heavy timber forests. They are handsome birds, with long legs and necks, weighing from four to six pounds, the cocks, especially, having very fine plumage, and they are easily identified by the unscientific observer by their all having but three toes. In favourite places—and such places are to be found wherever one may go—they are very numerous, and with a good dog one may kill from seven to ten brace during the heat of the day. At early dawn and evening they may be heard uttering the cry from which they take their name, and are then to be seen moving about over the plains in search of food; but at such times they are next to impossible to approach, as their long necks give them every advantage in observing coming danger, and they will run like greyhounds for several hundred yards, and then rise wild; but under the mid-day sun they become quite another bird; you may then walk over them, and if you do not absolutely tread upon them they will not rise, and this renders it impossible to find them without the assistance of a dog, the grass being so long and the ground to be beaten so extensive that it is otherwise the merest chance if one is stumbled upon. They are not difficult to kill, being slow flyers, and offering a large and easy mark, but anything under No. 4 shot would be of little use, and I should recommend and personally have always used No. 3. For the table they are unexceptionable, though, like other birds of the genus, they improve by keeping,—a thing not, however, very easy to accomplish, even in the so-called cold weather, in a tropical land. The most common and widely spread is *E. afra*, the *Otis afra* of Linnæus, and in the bush-country *Otis melangaster*, a handsome black-and-white bird, while on the up-country plains *Otis torquata* is more usually to be seen.

Closely allied to the bustard, if not absolutely one of them, is the little "dikkop," or "big-head" (*Ædicucenus maculosus*), truly spoken of by Baldwin as "the daintiest bird in Africa." To any one but a naturalist, it seems to be a miniature knorhaan, and is found, at certain seasons of the year only, for it appears to be migratory to a limited degree, on the table-lands and flats, where it can be shot in great numbers. It is easily flushed, though rarely rising out of range, and affords good sport with or without dogs. It particularly affects dry water-courses, or any slightly broken ground, in which also it generally forms its nest, as, in common with all the already mentioned birds, it lays its eggs on the bare ground, and is accompanied by its young brood as soon as they are hatched. Its colour is a pale rufous, mottled with dark brown blotches.

Among the larger birds of Africa, the wild turkey (*Geronticus cabrus*) is one of the most beautiful, as well as one of the most rare. Its colour is a dark, glossy, shining green, with a golden tinge on either shoulder, while, somewhat resembling our domesticated kind, its head and the upper part of the neck is nude of feathers, and a bright red; it has a long, slender, and slightly curved bill, with which it seizes the locusts and grasshoppers on which it principally feeds, and is a wild, shy bird, frequenting the open country, and difficult to approach, and it is but rarely that one is killed on the east coast. There is another bird which is often mistaken by the newcomer for it, a horn-bill, locally known as the "nsingisi," or snake-bird (*Bucornus Abyssinicus*). The point of resemblance is a large red bag under the head; its colour, however, is in no case bright, like that of the turkey, though of a lighter shade in young birds, but rather a dark, dull crimson, and so dark in old cocks as to nearly approach to purple. It is large, and of a blue-black colour, and one of its principal characteristics, in common with others of the same family to which it belongs, is its bill—a great serrated, crooked weapon, which it is not slow to use when wounded, and with which it destroys the snakes, lizards, etc., on which it lives. It is a dirty feeder, and after death emits an unpleasant smell, though not to the extent that is stated by Layard. It makes a loud droning noise, not unlike the sound of the Kaffir-drum, which is said to be an indication of wet weather, and it roosts and breeds in trees, the young ones not leaving the parent till the following year. The natives hold it in considerable reverence, both in the Cape Colony and Natal, believing it to be an unclean bird not unconnected with witchcraft, and one that it is most unlucky to kill. The Government of Natal, classing it with the secretary-bird as a destroyer of snakes, impose a fine of five pounds on any one taking its life, a needful precaution, as it is very common and anything but shy, and could easily be shot by any one so disposed.

Next on the list come the partridges, and the so-called pheasant; and although naturalists have discovered a wonderful number of different species of them on this continent—Smith, I think, mentions eleven kinds of francolins, and five of plerocles, while Layard has ten of the former and four of the latter—there are only three in Eastern Africa so far distinct as to deserve separate mention. These are the common red-legged partridge, called by the natives "Itendele;" a smaller kind called "Iswempe;" and the Natal pheasant (*Francolinus Natalensis*, where it is supposed to represent *F. clamator*), known as the "Inkwali." It is unnecessary to say much about the former, distributed as it is all over the world. In Africa it is found both on the plains and in the thorn jungles in sufficient quantities to afford very fair sport; twenty brace, or even more, being easily killed in many places. They never form large coveys, as our English birds do, and the young brood separates very soon after they have become independent. Horses, trained for the purpose, are generally used for shooting them, partly on account of the great extent of country which has to be gone over, necessitating very widely ranging dogs, and partly because colonial dogs are so unsteady that if they are kept long at their point, they are very apt to flush their birds.

The iswempe is a more rare and smaller bird, being about the size of a woodcock, and is found, almost exclusively, in damp rank bottoms where the grass is long, out of which it is difficult to flush them. It is very delicate eating, and therefore highly prized, though, numerically speaking, they do not afford much sport, a brace or two during a day being the average.

The inkwali is, on the contrary, an extremely fine bird, often weighing from three to four pounds, and measuring thirteen or fourteen inches, with dark mottled plumage and a brown back; being also capital eating, the flavour something resembling that of a grouse. Like others of the same genus, they are to be found in all jungle, whether forest or thorn, though they more usually frequent the former. It is difficult to flush them, as they prefer running into the nearest cover, and then squatting; and when once on the wing, they fly straight and strong, carrying away a heavy shot, and if not killed dead, they give an immense amount of trouble by the way in which they run and hide, more than two-thirds of those winged escaping when there is not a retriever at hand. When feeding about sunrise and sunset they utter a harsh cry, which renders it easy to find them, though little more than a chance shot will be got unless the sportsman be accompanied by a dog, while five or six brace will not be unusual if he is. It is utterly useless to go after them during the heat of the day, as they then retire into the shadiest and most impenetrable thicket they can find, where it is impossible to follow them. The moment the dog points, one should work up to them as rapidly as possible, so as to force them to flush, and should it be in a clump of trees, the lower branches ought to be watched, as they have a habit of hopping on to them out of reach of the dog, and composedly sitting there watching it. Their habits, like those of all francolins, much resemble those of the partridge, or, perhaps, even more so, those of the bird after which they are sometimes called,—the pheasant, to which, however, they bear no other resemblance.

There are two kinds of guinea-fowl found on the East coast, and, as they are mentioned by Layard in his catalogue of South-African birds, it is to be presumed that they are widely distributed. The first and common variety I shall not notice, as it is well known in this country; but the other (*Numida cristata*) is rare even in Africa. It is an extremely handsome bird, with a top-knot of black feathers, dark plumage mottled with blue spots, and the head and neck nude and of a bluish colour, while its throat is red; but it is so seldom seen that it affords no sport, though, as well as being a more beautiful, it is a larger and more delicate bird than the other. The latter, however, under some circumstances and in some spots, may be bagged in considerable numbers, but as a general rule they are so fleet and so shy and wary that though one may be passing through a country swarming with them, and may hear their peculiar kek, kek, kek, every morning and evening, days may often elapse without one being seen. In February and March, when the young broods are getting pretty strong, they may be treed by dogs accustomed to the work, and then are easily enough shot; and if the jungle is not too thick, and the birds at all plentiful, there should be no difficulty in killing more than one can carry. It is, however, neither a very sportsmanlike nor a very pleasant proceeding, as it must per force be done during the heat of the day, and the covers are often dense and difficult to penetrate. A far more agreeable plan is to go out during their feeding-time and stalk them, guided by their cry, and if possible to cut them off from the adjoining thickets, and if in that way one succeeds in breaking up a pack among the long grass, there is every chance of making a good bag, as they will keep on the move, squatting for a few minutes after every shot, and continually calling to each other; they may then, with the assistance of a dog, be flushed separately, and being heavy birds, slow at rising, and as easy to shoot as a pheasant, few ought to escape.

Besides the ones that I have enumerated, there are no other game birds to be found in the forests or thorns, unless it be some that from their rarity are seldom met with, and are therefore not to be counted upon for sport; but on the plains there are plovers and quails, while in some of the marshes snipe abound, and geese and ducks are to be got wherever there is water to float them. There are several varieties of plover, but the "Umbangaqua," the "Ititihoya," and the common golden species, are the most often met with. Of these, passing over the latter well-known bird with the remark that it exists far up the East coast, the Umbangaqua is most deserving of notice. It is a large bird, of a brown and reddish-white speckled colour, having a broad flat head, and a peculiar white bar across some of the wing feathers. It is found in small flocks or pairs among the broken banks of streams or dried-up water-courses, and lies close during the day, becoming wild towards dusk. It is easily killed, and is a most satisfactory bird to bag, having but few equals for the purposes of the table, and though it is not found in sufficient numbers to make it worth while to especially go out after it, yet when one happens to meet with it several couple may be killed.

The ititihoya, so called from its peculiar cry, is the most common and widely distributed of all, being found over the whole of South and Eastern Africa, and inhabiting the thorn country, as well as the treeless plains. It is much smaller than the former, and so much is lost in legs and wings that on the table it appears scarcely larger than a woodcock. There is no difficulty in shooting them, as they are far from shy; and even when fired at seldom do more than make a few circles in the air, and light again not many hundred yards off. Their cry is a loud and peculiar one, and as they do not utter it at night, unless disturbed, their voice is considered by the native hunters to be a warning that something is prowling about their camp, and, on one occasion, I became aware through it of the otherwise noiseless approach of a lion. I have personally killed but very few, though not from want of opportunity, but certainly from five to ten couple might be got on most days by any one who cared to shoot them.

Quails of two kinds are to be found, and on the upland flats and in the opens between the coast forests they afford fair sport, from ten to twenty brace being occasionally killed. The common quail (*Coturnix dactylisonans*) is somewhat rare, though arriving in considerable numbers from July to September according to locality, but they soon become scattered, and it is not usual to get more than three or four brace in a day. The smaller sort, however, which breeds in the colony of Natal, is more plentiful; and though next to impossible to flush the second time, exists in sufficient numbers to insure a respectable bag. They nearly always go in pairs, and are very partial to native footpaths or cattle tracks, along which they run till forced to rise, and no bird gives more trouble to the pointer, as, while emitting a strong scent, it keeps twisting in and out among the tufts of grass under the dog's very nose, utterly refusing to rise and be shot.

Both the common and painted snipe are not uncommon, and afford good sport in many of the low bottoms and marshes on the coast, bags of twenty-five and thirty couple not being unusual; while among the bays on the sea-shore wild-fowl of all kinds are abundant, and there is even better shooting in the small ponds and lagoons inland. There are, among others, the golden, the spur-winged, the black, and the grey goose, of which the black (*Nellapus Madagascariensis*), though black-green would be a better description, is the most common in Natal and up the east coast, while the spur-winged (*Plectropterus Gambensis*) is found further to the north.

The different species of duck are innumerable, but perhaps, besides the common yellow-billed kind (*Anas flavirostris*), the black duck (*A. sparsa*), and the tree duck (*Dendrocygna viduata*) are the two most often met with all over the east and north, the former being the most highly prized for the table; the muscovy is also pretty common, and there are widgeon and teal—the red-billed kind being the most numerous,—divers, coots, and water-rail. It is difficult to say what number of water-fowl might be killed, under favourable circumstances, during the course of a single day, but I fancy it would be very much a question of the ammunition holding out, and there hardly exists a stream where an occasional duck may not be picked up. In Zululand the black goose is often to be seen feeding in the maize-fields during early morning, sometimes not twenty yards away from the village fence. The one great necessity is a good retriever, though where there are crocodiles a boat must be used; many a wounded duck I have seen go down these insatiable brutes' throats, and they form the chief drawback to this description of shooting.

Pigeons always form a resource when everything else fails, and there are several different kinds of them. I have shot four, and a fifth, that I am not certain whether to class as a paroquet or as a pigeon, though I incline to the latter opinion. Commonest of all is the turtle-dove, found wherever there is a tree for it to perch upon, and in a land where the birds do not sing its soft cooing is one of the most pleasant sounds. Next stands the great blue rock-pigeon, a larger and far handsomer bird than the one known by the same name in this country. It is found in open, hilly districts, roosting and breeding among the rocks, and as far as I have seen never settling upon a tree. It flies in great flocks, and during harvest-time numbers may be killed in the maize and corn fields. I once got sixteen with my two barrels. Another bird, closely resembling this in plumage but found in the forests, inhabits the coast lands, though it is rare, and only occurs at intervals. There is also another little pigeon, or dove, which does not exist further south than the twenty-eighth degree of south latitude, though common higher up the coast. It is very small, scarcely half the size of a turtle-dove, with plumage of a light grey or drab colour, and a tail of several inches in length, and is a pretty little thing, very fearless, coming into the villages and picking up what it can find about the doors, even occasionally entering the huts. The bird which I above spoke of as being unable to decide its species, is commonly known as the green pigeon, and in shape, appearance, and colour exactly answers to its name, though its cry, a shrill whistle, is more characteristic of the paroquet; and were it possible for there to be a cross between the two, I should believe this to be it. It is found on the coast, its home being in the forests and in the clumps of trees which give such a park-like appearance to the more southern portion, and is sufficiently gregarious for twenty or more to take flight from a single tree. They fly wonderfully fast, and are as difficult a bird to shoot as I know, but are better eating than any of the true doves or pigeons, and are undoubtedly one of the handsomest birds in Africa.

There are still three birds remaining, which, though they cannot be classed among game—as, indeed, neither pigeons nor paroquets can—deserve mention from their value for the table. The first is a goat-sucker (*Caprimulgus Natalensis*), the native name being "Isavolo," of which the curious may find a most minutely correct plate in Smith's *Illustrations of the Natural History of South Africa*. Both in plumage and size, as well as in its mode of flying, it strongly resembles the woodcock, though when we approach the head the likeness ceases, its mouth being nearly as large and broad as the woodcock's bill is long, and being as applicable to its employment of catching flies as the latter is for boring into the ground. It was mere accident that taught me what a delicious bird it was. I had shot one when on my way home one evening, more out of curiosity to look at it than anything else, and it was taken in and sent up to dinner, and I then made the discovery, and never afterwards lost an opportunity of getting one. They are absolute pats of butter, sometimes even bursting in falling to the ground, and are, in my opinion, equal if not superior to any woodcock. They feed on flies and moths, which they catch at and after twilight, and, unless disturbed, are rarely seen during the day. According to Kaffir superstition, they are unclean birds, employed by witches for evil deeds, and are avoided accordingly, and the native shudders as he hears their soft and pleasant call in the twilight, which consists of a succession of sounds that he renders into "Come, come, come, and milk for my children," and into an invitation to its mate to come and suck their neighbours' cows, while it is curious that we should know it as the "goat-sucker." It is to be found, on the coast chiefly, in the long grass and scrub at the edge of thickets; and if such of my readers who may have the opportunity will only shoot one and taste it, I feel sure that they will not regret the experiment.

The common Cape lark (*Anthus Capensis*) is the next bird to which I would draw attention. It is capital eating, and has so strong a game-scent that the best pointer will scarcely pass it; and though they are small, yet being so very common, they are not altogether to be despised, even for the purposes of sport. Hundreds may be shot to points on any of the plains, and to a lesser degree on the more wooded coast-lands also.

Last, though by no means least in size, is the great crested crane, the Unohemu (*Balearica pavonina*). It is very large, second only to some of the bustards in size, and possesses the most beautiful plumage imaginable; its crest alone, of bristles marked with black and yellow bars standing out from a mass of the most glossy velvet down, flanked with white lobes, would be sufficiently noteworthy were the plumage of the rest of the body commonplace, and not, as it is, especially on the wings, extremely beautiful. It is a very shy and far from common bird, inhabiting the treeless districts, and seldom seen except in pairs, though I have come across small flocks of five or six; they may sometimes be heard on the uplands uttering the cry from which they take their name as they make for their roosting-place, and they are most often seen about autumn in the maize and millet fields, but if one kills half a dozen in a year it is as much as can be hoped for, though they are such good eating that no one who had once tasted them would lose a chance of doing so again.

APPENDIX I.

MAMMALS.

English or Common Name.	Kaffir or Native Name.	Scientific Name.
Aut-eater,	Isambane,	Orycteropus Æthiopicus.
Ard Wolf,	Isidawane,	Proteles cristatus.
Baboon,	Unoha,	Cynocephalus porcarius.
Blesbuck,	Inoni,	Damalis albifrons.
Bluebuck,	Ipete,	Cephalopus cæruleus.
Buffalo,	Inyati,	Bubalus caffer.
Bush-buck, { Male,	Nkonka,	Tragelaphus sylvaticus.
{ Female,	Imbabala,	
Cane rat, Northern Africa,	Far-eb-boos,	Aulacodus Swinderianus.
„ Southern Africa,	Ivondwe,	?
Duiker,	Impunzi,	Cephalopus mergens.
Eland,	Impofu,	Antilope oreas.
Elephant,	Indhlovu,	Elephas Africanus.
Gnu, Blue,	Inkonkone,	Catoblepas gnu.
„ Brindled,	Imbutuma,	Catoblepas gorgon.
Harness bush-buck,	Inyala,	
Hartebeest,	Inhluzele,	Antilope caama.
Hippopotamus,	Imvubu,	Hippopotamus amphibius.
Hyena,	Impisi,	Hyæna crocuta.
Jackal, Silver,	Inkanka,	
„ Black-backed,	Impungutye,	Canis mesomelas.
Klipspringer,	Ikoko,	Oreotragus satratrix.
Koodoo,	Ungangxa,	Antilope strepsiceros.

APPENDIX.

English or Common Name.	Kaffir or Native Name.	Scientific Name.
Leopard, Common,	Ingwe,	Felis leopardus.
,, Black-spotted,	,,	
,, Maned,	,,	
Lion,	Imbube,	F. leo.
Monkey, Common,	Inkau,	Cercopithecus pygerythus.
,, Grey,	Insimango,	C. samango.
Oribi,	Iula,	Oreotragus scoparius.
Oryx,	Uhlaza,	Oryx gazella.
Porcupine,	Ingugumbaue,	Hystrix Africæ australis.
Quagga,		Equus quagga.
Raebuck, Vaal,	Iza,	Pelea capreola.
,, Roi,	Inxala,	
Reed-buck,	Inhlango,	Eleotragus arundinaceus.
Red-buck,	Umkumbi,	Cephalopus Natalensis.
Rhinoceros, Black,	Upetyane,	R. bicornis.
,, ,,	Umkombe tovote,	R. Keitloa.
,, White,	Umkave,	R. simus.
,, ,,	Kulumane,	
,, ,,		R. Oswellii.
Roibuck,	Impalla,	Antilope melampus.
Sassabi,		Bubalus lunata.
Springbuck,	Umeqi,	Gazella euchore.
Steinbuck,	Iqina,	Caleotragus tragulus.
Water-antelope, South A.,	Ipeva,	Kobus ellipsiprymnus.
,, Central A.,		Antilope difassa.
Wild Dog,	Inkentyane,	Canis pictus seu venaticus.
Wild Pig,	Indhlovudawane,	Phacochœrus Æthiopicus.
,, Bush,	Ingulubi,	Potamochœrus Africanus.
Zebra,	Idube,	Equus zebra.
,, Burchell's,	,,	E. Burchellii.

APPENDIX II.

BIRDS.

English or Common Name.	Kaffir or Native Name.	Scientific Name.
Crane, Great Crested,	Unohemu,	Balearica pavonina.
Duck,	Idada,	Anas flavirostris.
„ Black,	„	A. sparsa.
„ Tree,	„	Dendrocygna viduata.
Goat-sucker,	Isavolo,	Caprimulgus Natalensis.
Goose,	Idada,	Nettapus Madagascariensis.
„ Spur-winged,	„	Plectropterus Gambensis.
„ Grey,	„	Chenalopex Ægyptiacus.
Hornbill, South African,	Insingizi,	Bucornus Abyssinicus.
Knorhaan,	Utekali,	E. Afra.
„	„	Otis melangaster.
„	„	Otis torquata.
Lark, Cape,		Anthus Capensis.
Natal Partridge,	Itendele,	Francolinus Natalensis.
Ostrich,	Intye,	Struthio Camelus.
Pauw, Crested,	Indhlantete,	Eupodis cristata.
„ Common,	„	E. caffra.
„ Coast,	„	E. Ludwigii.
Pigeon, Blue Rock,	Ivukuto,	Columba Guinea.
„ Green,	Ijubantonto,	
„ small species of interior,		
„ Bush,	Ihobe elimpofu,	C. Dalagorgui.

English or Common Name.	Kaffir or Native Name.	Scientific Name.
Plover,	Umbangaqua,	
„ Dikkop,	Iboya,	Ædicnemus maculosus.
„	Ititihoya,	Hoplopterus coronatus.
„ Golden,		Charadrius pluvialis.
Quail, Common,		Coturnix dactylisonans.
„	Isigwaca,	Turnix lepurana.
Natal Pheasant,	Inkwali,	Francolinus clamator.
Snipe, Common,		Gallinago Æquatorialis.
„ Painted,		Rhynchœa Capensis.
Turtle Dove,	Ijuba,	Turtor semitorquatus.
Rhinoceros or Buffalo bird,	Ihlalanyati,	Textor erythroryncbus.
Honey bird,	Ingede,	
Guinea fowl,	Impangele,	Numida coronata.
„ „		Numida cristata.

Edinburgh University Press:
THOMAS AND ARCHIBALD CONSTABLE, PRINTERS TO HER MAJESTY.

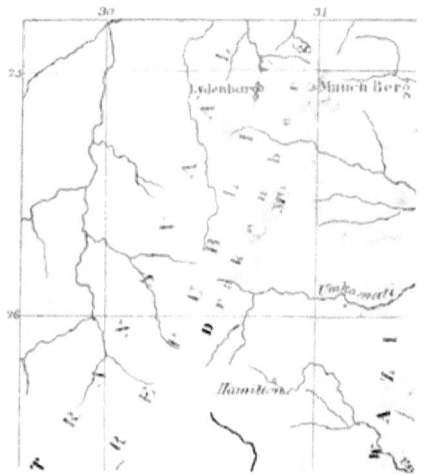

www.ingramcontent.com/pod-product-compliance
Lightning Source LLC
Chambersburg PA
CBHW022057300426
44117CB00007B/495